MANIAS, PANICS,

AND CRASHES

A History of Financial Crises

CHARLES P. KINDLEBERGER

Title-page illustration: "Scene in the Gold Room, New York City, on 'Black Friday' ", from Woodrow Wilson, *A History of the American People*, Vol. 5, *Reunion and Nationalization* (New York: Harper & Brothers, 1902)

© Basic Books, Inc. 1978

First published in the USA 1978
First published in the United Kingdom 1978
Reprinted in Papermacs 1981

Published by
THE MACMILLAN PRESS LTD
London and Basingstoke
Companies and representatives
throughout the world

Printed in Hong Kong

British Library cataloguing in Publication Data

Kindleberger, Charles Poor
    Manias, panics, and crashes
    1. Depressions – History
    2. Economic history
    I. Title
    338.5′4′0904

ISBN 0-333-25716-2 (hardcover)
ISBN 0-333-30832-8 (Papermac)

To the M.I.T. Old Guard of the 1940s

MAA, RLB, ECB, HAF, CAM, PAS, RMS, DST

and the memory of REF, WRMacL, and MFM

in gratitude for support and friendship

Much has been written about panics and manias, much more than with the most outstretched intellect we are able to follow or conceive; but one thing is certain, that at particular times a great deal of stupid people have a great deal of stupid money. . . . At intervals, from causes which are not to the present purpose, the money of these people —the blind capital, as we call it, of the country—is particularly large and craving; it seeks for someone to devour it, and there is a "plethora"; it finds someone, and there is "speculation"; it is devoured, and there is "panic."

—Walter Bagehot
"Essay on Edward Gibbon"

CONTENTS

ACKNOWLEDGMENTS

Inevitably, in working on a subject over a number of years, one accumulates valuable leads and ideas through conversation, correspondence, and discussion following seminars or lectures, without always recalling exactly what is owed to whom. The present circumstances constitute no exception. Martin Mayer put me on to the Minsky model. Hal Varian tried unsuccessfully to instruct me in catastrophe mathematics (which, for the most part, remains a blur). For discussion at M.I.T., I am especially indebted to Peter Diamond, to Rudiger Dornbusch, and to Stanley Fischer, who also read the manuscript. At Brigham Young University in January 1977, I had several discussions with Larry Wimmer and at Princeton with Lester Chandler and Dwight Jaffee. My files contain useful letters from Jacob Frenkel, the late Harry G. Johnson, Roland McKinnon, Edward S. Shaw, and Allan Sproul. Lectures on various aspects of the subject were given at the Eastern Economic Association, the Pacific Northwest Regional Economics Association, the Export-Import Bank conference on debts of developing countries, and seminars at the University of California, Brigham Young, Harvard, the Institute for Advanced Studies, Lewis and Clark College, Oregon, Princeton, Stanford, Utah, and Utah State.

Membership for four months at the Institute for Advanced Studies in Princeton, with its splendid facilities, provided an ideal place to work. Firestone Library at Princeton University proved rich in material. I have also taken advantage of academic visits to use the libraries of Brigham Young, Lewis and Clark, and the University of California. On the subject of financial crises, scholars owe a particular debt to Augustus

M. Kelley and Burt Franklin, who have reprinted much of the classic literature in the field.

"East-west, home's best." My greatest thanks, as always, I owe to the M.I.T. library system, and especially the Dewey Library, supplemented by the treasures of Widener, Baker, and Kress at Harvard.

Typing chores were performed partly at Princeton by the admirably efficient and agreeable staff of the Institute for Advanced Studies, under Mrs. Peggy Clark, and at M.I.T. by various staff members, but notably by Marie-Claire Humblet and Barbara Feldstein.

A final word of thanks goes to my friendly and creative economics editor, Martin Kessler.

CHARLES P. KINDLEBERGER

Massachusetts Institute of Technology
November 1977

Manias, Panics, and Crashes

CHAPTER 1

Financial Crisis:
A Hardy Perennial

There is hardly a more conventional subject in economic literature than financial crises. If few books on the subject have appeared since World War II, following the spate of the 1930s, it is because the industry of producing them is anti-cyclical in character, and recessions from 1945 to 1973 were few, far between, and exceptionally mild. More recently, with the worldwide recession of 1974–75, the industry has picked up. This work thus reflects a revived interest in an old theme.

Financial crises are associated with the peaks of business cycles. We are not interested in the business cycle as such, the rhythm of economic expansion and contraction, but only in the financial crisis that is the culmination of a period of expansion and leads to downturn. If there be business cycles without financial crises, they lie outside our interest. On the other hand, financial crises that prove so manageable as to have no effects on the economic system will also be neglected. The financial crises we shall consider here are major both in size and in effect and, as a rule, international in scope.

The issues to be probed are several. Are markets so rational that manias—irrational by definition—cannot occur? If, on the other hand, such manias do occur, should they be allowed to run their course, without governmental or other authoritative interference? Or is there a salutary role to be played by a "lender of last resort," who comes to the rescue and provides the public good of stability that the private market is unable to produce for itself? And if the services of a lender of last resort are provided nationally, by government or by such official institutions as a central bank, what agency or agencies can furnish stability to the international system, for which no government exists?

The reader is owed an immediate confession. In an earlier work, *The World in Depression, 1929–1939*, I reached the conclusion that the 1929 depression was so wide, so deep, and so prolonged because there was no international lender of last resort.[1] Exhausted by the war and groggy from the aborted recovery of the 1920s, Great Britain was unable to act in that capacity and the United States was unwilling to do so. This interpretation of the Great Depression has not gone unchallenged.[2] The present work is nonetheless an attempt to extend the analysis in time and space, back to the beginning of the eighteenth century and to Western Europe.

Speculative excess, referred to concisely as a mania, and revulsion from such excess in the form of a crisis, crash, or panic can be shown to be, if not inevitable, at least historically common. And the role of the lender of last resort is fraught with ambiguity and dilemma. Commenting on the behavior of the Bank of England in the crisis of 1825, Thomas Joplin said, "There are times when rules and precedents cannot be broken; others, when they cannot be adhered to with safety."[3] Of course. But breaking the rule establishes a precedent and a new rule, which should be adhered to or broken as occasion demands. In these circumstances, intervention is an art, not a science. General rules that the state should always intervene or that it should never intervene are both wrong, a fact abundantly demonstrated by contemporary questions of whether or not, or how, to rescue Lockheed, Penn Central, New York City, the Eastern bloc, and developing countries with their mountains of debt. This list of questions, moreover, suggests that the problem of financial crisis is still with us despite what the world has learned about economic stability from Keynes, so amply put into effect in the last thirty years.

This book, as already remarked, is not concerned with the business cycle, except insofar as failure to take action at the upper turning point may or may not prolong subsequent depression. Our concern is with speculative booms in the cycle and in the crises at the peak, and especially with their financial aspects. By no means is every upswing in business excessive, leading inevitably to mania and panic. But the pattern occurs sufficiently frequently and with sufficient uniformity to merit renewed study.

What happens, basically, is that some event changes the economic outlook. New opportunities for profits are seized, and overdone, in ways so closely resembling irrationality as to constitute a mania. Once the excessive character of the upswing is realized, the financial system experiences a sort of "distress," in the course of which the rush to reverse the expansion process may become so precipitous as to resemble panic. In the manic phase, people of wealth or credit switch out of money or borrow to buy real or illiquid financial assets. In panic, the reverse movement takes place, from real or financial assets to money, or repayment of debt, with a crash in the prices of commodities, houses, buildings, land, stocks, bonds—in short, in whatever has been the subject of the mania.

The monetary aspects of manias and panics are important, and we shall later examine them at some length. A monetarist view of the matter—that mania and panic would both be avoided if only the supply of money were stabilized at some fixed quantity, or at a regular growing level—is rejected. While better monetary policies would moderate mania and panic in all cases, and doubtless eliminate some, I contend that even optimal policies would leave a residual problem of considerable dimensions. Even if there were exactly the right amount of liquidity in the system over the long run, there would still be crises, and need in crisis for additional liquidity to be provided by a lender of last resort. This view can be generalized to commodity markets. Markets generally work, but occasionally they break down. When they do, they require government intervention to provide the public good of stability.

This position is widely at variance with the views at either of two extremes: that financial and commodity markets work perfectly in all times and places, or that they always work badly and should be replaced by planning or governmental assignments. On the contrary, I contend that markets work well on the whole, and can normally be relied upon to decide the allocation of resources and, within limits, the distribution of income, but that occasionally markets will be overwhelmed and need help. The dilemma, of course, is that if markets know in advance that help is forthcoming under generous dispensations, they break down more frequently and function less effectively.

It may be well to fix the limits in time and place of the panics we shall consider. We start with the South Sea bubble in London and the Mississippi bubble in Paris in 1719 and 1720. (Manias such as the Lübeck crisis 100 years earlier, or the tulip mania of 1634, are too isolated and lack the characteristic monetary features that come with the spread of banking after the opening of the eighteenth century.) Although I say "we start with the South Sea bubble," there will be no chronological history of crises. Rather, we shall attempt an analytical treatment using materials from crises going back to 1719 and coming up mainly to 1929, but in a few cases up to the recession of 1974–75.* In space, the major connected financial markets were Holland, Britain, Germany, and France in the eighteenth century; and Britain, Germany, France, and (beginning in 1819) the United States in the nineteenth century. Italy is of interest in connection with the crisis of 1866 and that of 1907, for which a particularly useful monograph exists.[4] For the rest, Italy plays only a modest role until after World War II.

Historical economics of a comparative sort relies on secondary sources, and cannot seek for primary material available only in archives. Accordingly, it follows the historical literature, which is most abundant for Britain and then for France, Germany, and the United States. The writer must confess, moreover, that his historical focus has been more on Europe than on the United States, at least for the period before World War I. To the extent that an abundance of work on a given country accurately reflects its importance in the international financial system, as it largely does, major attention to Britain is appropriate for the nineteenth century, if less so for the eighteenth, when Amsterdam matched or outstripped London in financial power. Inability to read Dutch has cut me off from most of at least one frequently cited monograph on the crisis of 1763,[5] but there is a considerable literature on Amsterdam in this period in more accessible languages, notably English.

This book is an essay in what is derogatively called today "literary economics," as opposed to mathematical economics,

---

* After 1720 there is a long gap until we come to the international crisis of 1763 at the end of the Seven Years War. A crisis and panic in London in 1745, when the Young Pretender landed in Scotland and advanced on England from the north until he was stopped at Carlisle, fall outside the interest of this work, since they were largely non-monetary and were limited to a single market. A number of well-known financial crises, such as that following the City of Glasgow Bank failure in 1878 or the panic of 1893 in New York will be explored for particular aspects but are too parochial to merit intensive examination for present purposes.

econometrics, or (embracing them both) the "new economic history." A man does what he can, and in the more elegant— one is tempted to say "fancier"—techniques I am, as one who received his formation in the 1930s, untutored. A colleague has offered to provide a mathematical model to decorate the work. It might be useful to some readers, but not to me. Catastrophe mathematics, dealing with such events as falling off a height, is a new branch of the discipline, I am told, which has yet to demonstrate its rigor or usefulness. I had better wait. Econometricians among my friends tell me that rare events such as panics cannot be dealt with by the normal techniques of regression, but have to be introduced exogenously as "dummy variables." The real choice open to me was whether or not to follow relatively simple statistical procedures, with an abundance of charts and tables. In the event, I decided against it. For those who yearn for numbers, standard series on bank reserves, foreign trade, commodity prices, money supply, security prices, rate of interest, and the like are fairly readily available in the historical statistics. My thesis does not rest on small differences in quantities, however —or so I believe. It seemed to me to bog the argument down, as well as involve an inordinate amount of work, with greater costs than benefits. The result is an essentially qualitative, not quantitative, approach.

Chapter 2 provides the background to the analysis. It consists of a model of speculation, credit expansion, financial distress at the peak, and then crisis, ending in panic and crash. It is patterned after early classical ideas of overtrading, followed by revulsion and discredit, as expressed by Adam Smith, John Stuart Mill, Knut Wicksell, Irving Fisher, and others, but most recently by Hyman Minsky, a monetary theorist who holds that the financial system is unstable, fragile, and prone to crisis. It is not necessary to agree with him about the current monetary system of the United States to recognize that his model may have great explanatory power for past crises in this country and especially in Western Europe.

The analysis itself, with copious historical illustration, begins with Chapter 3, which focuses on speculation, the mania phase of the subject. The central issue here is whether speculation can be destabilizing as well as stabilizing— whether, in other words, markets are always rational. The nature of the outside, exogenous shock which sets off the mania is examined in different historical settings: war, the end of war, a series of good harvests, a series of bad harvests, the opening of new markets, innovations, and the like. The objects of speculation are listed: commodity exports, commodity imports, agricultural land at home or abroad, urban building sites, new banks, discount houses, stocks, bonds (both foreign and domestic), glamour stocks, conglomerates, condominiums, shopping centers, office buildings. Moderate excesses burn themselves out without damage. A difficult question to answer is whether the euphoria of the upswing endangers financial stability only if it embraces two or more objects of speculation, a bad harvest, say, along with a railroad mania or an orgy of land speculation.

Chapter 4 deals with the monetary dimensions of both manias and panics. We shall note occasions when boom or panic has been set off by monetary events—a recoinage, a discovery of precious metals, a change in the ratio of the prices of gold and silver under bimetallism, and the like. More fundamentally, however, we shall stress the difficulty of getting the monetary mechanism right at any one time, and the impossibility of keeping it right. Money is a public good; as such, it lends itself to private exploitation. Banking, moreover, is notoriously difficult to regulate. Modern monetarists insist that much, perhaps most, of the cyclical difficulties of the past are the consequences of mistakes of understanding. That such mistakes were frequent and serious cannot be denied. The argument advanced in this chapter, however, is that even when the supply of money was neatly adjusted to the demands of an economy, and mistakes were avoided, the monetary mechanism did not stay right very long. When government produces one quantity of the public good, money, the public will proceed to make more, just as lawyers find new loopholes in tax laws as fast as legislation closes up old ones. The evolution of money from coins to include bank notes, bills of exchange, bank deposits, finance paper, and on and on illustrates the point. The Currency School may be right about the necessity for a fixed supply of money, but it is wrong about the possibility of achieving it.

In Chapter 5 we consider swindles and defalcations. It happens that crashes and panics are often precipitated by the revelation of some misfeasance, malfeasance, or malversation (the corruption of officials) engendered during the mania. It seems clear from the historical record that swindles are a response to the greedy appetite for wealth stimulated by the boom. And as the monetary system gets stretched, institutions lose liquidity, and unsuccessful swindles are about to be revealed, the temptation becomes virtually irresistible to take the money and run. It is difficult to write on this subject without permitting the typewriter to drip with irony. An attempt will be made.

Chapter 6 describes the crisis stage, with the emphasis on domestic aspects. One question is whether manias can be halted by official warnings—moral suasion or jawboning. By and large, the evidence suggests that it cannot, or at least that many crises followed warnings that were intended to head them off. The nature of the turning point is discussed: some bankruptcy, defalcation, or troubled area revealed or rumored, a sharp rise in the central-bank discount rate to halt the hemorrhage of cash into domestic circulation or abroad. And then there is the interaction of falling prices— the crash—and its impact on the liquidity of the system.

In Chapter 7 we turn to the international propagation of manias and crises. Connections run through many linkages, including trade, capital markets, flows of hot money, changes in central bank reserves of gold or foreign exchange, fluctuations in prices of commodities, securities, or national currencies, changes in interest rates, and direct contagion of speculators in euphoria or gloom. Some crises are local, others international. What constitutes the difference? Did, for example, the 1907 panic in New York precipitate the collapse of the Società Bancaria Italiana via pressure on Paris communicated to Turin by withdrawals? There is fundamental ambiguity here, too. Tight money in a given financial center can serve either to attract funds or to repel them, depending upon the expectations that a rise in interest rates generates. With inelastic expectations—no fear of crisis or of currency depreciation—an increase in the discount rate attracts funds from abroad, and helps provide the cash needed to ensure liquidity; with elastic expectations of change—of falling prices, bankruptcies, or exchange depreciation—raising the discount rate may suggest to foreigners the need to take more funds out rather than bring new funds in. The trouble is familiar in economic life generally. A rise in the price of a commodity may lead consumers to postpone purchases, awaiting the decline, or to speed them up against future increases. And even where expectations are inelastic, and the increased discount rate at the central bank sets in motion the right reactions, lags in responses may be so long that the crisis supervenes before the Marines arrive.

Crisis management at the domestic level is treated in Chapters 8 and 9. The first of these is devoted to no management on the one hand, and a host of miscellaneous devices on the other. No management is the remedy of those who think that the market is rational and can take care of itself; according to one formulation, it is healthy for the economy to go through the purgative fires of deflation and bankruptcy that get rid of the mistakes of the boom. Among the miscellaneous devices are holidays, bank holidays, the issuance of scrip, guarantees of liabilities, issuance of government debt, deposit insurance, and the like. Chapter 9 addresses questions related to a lender of last resort—whether there should be one, who it should be, how it should operate—and the dilemmas posed for the system by the discharge of such a role. If the market is sure it will be saved by a lender of last resort, its self-reliance is weakened. On the other hand, one may choose to halt a panic for the sake of the system today, rather than worry about effects on incentives tomorrow. If there is a lender of last resort, however, whom should it save: insiders? outsiders and insiders? only the solvent, if illiquid? But solvency depends upon the extent and duration of the panic.

The penultimate chapter moves from the domestic scene, in which there is responsible government, to the international arena, where no agency or government has de jure responsibility for providing the public good of monetary stability.

A final chapter sums up the argument. In a word, our conclusion is that money supply should be fixed over the long run but be elastic during the short-run crisis. The lender of last resort should exist, but his presence should be doubted. For example, uncertainty about whether New York City would be helped, and by whom, may have proved just right in the long run, so long as help was finally provided, and so long as there was doubt right to the end as to whether it would be. This is a neat trick: always come to the rescue, in order to prevent needless deflation, but always leave it uncertain whether rescue will arrive in time or at all, so as to instill caution in other speculators, banks, cities, or countries. In Voltaire's *Candide*, the head of a general was cut off "to encourage the others." What I am urging is that some sleight of hand, some trick with mirrors be found to "encourage" the others (without, of course, cutting off actual heads) because monetarist fundamentalism has such unhappy consequences for the economic system.

Let me close this introduction with a word of caution. This book has few new themes. Insofar as it fits into an intellectual pattern, it is against revisionism. A considerable portion of the economic writing of the last thirty years has been devoted to attacking old-fashioned modes of analysis that I happen to believe are valid. The monetarist school of Milton Friedman, for example, holds that there is virtually no destabilizing speculation, that markets are rational, that governments make mistake after mistake. I hope to suggest that such views, although not necessarily wrong, are too emphatic and leave too little room for exceptions. Both Keynesians and monetarists tend to disregard the macro-economic impact of price changes, on the ground that gains from price changes for producers or consumers are matched by losses to consumers or producers, with no net effect on the system except where there is money illusion, i.e., when a consumer or producer fails to see that his income has changed when prices change while nominal monetary aggregates remain unchanged. This disregard is often mistaken, in my judgment, as when the decline of prices leads to industrial, mercantile, and investor bankruptcy, financial disintermediation, bank failure, and spreading deflation before the benefits, if any, from lower prices have a chance to make themselves felt. The net effects of rising prices in today's world may be limited by offsetting gains and losses, without letting loose dynamic reactions. I would argue, however, that the pre-Keynesians were right in paying attention to price movements, now so cavalierly discarded. A study of manias, bubbles, crashes, panics, and the lender of last resort helps us to move from classical thesis through revisionist antithesis to a more balanced synthesis. Or so I claim.

CHAPTER 2

Anatomy of
a Typical Crisis

History vs. Economics

For historians each event is unique. Economics, however, maintains that forces in society and nature behave in repetitive ways. History is particular; economics is general. In the chapters that follow, we shall set out various phases of speculative manias leading to crisis and collapse, with a wealth of historical explanation. In this chapter we are interested in the underlying economic model of a general financial crisis.

Note that we are not presenting here a model of the business cycle. The business cycle involves a full revolution of the economic wheel, while boom and bust deal only with that portion of the cycle covering the final upswing and the initial downturn. Nor are we concerned with the periodicity of both cycles and crises. Such a discussion would broaden the subject to different kinds of cycles: the Kitchin cycle of thirty-nine months, based on the rhythm of fluctuations in business inventories; the Juglar cycle of seven or eight years, related to business investment in plant and equipment; the Kuznets cycle of twenty years, from population changes from generation to generation and the resultant rise and fall in the construction of housing; and possibly the more dubious and elusive Kondratieff cycle, set off by major inventions such as the railroad and the automobile.[1] Along with other observers, we note the spacing of crises ten years apart in the first half of the nineteenth century (1816, 1826, 1837, 1847, 1857, 1866) before the timing became more ragged. We make no attempt to explain this rhythm, beyond suggesting that some time must elapse after one speculative mania that ends in crisis before investors have sufficiently recovered from their losses and disillusionment to be willing to take a flyer again.

The Model

We start with the model of Hyman Minsky, a man with a reputation among monetary theorists for being particularly pessimistic, even lugubrious, in his emphasis on the fragility of the monetary system and its propensity to disaster.[2] Although Minsky is a monetary theorist rather than an economic historian, his model lends itself effectively to the interpretation of economic and financial history. Indeed, in its emphasis on the instability of the credit system, it is a lineal descendent of a model, set out with personal variations, by a host of classical economists including John Stuart Mill, Alfred Marshall, Knut Wicksell, and Irving Fisher.

According to Minsky, events leading up to a crisis start with a "displacement," some exogenous, outside shock to the macroeconomic system. The nature of this displacement varies from one speculative boom to another. It may be the outbreak or end of a war, a bumper harvest or crop failure, the widespread adoption of an invention with pervasive effects—

canals, railroads, the automobile—some political event or surprising financial success, or a debt conversion that precipitously lowers interest rates. But whatever the source of the displacement, if it is sufficiently large and pervasive, it will alter the economic outlook by changing profit opportunities in at least one important sector of the economy. Displacement brings opportunities for profit in some new or existing lines, and closes out others. As a result, business firms and individuals with savings or credit seek to take advantage of the former and retreat from the latter. If the new opportunities dominate those that lose, investment and production pick up. A boom is under way.

In Minsky's model, the boom is fed by an expansion of bank credit which enlarges the total money supply. Banks typically can expand money, whether by the issue of bank notes under earlier institutional arrangements, or by lending in the form of additions to bank deposits. Bank credit is, or at least has been, notoriously unstable, and the Minsky model rests squarely on that fact. This feature of the Minsky model is incorporated in what follows, but we go further. Before banks had evolved, and afterward, additional means of payment to fuel a speculative mania were available in the virtually infinitely expansible nature of personal credit. For a given banking system at a given time, monetary means of payment may be expanded not only within the existing system of banks, but also by the formation of new banks, the development of new credit instruments, and the expansion of personal credit outside of banks. Crucial questions of policy turn on how to control all these avenues of monetary expansion. But even if the instability of old and potential new banks were corrected, instability of personal credit would remain to provide means of payment to finance the boom, given a sufficiently thoroughgoing stimulus.

Let us assume, then, that the urge to speculate is present, and is transmuted into effective demand for goods or financial assets. After a time, increased demand presses against the capacity to produce goods or the supply of existing financial assets. Prices increase, giving rise to new profit opportunities and attracting still further firms and investors. Positive feedback develops, as new investment leads to increases in income that stimulate further investment and further income increases. At this stage we may well get what Minsky calls "euphoria." Speculation for price increases is added to investment for production and sale. If this process builds up, the result is often, though not inevitably, what Adam Smith and his contemporaries called "overtrading."

Now overtrading is by no means a clear concept. It may involve pure speculation for a price rise, an overestimate of prospective returns, or excessive "gearing."[3] Pure speculation, of course, involves buying for resale rather than use in the case of commodities, or for resale rather than income in the case of financial assets. Overestimation of profits comes from euphoria, affects firms engaged in the productive and distributive processes, and requires no explanation. Excessive gearing arises from cash requirements which are low relative both to the prevailing price of a good or asset and to possible changes in its price. It means buying on margin, or by installments, under circumstances in which one can sell the asset and transfer with it the obligation to make future payments. As firms or households see others making profits from speculative purchases and resales, they tend to follow. When the number of firms and households indulging in these practices grows large, bringing in segments of the population that are normally aloof from such ventures, speculation for profit leads away from normal, rational behavior to what have been described as "manias" or "bubbles." The word "mania" emphasizes the irrationality; "bubble" foreshadows the bursting.

As we shall see in the next chapter, the object of speculation may vary widely from one mania or bubble to the next. It may involve primary products, especially those imported from afar (where the exact conditions of supply and demand are not known in detail), or goods manufactured for export to distant markets, domestic and foreign securities of various kinds, contracts to buy or sell goods or securities, land in the country or city, houses, office buildings, shopping centers, condominiums, foreign exchange. At a late stage, speculation tends to detach itself from really valuable objects and turn to delusive ones. A larger and larger group of people seeks to become rich without a real understanding of the processes involved. Not surprisingly, swindlers and catchpenny schemes flourish.

Although Minsky's model is limited to a single country, overtrading has historically tended to spread from one country to another. The conduits are many. Commodity prices may rise, and so may the prices of securities that are traded internationally. Speculation in exports, imports, or foreign securities furnishes direct links between markets of countries. By these means euphoria and overtrading in one country can be fed by capital inflows from foreign purchases of particular goods or assets. And if these capital flows lead to inflows of gold or silver, monetary expansion in the original country is enhanced, as the boom is fueled by additional supplies of money on which higher pyramids of credit can be supported. In an ideal world, of course, a gain of specie for one country would be matched by a corresponding loss for another, and the resulting expansion in the first case would be offset by the contraction in the second. In the real world, however, while the boom in the first country might gain speed from the increase in the supply of reserves, or "high-powered money," it might also rise in the second despite the loss in monetary reserves, as investors respond to rising prices and profits abroad by joining in the speculative chase. In other words, the potential contraction from the shrinkage on the monetary side might be overwhelmed by the increase in speculative interest and the rise in demand. For the two countries together, in any event, the credit system is stretched tighter.

As the speculative boom continues, interest rates, velocity

of circulation, and prices all continue to mount. At some stage, a few insiders decide to take their profits and sell out. At the top of the market there is hesitation, as new recruits to speculation are balanced by insiders who withdraw. Prices begin to level off. There may then ensue an uneasy period of "financial distress." The term comes from corporate finance, where a firm is said to be in financial distress when it must contemplate the possibility, perhaps only a remote one, that it will not be able to meet its liabilities.[4] For an economy as a whole, the equivalent is the awareness on the part of a considerable segment of the speculating community that a rush for liquidity—to get out of other assets and into money—may develop, with disastrous consequences for the prices of goods and securities, and leaving some speculative borrowers unable to pay off their loans. As distress persists, speculators realize, gradually or suddenly, that the market cannot go higher. It is time to withdraw. The race out of real or long-term financial assets and into money turns into a stampede.

The specific signal that precipitates the crisis may be the failure of a bank or firm stretched too tight, the revelation of a swindle or defalcation by someone who sought to escape distress by dishonest means, or a fall in the price of the primary object of speculation as it, at first alone, is seen to be overpriced. In any case, the rush is on. Prices decline. Bankruptcies increase. Liquidation sometimes is orderly, but more frequently degenerates into panic as the realization spreads that there is only so much money, and not enough to enable everyone to sell out at the top. The word for this stage—again, not from Minsky—is "revulsion." Revulsion against commodities or securities leads banks to cease lending on the collateral of such assets. In the early nineteenth century this condition was known as "discredit." "Overtrading," "revulsion," "discredit"—all these terms have a musty, old-fashioned flavor. They are imprecise, but they do convey a graphic picture.

Revulsion and discredit may go so far as to lead to panic (or

put it, *Torschlusspanik*, door-shut-panic), with
g to get through the door before it slams shut.
on itself, as did the speculation, until one or
ings happen: (1) prices fall so low that people
are again tempted to move back into less liquid assets; (2)
trade is cut off by setting limits on price declines, shutting
down exchanges, or otherwise closing trading; or (3) a lender
of last resort succeeds in convincing the market that money
will be made available in sufficient volume to meet the demand
for cash. Confidence may be restored even if a large volume
of money is not issued against other assets; the mere knowledge that one can get money is frequently sufficient to
eliminate the desire.

Whether or not there should be a lender of last resort is a
matter of some debate. Those who oppose the function argue
that it encourages speculation in the first place. Supporters
worry more about the current crisis than about forestalling
some future one. There is also a question of the place for an
international lender of last resort. In domestic crises, government or the central bank (when there is one) has responsibility. At the international level, there is neither a world
government nor any world bank adequately equipped to serve
as a lender of last resort, although some would contend that
the International Monetary Fund since Bretton Woods in 1944
is capable of discharging the role.

Dilemmas, debates, doubts, questions abound. We shall
have more to say about these questions later on.

The Validity of the Model

The general validity of the Minsky model will be established
in detail in the chapters that follow. At this stage we simply
want to argue against two contrary positions. The first main-

tains either that each crises is unique, a product of a unique set of circumstances, or that there are such wide differences among economic crises as a class that they should be broken down into various species, each with its own particular features. The second position is that while the Minsky model may have been true of some earlier time, today things are different. This argument cites structural changes in the institutional underpinnings of the economy, including the rise of the corporation, the emergence of big labor unions and big government, modern banking, speedier communications, etc., etc. These changes, it is alleged, make a model of crises based on the instability of credit uninteresting except to antiquarians.

The issue cannot of course be resolved to the satisfaction of everyone. Truth is multidimensional, and on issues of this kind, differences of approach to truth can be justified on the basis of taste or depth of perception. The argument here is that the basic pattern of displacement, overtrading, monetary expansion, revulsion, and discredit, generalized in modern terms by the use of the Minsky model, describes the nature of capitalistic economies well enough to direct our attention to crucial problems of economic policy.

Take first the contrary view that each crisis is unique, a product of a series of historical accidents. This has been said about 1848 and about 1929,[5] and is implied by the series of historical accounts of separate crises referred to throughout the text below. There is much to support the view. Individual features of any one crisis will differ from those of another: the nature of the displacement, the object or objects of speculation, the form of credit expansion, the ingenuity of the swindlers, the nature of the incident that touches off revulsion. But if one may borrow a French phrase, the more something changes, the more it remains the same. Details proliferate; structure abides. Our interest in this chapter is structure; details engage us below.

More compelling is the suggestion that the genus "crises"

should be divided into species labeled commercial, industrial, monetary, banking, fiscal, financial (in the sense of financial markets), and so on, or into groups called local, regional, national, and international. Taxonomies along such lines abound. Although there is something to be said for such classification, we reject it for two reasons. In the first place, we are concerned primarily with international financial crises involving a number of critical elements—speculation, monetary expansion, a rise in the prices of assets followed by a sharp fall, and a rush into money. Crises that fall outside these dimensions do not, on the whole, concern us, and there are enough within the category to suggest that the broad genus is worthy of study. Second, this book is sufficiently occupied with general features; to penetrate to deeper levels would overburden the analysis by burying it in detail.

A more cogent attack on the model used here comes from the late Alvin Hansen, who claimed that something closely akin to it applied satisfactorily to the world economy prior to the middle of the nineteenth century but then underwent sea-change:

Theories based on uncertainty of the market, on speculation in commodities, on "overtrading," on the excesses of bank credit, on the psychology of traders and merchants, did indeed reasonably fit the early "mercantile" or commercial phase of modern capitalism. But as the nineteenth century wore on, captains of industry . . . became the main outlets for funds seeking a profitable return through savings and investments.[6]

In the book from which this quotation is drawn, Hansen was setting out to explain the business cycle. Before getting to the Keynesian analysis, of which he was the foremost expositor, he wanted to clear away earlier explanations. In my judgment, he was wrong—not about the rise of the modern corporation or the importance of savings and investment, but on the corollary that these required the dismissal of the earlier views on speculation in commodities and securities and on instability in credit and prices. It is understandable that

Hansen's attention was drawn to savings and investment and the forces that lay behind them, but ignoring uncertainty, speculation, and instability does not mean that they have disappeared.

The heart of this book is that the Keynesian theory is incomplete, and not merely because it ignores the money supply. Monetarism is incomplete, too. A synthesis of Keynesianism and monetarism, such as the Hansen-Hicks IS–LM curves that bring together the saving-investment (IS) and liquidity-money (LM) relationships, remains incomplete, even when it brings in production and prices (as does the most up-to-date macroeconomic analysis), if it leaves out the instability of expectations, speculation, and credit. The Keynesian and Friedmanite schools, along with most modern macroeconomic theories that synthesize them, are perhaps not so much wrong as incomplete. At the same time, the omissions under particular circumstances may be so critical as to make both Keynesianism and monetarism misleading.

The Model's Relevance Today

One place where the model surely applies today is foreign-exchange markets, in which prices rise and fall in wide swings, despite sizable intervention in the market by monetary authorities, and in which exchange speculation has brought large losses to some banks. Financial crisis has been avoided, but in the opinion of some observers, not by much.

Again, contemplate the enormous external debt of the developing countries, built up not only since the rise of oil prices but importantly—a widely ignored fact—in the several years before that time, as multinational banks swollen with dollars tumbled over one another in trying to uncover new foreign borrowers and practically forced money on the less-developed countries (LDCs). Some of the chickens have already come home to roost, in defaults by Zaïre and Peru; others, such as Pertamina in Indonesia, have had close calls. In this area the world remains in "distress" as it contemplates uneasily the possibility of widespread default, euphemistically called "debt-rescheduling" and demanded by at least some LDCs, though the more important debtors have thought better of it.

The model also applies in part in the domestic sphere. The biggest economic problem, to be sure, is how to expand employment without inflation, and here the model helps no more than do pure Keynesianism or pure monetarism. But mere mention of Billie Sol Estes and Bert Lance is sufficient to indicate that speculation and expansive bankers are not relics of a distant past, and West Coast speculation in housing has raised prices to giddy heights from which sharp falls, speculator bankruptcies, and even bank failures are not impossible, though the problem is regionally limited. The real domestic concern is not over speculative upswings but over revulsion and discredit without the antecedent overtrading. A number of analysts darkly forecast persistent movements from stocks into bonds, from bonds into money, and even from money into goods.

Beyond insisting, however, that the model cannot be dismissed out of hand, as Hansen tried to do, I take no position on its present applicability to the domestic financial picture in the United States, as opposed to the international monetary sphere, where it clearly does apply. This is a work in history, not economic forecasting.

CHAPTER 3

Speculative Manias

Rationality of Markets

The word "mania" in the chapter title connotes a loss of touch with reality or rationality, even something close to mass hysteria or insanity. It is used continuously in economic history, which is replete with canal manias, railroad manias, joint stock company manias, land manias, and a host of others. Yet economic theory, along with social science generally, adopts the assumption that man and men are rational. How can the two views be reconciled?

At one level of discourse, "rational expectations" is a technical assumption used in econometric testing of models. Instead of assuming that tomorrow will be like today as today was like yesterday—simple lagging of variables—econometricians using "rational expectations" assume that markets will react to changes in variables in the way that economic theory would regard as rational, i.e., in conformity with standard economic models.

As a more general assumption, what does it mean to say that markets are rational?[1] Is it assumed that most markets behave rationally, or that all markets behave rationally most of the time, or that all markets behave rationally all the time? Which formulation one adopts makes a difference. It is much easier to agree that most markets behave rationally most of the time than that all markets do so all the time. Frequently the argument seems to be between two polar positions, one which holds that no market is ever rational, the other that all markets are always so. In a meeting on the influence of expert networks, Harry G. Johnson offered this description of the difference between the "Bellagio group" of older economists, interested in international monetary reform, and a younger one from Chicago-Rochester-Manchester-Dauphine-Geneva:

The difference can be encapsulated in the proposition that whereas the older generation of economists is inclined to say "the floating rate system does not work the way I expected, therefore the theory is wrong, the world is irrational and we can only regain rationality by returning to some fixed rate system to be achieved by cooperation among national governments," the younger generation is inclined to say "the floating rate system is a system that should be expected to operate rationally, like most markets; if it does not seem to work rationally by my standards, my understanding of how it ought to work is probably defective; and I must work harder at the theory of rational maximizing behavior and the empirical consequences of it if I am to achieve understanding." This latter approach is the one that is being disseminated, and intellectually enforced, through the [younger] network.[2]

Rationality is thus an a priori assumption rather than a description of the world.

There can be no doubt that rationality in markets in the long run is a useful hypothesis. It is a "pregnant" hypothesis, to use the terminology of Karl Popper, one which illuminates understanding. The world more or less acts as if men were rational in the long run, and we should analyze economic affairs as if the hypothesis holds.

Milton Friedman, however, has gone further. He has claimed that there can be no destabilizing speculation. A destabilizing speculator who bought as prices rose, and sold as they fell, would be buying high and selling low, thereby losing money.

In a Darwinian sense, therefore the destabilizing speculator would fail to survive, so there can be no destabilizing speculation.[3] Even a fellow monetarist like Harry Johnson claims this analysis makes him uneasy.[4] I submit that history and a more refined theory demonstrate it to be wrong.*

The a priori assumptions of rational markets and consequently the impossibility of destabilizing speculation are difficult to sustain with any extensive reading of economic history. The pages of history are strewn with language, admittedly imprecise and possibly hyperbolic, that allows no other interpretation than occasional irrational markets and destabilizing speculation. Here are some phrases culled from the literature: *manias . . . insane land speculation . . . blind passion . . . financial orgies . . . frenzies . . . feverish speculation . . . epidemic desire to become rich quick . . . wishful thinking . . . intoxicated investors . . . turning a blind eye . . . people without ears to hear or eyes to see . . . investors living in a fool's paradise . . . easy credibility . . . overconfidence . . . overspeculation . . . overtrading. . . .*

The firm of Overend, Gurney, which crashed on Black Friday in May 1866, was said to consist of "sapient nincompoops."[6] "These losses," said Bagehot, "were made in a manner so reckless and so foolish that one would think a child

---

* On one occasion, Friedman moved to a different position, saying, "Destabilization speculation is a theoretical possibility, but I know of no empirical evidence that it has occurred even as a special case, let alone as a general rule."[5] In commenting to me privately on this statement, William Poole observed that Friedman might have had in mind some definition of destabilizing speculation that limited it to those positions taken in a market that were evidently irrational in light of the information available to the speculator at the time. Friedman has told me that this was not his definition. Poole's interpretation serves nonetheless to illustrate the connection between rationality of markets and destabilizing speculation. Rational markets are always (mostly?) governed by stabilizing speculation, which takes available information as it comes along and calculates an appropriate set of prices. If markets were sometimes irrational in the short run, prices might move excessively up or down relative to long-run values, even occasionally producing dynamic changes that would not have occurred in completely rational markets.

who had lent money in the City of London would have lent it better."[7]

Clapham's description of the Baring firm in 1890 is understated in characteristic British fashion: "They had not considered these enterprises or the expected investors in them coolly or wisely enough [but had] gone far beyond the limits of prudence."[8]

Or consider the rich language of Adam Smith on the South Sea bubble: "They had an immense capital dividend among an immense number of proprietors. It was naturally to be expected, therefore, that folly, negligence, and profusion should prevail in the whole management of their affairs. The knavery and extravagance of their stock-jobbing operations are sufficiently known [as are] the negligence, profusion and malversation of the servants of the company."[9]

Rationality of the Individual, Irrationality of the Market

Manias and panics, I contend, are associated on occasion with general irrationality or mob psychology. Often, the relationship between rational individuals and the irrational whole is more complex. After (1) mob psychology, we can distinguish a series of related cases: (2) people will change at different stages of a continuing process, starting rationally, and, gradually at first, then more quickly losing contact with reality; (3) rationality will differ among different groups of traders, investors, or speculators, including those at the earlier stages and those at the later; (4) all will succumb to the fallacy of composition, which asserts that from time to time the whole is other than the sum of its parts; (5) there will be failure of a market with rational expectations as to the *quality* of a reaction to a given stimulus to estimate the right *quantity*, especially when there are lags between stimulus and reaction; (6) irrationality may exist insofar as economic actors choose the wrong model, fail to take account of a particular and crucial bit of information, or go so far as to suppress information that does not conform to the model implicitly adopted. The irrationality of the gullible and greedy in succumbing to swindlers and defalcators we leave to a later chapter.

Mob psychology or hysteria is well established as an occasional deviation from rational behavior. We have its elements in many economic models: the demonstration effect, which leads developing countries to adopt consumption standards beyond their capacity to produce for themselves; keeping up with the Joneses in consumption; refusing, when income declines, to cut consumption symmetrically with the increase in consumption that occurred when income rose (the Duesenberry effect). In politics, it is known as the bandwagon effect, when people back winners, or as "rats deserting the sinking ship," when they turn from losers—though if the ship is really sinking, it is rational for the rat to leave. The subject is discussed generally by the French historian Gustave LeBon in *The Crowd*[10] and has been applied to the South Sea bubble by Charles McKay in his *Memoirs of Extraordinary Delusions and the Madness of Crowds.*[11] For a neat example, take the case of Martin, the banker who subscribed to £500 worth of South Sea stock in the third subscription list of August 1720, saying "When the rest of the world are mad, we must imitate them in some measure."[12]

The modern proponent of irrationality in this sense is Hyman Minsky, who emphasizes a mild form in his discussion of "euphoria" in markets. In an earlier day, such waves of excessive optimism (perhaps followed by excessive pessimism) might have been tied to sunspots or the path through the heavens of Venus or Mars. In Minsky's formulation they start with a "displacement," some structural characteristics of the system, and human error. Some event increases confidence. Optimism sets in. Confident expectations of a steady stream of prosperity, and of gross profits, make portfolio plunging more appealing. Financial institutions accept liability structures that decrease liquidity, and that in a more sober climate they would have rejected. The rise is under way, and may feed on itself until it constitutes a mania.

The alternative explanation of the unsober upswing goes back to Irving Fisher, his colleague Harry Gunnison Brown, and ultimately to Knut Wicksell, and emphasizes that the real rate of interest was too low.[13] Prices rise on the upswing, while interest rates lag. This implies a fall in the real rate of interest. Lenders have money illusion, i.e., they ignore the price rise and are content with the nominal rate of interest. Borrowers do not have money illusion, i.e., they recognize that the real rate of interest has fallen. With real interest rates falling, and profit prospects either rising or steady, rational investors expand. The picture is not persuasive. It is doubtful that one group of financial actors will have money illusion and another not. Moreover, euphoria is seldom general but usually focuses on one or two objects of speculation, implied by the displacement.

Speculation often develops in two stages. In the first, sober stage of investment, households, firms, investors, or other actors respond to a displacement in a limited and rational way; in the second, capital gains play a dominating role. "The first taste is for high interest, but that taste soon becomes secondary. There is a second appetite for large gains to be made by selling the principal."[14] In the United States, land was initially bought in the 1830s for extending the cultivation of high-priced cotton, and thereafter for resale. In the 1850s, according to Van Vleck, farmers and planters both "consumed" land and speculated in it. In ordinary times they bought more land than they cultivated, as a hedge against the declining value of the acres they planted; in boom, this more or less sound basis was discarded, and farms were heavily mortgaged to buy land, which in turn was mortgaged to buy still more so as to benefit from speculative price rises.[15]

The 1830s railway boom in Britain also had two stages: a first, prior to 1835, when the projects were not bubbles, and a second, after 1835, when they were. In the first phase, shares were sold by promoters to local chambers of commerce, Quaker capitalists, and hard-headed Lancashire businessmen, both merchants and industrialists—that is, to men of substance expecting to benefit from the building of the railroad and known to be in a position to meet not only the initial 5 to 10 percent payment but any subsequent calls for payment as the work progressed. In the second phase, professional company promoters—many of them rogues interested only in quick profits—tempted a different class of investors, including ladies and clergymen.[16]* The same stages are observed in the

---

* The ladies and clergymen—in American parlance, "widows and orphans"—may more properly belong to a third stage when the securities have become seasoned in the market. The French call such investments suitable for "the father of a family." Charles Wilson in *Anglo-Dutch Commerce and Finance in the Eighteenth Century* (Cambridge: Cambridge University Press, 1941) produces a number of variations on investor groups in the Netherlands:

> "spinsters, widows, retired naval and army officers, magistrates, retired merchants, parsons and orphanages" (p. 118); "hundreds of other merchants . . . as well as thousands of civil servants, magistrates, widows and orphans and charitable institutions" (p. 135); "widows, parsons, orphanages, magistrates and civil servants" (p. 162); "country gentry, wealthy burghers and officials of Amsterdam, widows and wealthy spinsters" (p. 181); "spinsters, theologians, admirals, civil servants, merchants, professional speculators, and the inevitable widows and orphans" (p. 202).

In the quotation from Bagehot that constitutes the epigraph of this book, the owners of the blind capital who lacked the wisdom to invest it properly were characterized in the excised portion as "quiet ladies, rural clergymen and country misers" and again as "rectors, authors, grandmothers." See Bagehot, "Essays on Edward Gibbon," quoted in Theodore E. Burton, *Financial Crises and Periods of Industrial and Commercial Depression* (New York: Appleton, 1902), pp. 321-2. Today's class of unskilled investors includes especially doctors.

The opening shot in Bismarck's financial war against Russia in 1887 that culminated in the November *Lombardverbot*, forbidding the acceptance by the Reichsbank of Russian securities as collateral for loans, was an instruction to the Orphan Courts to discriminate against Russian securities in the portfolios of their wards (*Allgemeine Zeitung*, July 28, 1887).

early 1870s for building sites in Vienna, initially bought for construction, later as speculative poker chips for profitable resale.[17] Or follow Ilse Mintz' two-stage process in foreign bonds marketed in New York: sound prior to 1924 and the Dawes loan (which touched off the boom) and inferior thereafter.[18] Today there is a market in just-built and unfinished houses in southern California, sold from one person to another at rising prices with the help of a lively push in second mortgages.

The fact of two stages raises the question of two groups of speculators, the insiders and the outsiders. These have served as some economists' answer to Friedman's a priori demonstration that destabilizing is impossible.[19] The insiders destabilize by driving the price up and up, selling out at the top to the outsiders, who buy at the top, and sell out at the bottom when the insiders are driving the market down. The losses of the outsiders are equal to the gains of the insiders, and the market as a whole is a standoff. In a technical article, Johnson has pointed out that for every destabilizing speculator there must be a stabilizing one, and vice versa.[20] But the professional insiders initially destabilize by exaggerating the upswings and the falls, while the outsider amateurs who buy high and sell low are less price manipulators than the victims of euphoria, which infects them late in the day. When they lose, they go back to their normal occupations to save up for another splurge.

A recent paper by Larry Wimmer on the Gold Panic of 1869 in the United States purports to demonstrate that there was no destabilizing speculation. The paper is helpful in correcting a host of misconceptions about the episode, particularly among general historians, but he and I have agreed that the evidence is consistent with a hypothesis that Gould and Fisk destabilized on balance by first driving the price up and then, having converted the outside speculators from stabilizers to destabilizers, selling out at the top (at least Gould did).[21] The information available to the two groups differed. In the early stage, Gould was trying to persuade the government of the desirability of forcibly depreciating the dollar by driving up the agio (premium) on gold in order to raise grain prices, while the outsider speculators were still operating on the expectation derived from past performance that the government's policy was to drive the agio down and resume convertibility of greenbacks into gold. On September 16, the outsiders abandoned this expectation and adopted Gould's, buying heavily and driving the gold price up. On September 22, on the other hand, Gould learned from his associate, President Grant's brother-in-law, that the outsiders had originally been right, and that his plan was not going to be adopted. He sold. Belatedly the outsiders saw they were wrong. The result was the Black Friday of September 24, 1869, one of three Black Fridays which take their place alongside Black Tuesday and Black Thursday of 1929.

Another case involving two sets of speculators, insiders and outsiders, is the "bucket shop." This term has practically disappeared from the language since the Securities and Exchange Commission stamped it out after 1933 as an illegal practice. Nor is it discussed in the economic literature known to me.* To learn about bucket shops, one has to turn to novels, from which in truth one can learn a great deal of historical detail about manias, panics, swindles, and financial aberrations generally. A classic picture of a bucket shop is given in Christina Stead's excellent *House of All Nations*.[22] In a bucket shop, insiders take orders from the outsider public to buy and sell securities, but do not execute them, assuming what is usually the case, that the outsider's bet will prove to have been wrong. And the bucket shop has the advantage of a hedge:

* There is a useful discussion of bucket shops, with their "boiler rooms" (sales area) set aside for "dynamiters" (salesmen), in Watson Washburn and Edmund S. DeLong, *High and Low Financiers: Some Notorious Swindlers and Their Abuses of our Modern Stock Selling System*, (Indianapolis: Bobbs-Merrill, 1932). Washburn and DeLong were lawyers in the state attorney-general's office in New York in the 1920s.

if the outsider should turn out to be a stabilizing speculator and right—buying low and selling high—the bucket-shop operator turns swindler and decamps. In *House of All Nations,* Jules Bertillon in 1934 fled to Latvia; today the destination would be Brazil or Costa Rica.

For a further example of an outside destabilizing speculator who bought high and sold low, there is the edifying history of a great Master of the Mint, Isaac Newton, a scientist and presumably rational. In the spring of 1720, he stated: "I can calculate the motions of the heavenly bodies, but not the madness of people." On April 20, accordingly, he sold out his shares in the South Sea Company at a solid 100 percent profit of £7,000. Unhappily, a further impulse later seized him, an infection from the mania gripping the world that spring and summer. He reentered the market at the top for a larger amount, and ended up losing £20,000. In the irrational habit of many of us who experience disaster, he put it out of his mind, and never, for the rest of his life, could he bear to hear the name South Sea.[23]

Yet euphoric speculation, with stages or with insiders and outsiders, may also lead to manias and panics when the behavior of every participant seems rational in itself. This is the fallacy of composition, in which the whole differs from the sum of its parts. The action of each individual is rational—or would be, were it not for the fact that others are behaving in the same way. If a man is quick enough to get in and out ahead of the others, he may do well, as insiders do, even though the totality does badly. On the South Sea bubble, Carswell quotes a rational participant:

The additional rise above the true capital will only be imaginary; one added to one, by any stretch of vulgar arithmetic will never make three and a half, consequently all fictitious value must be a loss to some person or other first or last. The only way to prevent it to oneself must be to sell out betimes, and so let the Devil take the hindmost.[24]

"Devil take the hindmost," *sauve qui peut*, and the like are recipes for a panic. The analogy of fire in a theater comes to mind.* Or try the chain letter, which presumably I do not need to describe: not everyone can get out in time unless the chain expands infinitely. It is rational to participate so long as one knows one is in on the early stages of the chain, and believes all others will think they are, too. The Ponzi scheme, discussed in Chapter 5, was a sort of chain letter in which the 50 percent profit in forty-five days guaranteed to purchasers of his notes in Boston in 1920 was paid to the early buyers, most of whom regrettably put their earnings back in for pyramiding, out of money paid by late buyers. When the late buyers suspected they might not get their money back, the system collapsed. There is never enough money for all because the swindlers—the organizers of the South Sea Company, Ponzi, and the smart ones who get out early— have taken it, and the inflow of new money must ultimately dry up.

Closely akin to the fallacy of composition is the standard "cobweb" demonstration in elementary economics, in which demand and supply are linked not simultaneously, as in an auction that clears the market at each moment of time, but with a lag. "Displacement" consists of events which change the situation, extend the horizon, and alter expectations. In such cases, otherwise rational expectations fail to take into account the strength of similar responses by others. Too many young people respond to the demand for physicists, mathematicians, schoolteachers, or whatever. But this fact is revealed only when, after a delay, the supply comes on the

* In the economic literature the only reference to theaters I find, unless it be implied in *Torschlusspanik*, is Clapham on the money-market panic of December 1, 1825, when there was a rush "like that for the pit of a theatre on the night of a popular performance," a positive instead of a negative simile (Sir John Clapham, *The Bank of England: A History* [Cambridge: Cambridge University Press, 1945], vol. 2, p. 98.).

market and job opportunities are scarce instead of abundant. Response to a shortage of coffee, sugar, cotton, or some other commodity may be similarly excessive: the price goes way up and then comes way down.

The history of manias and panics is replete with examples of destabilizing "cobweb" responses to exogenous shocks. When Brazil opened up as a market in 1808 after the Portuguese royal family fled there during Wellington's campaign in the peninsula, more Manchester goods were sent to the market in a few weeks than had been consumed there in twenty years, including the ice skates and warming pans that, as Clapham noted, proved to be the accepted illustration of commercial madness among nineteenth-century economists.[25]* In the 1820s, independence for the Spanish colonies initiated an excessive boom in lending to new Latin American governments, investing in mining shares, and exporting to the area. "The demand is sudden, and as suddenly stops. But too many have acted as if it were likely to continue."[26]

In the 1830s, says Matthews, there was a cobweb fluctuation of two-year periodicity. "Each merchant would be ignor-

---

* Hyndman, a socialist, sarcastically ascribes this example to the 1820s: "The most ridiculous blunders were made by the class which was supposed to be carrying on business for the general benefit. Warming-pans were shipped to cities within the tropics, and Sheffield carefully provided skaters with the means of enjoying their favorite pastime where ice had never been seen. The best glass and porcelain were thoughtfully provided for naked savages, who had hitherto found horns and cocoa-nut shells quite hollow enough to hold all the drink they wanted." (See H. M. Hyndman, *Commercial Crises of the Nineteenth Century* [1892; 2nd ed. (1932), reprinted, New York; Augustus M. Kelley, 1967], p. 39). Clapham is right and Hyndman wrong. The source for both is J. R. McCullough, *Principles of Political Economy*, 2nd ed. (Edinburgh, 1830), which refers to 1810, not 1825.

The announcement of the formation of the South Sea Company in May 1711 produced expectations of a strong demand for British goods in Latin America that would provide "a triumphant solution to the [British] financial problem and need for expansion for the support of our way of life." Booming markets were anticipated in "Colchester bays, silk handkerchiefs, worsted hose, sealing wax, spices, clocks and watches, Cheshire cheese, pickles, scales and weights for gold and silver." (See John Carswell, *The South Sea Bubble* [London: Cresset Press, 1960], p. 55.)

ant of the amount other merchants would be bringing forward by the time his own merchandise was on the market."[27] The same was true in the United States in the 1850s, following the discovery of gold in California:

The extraordinary and undue expectations entertained not only in the United States but in this country [Britain] as to the capability of California—after the 1849 gold discovery—unquestionably aided in multiplying and extending the disaster consequent on the American crisis. When it was again and again stated, both in London and in Boston, in regard to all shipments to San Francisco, that six, or at most eight, moderately-sized or assorted cargos per month were all that were required or could be consumed; instead of that eastern shippers dispatch twelve to fifteen first-class ships a month, fully laden.[28]

A rather farfetched line of reasoning led from phylloxera, which ruined many vineyards and set back wine production in France, to the 1880s boom in brewery shares in Britain, as one after another private brewery went public in the public-companies mania. Among them, Arthur Guinness and Co. was bought for £1.7 million and sold for £3.2 million.[29]

Nearer to the present was the boom in Britain at the end of World War I, when businessmen thought victory would ensure the elimination of German competition in coal, steel, shipping, and even cotton textiles. Prices of industrial assets, ships, equities, even houses increased. Companies were merged and took on heavy loads of debt. Then from the summer of 1920 to the coal strike of the second quarter of 1921, sober realization grimly set in.[30]

On the borderline of rationality are three more cases. The first deals with target workers, so to speak—people who get used to a certain income and find it difficult to adjust downward when rationality calls for it. In consumption theory, this is the Duesenberry effect already referred to. In labor supply, it constitutes the "backward-bending supply curve," which suggests that higher wages or salaries produce not more work but less, and that the way to increase effort is to lower the return per unit time. In economic history books, this principle is known as "John Bull can stand many things but he cannot stand 2 percent." John Stuart Mill put it thus:

Such vicissitudes, beginning with irrational speculation and ending with a commercial crisis, have not hitherto become less frequent or less violent with the growth of capital and the extension of industry. Rather they may be said to have become. more so: in consequence, it is often said, of increased competition; but, as I prefer to say, of a low rate of profit and interest, which makes the capitalists dissatisfied with the ordinary course of safe mercantile gains.[31]

In France at the end of the Restoration and the beginning of the July monarchy, i.e., between 1826 and 1832, speculation was rife despite the "distrust that the French always feel toward ill-gotten money." Landowners earned 2.25 to 3.75 percent on their assets; industrialists tried to do better than the long-run interest rate on their fixed investment by 2 to 4 percent, i.e., to earn 7 to 9 percent overall. Merchants and speculators in raw materials sought to realize 20 to 25 percent on the money they had engaged for several years when they succeeded in mounting an operation.[32] Earlier, notes Charles Wilson, the Dutch were converted from merchants into bankers (accused of idleness and greed), and developed habits of speculation, because of the decline in the rate of interest in Amsterdam to 2.5 and 3 percent.[33] Large-scale conversions of public debt in 1822 and 1824, and again in 1888, were associated with a decline in the rate of interest and stimulated appetites of investors for foreign securities.[34] As Andréadès observed of England, "When interest goes down, the English commercial world, unable to reduce its mode of life, deserts its usual business in favour of the more profitable, but on that very account more risky undertakings . . . speculation leads to disaster and ultimately must be borne by the central bank."[35]

The second borderline case involves hanging on in the hope of some improvement, or failing to take a specific type of action when changes in circumstances occur. On the first score, note the failures of the New York Warehouse and Security Company, of Kenyon, Cox & Co., and of Jay Cooke and Co. on September 8, 13, and 18, 1873, because of advances made to railroads (respectively, the Missouri, Kansas and Texas, Canada Southern, and Northern Pacific) with which they were associated, when because of the tight condition of the bond market those railroads were unable to sell bonds for funds needed to complete construction already under way.[36] Similarly, when long-term lending to Germany stopped in 1928, as financial preoccupation in New York turned from bonds to the stock market, New York banks and investment houses kept on lending at short term. When riding a tiger, or holding a bear by the tail, it seems rational—but may not be —to hang on. The model is apposite today, as the world banking community contemplates its large volume of loans to developing countries and to the Socialist bloc.

For an error of omission, note the plight of Hamburg banks which opened large credits during the Crimean War in favor of Swedish houses engaged in smuggling goods into Russia, but neglected to cancel them when peace came. The Swedes used the credits to speculate in shipbuilding, factories, and mining, which helped embroil Hamburg in the world crisis of 1857.[37]

The third borderline case is to have a rational model in mind, but the wrong one. The most famous example in another field is the French "Maginot Line psychology," though this may be thought of less as a case of irrational expectations than one of undistributed lag. " 'When a man's vision is fixed on one thing,' thought Ponzi, 'he might as well be blind.' "[38] In the 1760s, Hamburg merchants were not hurt by the fall in commodity prices until the end of the Seven Years War. Thus, in 1799, when the Napoleonic Wars were continuing, they were unprepared for the decline in prices which came with penetration of the blockade of Napoleon's 1798 Continental system.[39] Or take the French bankers and industrialists who formed the copper ring in 1888, patterned after the cartel movement in iron and steel, steel rails, coal, and sugar in the early part of the decade, bemused as they were by the successes of the diamond syndicate in South Africa and of the Rothschilds' mercury monopoly in Spain. (One notes today economists who extrapolate from the triumph of the Organization of Petroleum Exporting Countries, or OPEC, to assume successful price fixing at higher levels in practically every other raw material and foodstuff.) By 1890 the French syndicate held 160,000 tons of high-priced copper, plus contracts to buy more, with old mines being reworked, scrap processing being initiated everywhere, and the price sinking like a stone. From £80 a ton at the top to £38, the collapse almost took with it in 1889 the Comptoir d'Escompte, which was saved by an advance of 140 million francs from the Bank of France, reluctantly guaranteed by the Paris banks.[40]

For the purely irrational cases, two examples may suffice: a society pinning its hopes on some outstanding event of no possible relevance to the situation, on the one hand; and a society ignoring evidence it would prefer not to think about, on the other. As an instance of the first consider the faith placed in the World Exhibition that opened in Vienna on May 1, 1873. Already by the first of the year, says Wirth, the liquid assets of enterprises were widely exceeded by their liquid liabilities, producing acute "distress": credit at banks was stretched to the limit, a move from commodities, land, shares, and debt back into money was under way, the chain of accommodation bills was extended as far as it would go. Nonetheless, the system hung on, waiting for the opening of the exhibition which, it was thought (or at least hoped), would like a *deus ex machina* save the situation by some unknown means. When the opening of the exhibition produced no change, the market collapsed on May 5 and 6.[41]

As an illustration of repression of contradictory evidence, consider J. W. Beyen's analysis of the German failure to restrict short-term borrowing from abroad at the end of the

1920s. He suggested that the dangers were not faced, even by Schacht, and added: "It would not have been the first nor the last time . . . that consciousness was being 'repressed.' "[42]

On this showing, I conclude that despite the general usefulness of the assumption of rationality, markets can on occasions—infrequent occasions, let me emphasize—act in destabilizing ways that are irrational overall, even when each participant in the market is acting rationally. It behooves us now to turn to displacements, to the objects of speculation, and to national differences, if any, in the propensity to speculate. On the first two issues the historical illustrations offer considerable material.

Displacements

Displacement is some outside event that changes horizons, expectations, profit opportunities, behavior—"some sudden advice many times unexpected."* The event must be of significant size. Each day's events produce some changes in outlook, but few significant enough to qualify as displacements.

In the first place comes war. In some systems, perhaps including the Marxian, war may be regarded as an endogenous product of the politico-economic system, say, of nationalist capitalism. The question lies outside our interest. Wars are

* The full quotation is from Gerard Malynes, writing in 1686: "And this bargaining is most proper for such and the like commodities, the price whereof doth quickly rise and fall, and are also commodious when a man's money is not so ready to buy much, and to make a great employment with little money, which happeneth upon some sudden advice many times unexpected, whereupon men are very hot to buy or sell; which is much used in buying of Herring before they are catched, by 'stellegelt,' as they call it, that is by a summe of money agreed upon to be paid, if the partie doth repent himselfe of the bargaine. . . ." The passage is quoted by Violet Barbour, *Capitalism in Amsterdam in the 18th Century* (Ann Arbor: University of Michigan Press, 1963), p. 74.

assumed to be external to the system, whether or not, at some level of abstraction, they actually are.

Some crises occur immediately at the beginning or end of a war, or soon enough after the end to permit a few expectations to be falsified. For beginnings, the most notable is the crisis of August 1914. At the end, there are the crises of 1713, 1763, 1783, 1816, 1857, 1864, 1873, and 1920. Moreover, seven to ten years after a war, long enough for expectations formed at the end of the original crisis to be falsified, come an impressive series of crises: 1720, 1772, 1825, 1873 in the United States (if it be connected to the Civil War), and of course 1929.

Far-reaching political changes may also act to jar the system and displace expectations. The Glorious Revolution of 1688, for example, gave rise to a boom in company promotion: by 1695 there were 140 joint-stock companies with a total capital of £4.5 million, of which fewer than one-fifth had been founded before 1688. By 1717 total capitalization had reached £21 million.[43] In July 1720 the Bubble Act forbade formation of further joint-stock companies without explicit approval of Parliament, a limitation that lasted until 1856. This has normally been interpreted as a reaction against the South Sea Company speculation. Carswell, however, makes clear that it was undertaken in support of the South Sea Company, as king and Parliament sought to repress rival bubbles that might divert capital subscriptions in cash intensely needed by the South Sea promoters as the bubble stretched tighter.[44]

The events of the French Revolution, Terror, Directorate, Consulate, and Empire, along with incidents of the Napoleonic Wars themselves, similarly served as displacements, setting in motion large-scale specie movements in 1792–93 and 1797 and opening and closing markets in Europe and elsewhere for British and colonial goods. Further political events of the kind in France were the Restoration (1815), the July Monarchy (1830), the February 1848 revolution, and the Second Empire (1852). The Sepoy Mutiny in India in May 1857, followed by a Hindustan military revolution, contributed to the distress of London financial markets.[45] They afford a precedent for the Invergorden disorder of September 1931, when a contingent of British sailors came close to striking over pay reductions decreed by the new national government. This was interpreted by continental Europe as mutiny on the part of one great British institution, the navy, and had some role in humbling one other great institution, the Bank of England, by pushing Britain off gold.[46]

War, revolution, restoration, change of regime, and mutiny are taken here to come largely from outside the system, the model being designed to exclude them. Monetary and financial displacements are more difficult to describe as exogenous. But maladroit recoinage, tampering with gold/silver ratios under bimetallism, conversions undertaken to economize on government revenue which unexpectedly divert investor attention to other avenues, new lending which proves successful beyond all anticipation—these can also be regarded as displacements.

Two German recoinages provide a study in contrast. In the first, in 1763, Frederick II of Prussia bought silver in Amsterdam on credit to provide for a new coinage to replace that which had been debased during the Seven Years' War, and withdrew the old debased money from circulation before the new money was issued. This precipitated a deflationary crisis and the collapse of the chain of discounted bills.[47] More than 100 years later, after the Franco-Prussian indemnity, German authorities issued new money but this time before the old was withdrawn, in order to save interest. In three years the circulation of coins rose threefold from 254 million thalers (762 million marks). The result was inflation.[48]

The crises of 1893 in the United States, arising from the threat to gold convertibility from the Sherman Silver Act of 1890, has already been noted. So have the British debt conversions of 1822, 1824, 1888, and 1932, though the last was associated with a boom in housing that did not lead to crisis. In France, conversion of the 5 percent rente was dis-

cussed after 1823 as the money supply expanded, and the rate
of interest would have fallen had investors not been reluctant
to buy rentes at a premium. Each of three bankers had a
different idea of the purpose of the conversion: Rothschild
wanted to sell more rentes; Greffuhle (and Ouvrard) hoped to
attract investors into canals; Laffitte wanted to ensure the
development of industry. In the event, political obstacles prevented passage of the necessary legislation, and the market
finally gave up its objection to maintaining the rente at a
premium. This sharp decline in interest rates touched off
speculation.[49] Canals were built by the government with private
money,[50] and the faint glow of a railroad boom could be seen
in France along the Loire, the Rhone, and the Seine. But the
main object of speculation was building in and around the
major cities—Paris, Mulhouse, Lyons, Marseilles, Le Havre.[51]
Honoré de Balzac's novel *César Birotteau*, written in 1830 and
recounting the doleful story of a perfumer who was enticed
into buying building lots in the vicinity of the Madeleine on
borrowed money for "one quarter of the value they were sure
to have in three years," was inspired by this experience.[52]

The successes of loans in recycling indemnities after the
Napoleonic and Franco-Prussian wars and World War I have
been mentioned. Any surprising success of a security issue,
with a large multiple oversubscription and a quick premium
for subscribers, attracts borrowers, lenders, and especially investment bankers. The Baring loan of 1819—"the first important foreign loan contracted by a British house"[53]—led
quickly to a series of issues for France, Prussia, Austria, and
later, after independence for the colonies, the Spanish
American republics. The Thiers rente made French banking
houses salivate in the hope of foreign loans, a hunger that
received a further fillip from the 1888 conversion loan for
czarist Russia which bailed out German investors and sent
French investors down a trail that was to end, after revolution
in 1917, with a whimper rather than a bang. The Dawes loan
in 1924, opened the eyes of American investors to the delights

of foreign lending, from which they were to turn away in half a decade. The Thiers rente was oversubscribed fourteen times, and the Dawes loan eleven. Far more important than the size of the multiple, however, was its relation to expectation. Rosenberg called three French loans of 1854 and 1855 sensational, since they were oversubscribed almost two-to-one (468 million francs on an offering of 250 million), four-to-one (2,175 million francs for an issue of 500 million), and five-to-one (3,653 million against 750 million). In Austria and Germany, however, when the speculative boom of the 1850s was under way, the Kredit Anstalt opening stock sale was oversubscribed forty-three times, largely by people who had stood in line all night; and when the Brunswick Bank sought 2 million thalers in May 1853, it was offered 112 times that amount in three hours.[54]

Objects of Speculation

The objects of speculation will differ from boom to boom and crisis to crisis. It would be impossible to furnish an exhaustive catalogue of what goods and assets attract the play where and when. A short list is furnished in the stylized table of cycles presented in the appendix. A somewhat more detailed listing, in roughly chronological order, is perhaps worth offering here. The list shows the tendency for these objects to move from a few favored items at the beginning of our period to a wide variety of commodities and other assets and instruments at the end.

The list is partial, suggestive:

British Government debt: Amsterdam, 1763.
Selected companies: South Sea Company, Compagnie d'Occident, Sword Blade Bank, Banque Générale, Banque Royale, 1720;

British East India Company, 1772; Dutch East India Company, 1772, 1783.

Import commodities: sugar, coffee, 1799, 1857 in Hamburg; cotton in Britain and France, 1836, 1861; wheat in 1847.

Country banks: England, 1750s, 1793, 1824.

Canals: 1793, 1820s in Britain; 1823 in France.

Export goods: 1810, 1816, 1836 for Britain.

Foreign bonds: 1825 in London; 1888 in Paris; 1924 in New York.

Foreign mines: Latin American in Britain, 1825; German in Britain and France, 1850.*

Foreign direct investment: by U.S. companies, 1960s.

Building sites: 1825 in France; 1857 in the United States; 1873 in Austria and Germany; 1925 in Florida; 1970s in Florida, Arizona, and New Mexico.

Agricultural land: *biens nationaux* (noble land confiscated during the Revolution in France), speculated in from 1815 to 1830s.

Public lands: United States, 1836, 1857; Argentina, 1888–90.

Railroad shares: 1836, 1847 in Britain; 1847, 1857 in France; 1857, 1873 in the United States.

Joint-stock banks: Germany, 1850s and early 1870s.

Joint-stock discount houses: Britain in the 1860s.

Private companies going public: 1888 in Britain; 1928 in the United States.

Existing and merged companies: 1920 in Britain; 1928 in the United States; conglomerates in the United States, 1960s.

Copper: 1888 in France; 1907 in the United States.

Foreign exchange: the mark in 1921–23; the franc in 1924–26; sterling in 1931, 1964, etc.; the dollar in 1973.

Gold: 1960s, 1970s.

New industries: the United States in 1920s, 1960s.

Buildings: hotels, condominiums, office buildings, nursing homes, retirement villages.

Commodity futures.

Stock puts and calls (options).

It is necessary now to move to a critical question, one which probably cannot be resolved. Assume that we have demon-

---

* Referring to the mania in domestic mines in 1873, Ludwig Bamberger, the German banker and deputy, said: "The exchange is now caught up in mining companies, and mining, as my experience teaches, is the last act of the drama" (quoted by Felix Pinner, *Die grossen Weltkrisen*, [Zurich and Leipzig: Max Niehans Verlag, 1937], p. 208).

strated that destabilizing speculation can occur in a world of individuals whom it is convenient and fruitful to consider as normally rational. Permit this world to be perturbed by a "displacement" of one sort or another, largely from outside the system, giving rise to prospects which individuals misjudge, either for themselves or for others. At some stage, investment for use gives way to buying and selling for profit. How likely is the speculation to lead to trouble?

No answer, however tentative, can be given until we explore the credit and money mechanism in Chapter 5. There is, however, a philosophical riddle as to whether two or more objects of speculation must be (are likely to be?) involved before "overtrading" reaches sufficient dimensions to result in crisis. Let us take a few occasions when there seem to have been two or more objects.

The 1720 South Sea and Mississippi bubbles were related, as Chapter 7 will explain, and powerfully stoked by monetary expansion in the two countries that supported a high head of speculative steam. Speculation starting in the securities of the South Sea Company and the Sword Blade Bank in England, and in those of the Mississippi Company and John Law's *Banques* in France, spread rapidly to other ventures, mostly swindles, and to commodities and land. The South Sea Company was brought down by its attempt to suppress rival speculations, bringing proceedings under the Bubble Act of June 1720 against York Buildings, Lustrings, and Welsh Copper. The effort boomeranged.[55] The spread of speculation from one object to another, to generalize the rise of prices, is illustrated by the fact that speculators who were forehanded enough to cash their profits in South Sea stock moved on to purchase bank and insurance stocks or country houses.[56] So closely linked were the several markets that in time the price of land began to move with South Sea bubble quotations.[57]

The 1763 boom seems to have had no particular focus; rather, it was based exclusively on government war expenditure and its finance through chains of discount bills. The

DeNeufville Brothers, whose failure set off the panic, sold "commodities, ships, and securities like so many Dutch firms,"[58] with hundreds of thousands of florins in acceptance liabilities against which they rarely kept more than a few thousand guilders in cash reserves. Some contribution to the downturn in business may have been brought on by an un-paralleled drought in England in 1762, with a shortage of hay and scarcities of meat, butter, and cheese.[59] Nevertheless, speculation leading up to the crisis seems not to have been concentrated.

The crisis of 1772 was precipitated by speculation in Amsterdam and London in the stock of the East India Company, and by the collapse of the Ayr Bank (Douglas, Heron & Co.). Numerous complex details are involved, including the political reverses of the East India Company, its credit being restricted by the Bank of England; the practice of the thrusting new Ayr Bank (which was left the bad loans by the established banks) in borrowing from London when its acceptances came due; and the flight in July 1772 of Alexander Fordyce, who had lost his firm's money selling East India Company stock prematurely. When the stock actually fell in the fall of the year, Clifford & Co., the Dutch banker which had headed a syndicate trying to push the price up, went under. These phenomena seem superficial, however. Heavy investment in Britain in houses, turnpikes, canals, and other public works had put a strain on resources and unleashed the excess credit.[60] A source I have been unable to check relates the fall in coffee prices beginning in 1770 to the financial crisis of 1772–73,[61] but this is not mentioned by Wilson, the standard source, or by Ashton, Clapham, or Buist.[62]

In 1793 there were several causes: country banks, canals, the Reign of Terror that stimulated an initial flow of capital to Britain, and bad harvests. In 1799 there was one cause, the tightening and loosening of the blockade. Contrarywise, the crisis of 1809–10 is said to have had "two separate causes:

a reaction from the speculation in South America and a loosening and then tightening of the continental blockade."[63]

In 1815–16 came a postwar boom of exporting to Europe and the United States which exceeded all possibility of sales, plus a fall in the price of wheat. Canals and South American government bonds and mines combined in 1825; British exports, cotton, land sales in the United States, and the beginning of the railroad mania contributed to the crisis in the mid-1830s. The crisis of 1847 had the railway mania, the potato disease, a wheat crop failure one year and a bumper crop the next, followed on the Continent by revolution.

One could go on, but the recital is wearisome. In most of the significant crises at least two objects of speculation were involved, and (as will be seen in Chapter 7) at least two markets. Just as the national markets were interconnected, so the speculation was likely to be, if only by the underlying credit conditions. But when a crisis like that of 1847 arises from objects as disparate as railroads and wheat, there is some basis for suggesting that the crisis is accidental in origin, unless the monetary weakness which feeds it is systematic.

National Differences in Speculative Temperament

Before we close our discussion of speculative manias, we should perhaps nod to the suggestion that one country is more inclined to speculate than another. The proposition is dubious, rather on a level with the view in Europe of venereal diseases as characteristic of a neighboring nation, e.g., "the French disease," "the English disease," "the Italian disease," etc. There may be something to the notion that banking institutions give more play to speculation in one country than in another. Juglar for example claims the French crises in the eighteenth century were less abrupt and less violent than those of Great Britain because (after the John Law affair) credit in France was less used and less abused.[64] A different view ascribes French experience to a severe bankruptcy law:

Whether by the educating forces of law and established institutions, or by tradition, a high standard of business honesty prevails in France. The act of sons in toiling for years to pay the debts of their fathers, and of notaries in paying for the defalcations of one of their number, for the sake of the profession, although without personal association with him, indicates a standard of compliance with business obligations which cannot be without influence upon the material prosperity of a people. It may be surprising that the nation whose soldiers are so noted for dash in war should furnish financiers and business men who are the embodiment of conservatism in their methods, but such is clearly the case.

This same author goes on to say:

England is the country in which a spirit of adventure and speculation has done most to promote crises and depressions.[65]

A common view is that the United States is "the classic home of commercial and financial panics," presumably because of wildcat banking.[66] But apart from especially permissive institutions, it is easy to find abundant and contradictory views on the demand side for other countries also: love of gambling lies deep in the Dutch character.[67] "The French nation is prudent and economical, the English nation is enterprising and speculative."[68] "The character of this nation [Britain] is in carrying everything to excess . . . virtue, vice."[69] After 1866, a new arrogance was said to have taken hold of the Germans, but they surpassed the French only in "stockmarket swindling and speculation horrors."[70] Morgenstern finds ten panics in France, exceeding by two even the United States, which is "not surprising, given the unstable character of French politics."[71] (To be sure, this addresses displacements rather than love of speculation.) Contrast, however, the opinion of a French financier who claims that "the French love money not for the possibilities of action which it opens, but for the income it assures."[72] Or consider two views, at the level of a Harvard-Yale debate, from a fictional Frenchman and an Englishman in 1931:

WILLIAM BERTILLION: England's such a Christmas tree for share-pushers. Noble lords will sit on the board of any company for a couple of quid a sitting. And the public. Loco or idiotic. God, I've never heard of such people, except perhaps some peasants in Bessarabia, or the niggers in the Cameroons, who believe in what they believe in. Magic. Put up any sort of business that sounds utterly impossible and they gulp it down.[73]

STEWART: England's the world's banker. Never failed yet, never failed yet. She keeps her word, that's why. . . . None of this—none of this speculation you get in the American stock market. Every Tom, Dick and Harry trying to make a pile—like in France.[74]

It's a standoff. The speculative temperament may differ among countries. One thinks of the Danes, for example, as phlegmatic and not particularly inclined to take risks. Levels of speculation may also differ from time to time for a given country, say, in moods of national elation or depression. We recognize the possibilities, but abstain from trying to fit them into our framework.

CHAPTER 4

Fueling the Flames:
Monetary Expansion

Speculative manias gather speed through expansion of money and credit or perhaps, in some cases, get started because of an initial expansion of money and credit. One can look back at particular manias followed by crashes or panics and see what went wrong. In the Lübeck crisis early in the seventeenth century—too early for us to pay it any but passing attention —the monetary expansion came from clipping and counterfeiting, the so-called *Kipper und Wipper* period.[1] John Law had his Banque Générale, later the Banque Royale; the South Sea Company the Sword Blade Bank. In 1763, Dutch expansion was financed by the unpronounceable *Wisselruitij*, or chains of accommodation bills; the canal mania of 1793 in Britain, by a sudden explosion of country banks. In 1825 it was country banks again. The 1830s saw the formation of joint-stock banking in Britain, after the banking legislation of 1826 and 1833. In the United States, monetary expansion came less from operations of the Second Bank of the United States, it is claimed, than from substitution of bills of exchange for silver in triangular trade between the United States, China, and Britain. Instead of buying silver from Mexico and shipping it to China, which sent it on to Britain, thus paying in turn for U.S. net imports from China and Chinese net imports from England, American merchants sent sterling bills to the Orient in payment for goods, releasing silver to add to monetary stocks and stimulating inflation in the United States.[2]

The boom of the 1850s was built on gold discoveries, banking formation in Britain, France, Germany, and the United States, and the institution of a clearinghouse in New York and extension of an existing one in London. Additionally, the Bank Act of 1844 went wrong when it failed to limit deposits as well as currency. In 1866 in Britain, the problem was extension of the discount market through joint-stock discount houses. Boom in Central Europe rested on gold payments in the Franco-Prussian indemnity, creation of *Maklerbanken* (brokers' banks) in Germany, which then spread into Austria, and *Baubanken* (construction banks) in Austria, which then pushed their way into Germany.

In 1882 in France, expansion came from a system of fortnightly clearing of stock-exchange transactions; this gave speculators credit through a system of *reportage*, much as the call-money market in New York helped finance the stock market boom in 1929.[3] In 1893 in the United States, the catalyst was silver coinage; in 1907, expansion of trust companies. In the years before and after World War I, the international credit base was expanded by the gold-exchange standard. The 1920s also saw development of installment credit. After World War II, new bases for credit were found in credit, negotiable certificates of deposit (CDs), the Euro-currency market, and, more generally, what came to be known as "liability management" in contrast to the management of bank assets.[4] (Actually, something very much akin to the negotiable CD was issued by Austrian banks in the 1870 boom: the so-called *Cassenscheine*, which bore interest and permitted further expansion on the same reserve base.)[5]

When the list is assembled in this fashion, we can see that what we have is not just a series of accidents. The form each event takes may be accidental—the substitution of commercial acceptances for silver in payment to China, or the development of deposits after the Bank Act of 1844 to frustrate the intention of the Currency School to limit the money supply—but the continuous process is not. Monetary expansion is systematic and endogenous rather than random and exogenous.

The fact of the matter is that money, defined as means of payment in actual use, has been continuously expanded, and existing money has been used ever more efficiently in periods of boom to finance expansion, including speculation. This has occurred despite efforts of banking authorities to control and limit the money supply. Such efforts have a long history. They include the resumption of specie payments and convertibility after wars (until the period of floating that began in 1973). Then there is the demonetization of lesser metallic monies—copper displaced by silver and silver displaced by gold. Again, central banks sought and obtained a monopoly of the note issue, restricting and finally eliminating the right of private, country, and joint-stock (corporate) banks to issue currency. Legislation and custom limited the amounts of deposit money that could be issued against primary reserves, starting shortly after the Bank Act of 1844 and continuing through the application by the Federal Reserve System of reserve requirements against not only demand and time deposits (as embodied in the original Reserve Act of 1913) but ultimately also certificates of deposit and borrowings by U.S. banks from the Eurocurrency market. The process is Sisyphean, a *perpetuum mobile*, akin to efforts at tax reform in which lawyers seek out tax loopholes, Congress and the IRS block them up, and the tax lawyers carve out new ones.

Currency School vs. Banking School

In the history of monetary theory, a running battle has taken place between the Currency School and the Banking School, as they were called when the argument blew up in 1810 over the Bullion Report. Today the Currency School is roughly that of the "monetarists," while the Banking School is even more loosely congruent with the Keynesians. In the 1890s in the United States, more or less the same breakdown in ideology and economic analysis separated the hard-money school from the Populists. In the eyes of most economists, the Currency School of 1810 won a clear intellectual victory over its opposition. In the present context, however, this is an oversimplification. The two schools are locked in dialectical symbiosis. Coexisting at least since the seventeenth century, and probably even earlier, the conflict continues today.

The distinction, and sometimes the clash, between forces seeking to limit the money supply (the Currency School) and those wanting or at least acting to expand it (the Banking School) goes back at least 100 years before the opening of our period of interest, and 200 years before the two schools were recognized as antithetical. Some institutions rendered a given supply of money more efficient. Others expanded it. For example, the Bank of Amsterdam, started in 1609, was a giro-bank. It issued notes against deposits of metal, but performed no credit operations until finally in the next century it misguidedly and fatally came to the rescue of the Dutch East India Company. In 1614 a Bank of Lending (*Huys van Leening*) was established by the Municipality of Amsterdam, but it was relatively inactive and unimportant. The Bank of Amsterdam was not only a giro-bank: it was also a *Wisselbank*, where bills of exchange (*Wissel* in Dutch, *Wechsel* in German) were paid. Merchants had to keep deposits there to meet bills presented for collection. Deposits in precious metal enabled the Bank of Amsterdam to earn seignorage on mint-

ing, so that it paid a low rate of interest on deposit. The
Bank issued no credit, and the *Huys van Leening* very little,
but they enabled merchants efficiently to establish their own
credit.[6] It was this credit of merchants, expanding excessively
in the *Wisselruitij*, that brought down the DeNeufville firm in
1763 when the chain of bills of exchange snapped.

The Swedish Riksbank, established in 1668, foreshadows
the Bank Act of 1844 in Britain, since it had two departments,
a Bank of Exchange patterned after the Bank of Amsterdam
(*Wisselbank*) and a Bank of Lending (*Länebank*).[7] In the
Bank of England in 1844 these became the Issue Department,
which issued bank notes against deposits of coin or bullion,
above a specified fiduciary issue representing government
debt, and the Banking Department, which made loans and
discounts up to a multiple of its reserves of bank notes put
out by the Issue Department. The whole represented a compromise between the Currency and Banking schools. The Issue
Department was a victory for the Currency School, which had
criticized the Bank of England's granting of loans and issuance
of bank notes during the period of suspension of the gold
standard after 1797. (The Bank's defense, that in giving loans
to finance trade it was not increasing inflation, was scathingly
rejected by Ricardo and the Currency School.) The Banking
Department meant a limited victory for the Banking School,
and for those who agree with it that credit is needed in the
early stages of a recovery to finance at least the initial
upswing.

If the Banking School was right on the need for credit expansion to make a start in economic expansion, the Currency
School was surely correct in observing that credit creation
based thereafter on ongoing business opportunities is a
formula for disaster. The "real-bills" doctrine urged that
discounts be limited to acceptances covering actual commercial
transactions, so as to forestall the expansion of promissory
notes. The more commerce, the more discounting and the more
inflation. The Currency School recognized the need for a limit.

We leave until later the rather muddy issue between the two schools over whether it was useful to lend in a crisis. The present question is whether it is practicable, once expansion of credit has started, to decree a stopping place, and whether this can be done by automatic rule.

The Currency School said yes, it wanted a simple rule just as monetarists today want a simple rule that would fix the growth rate of the money supply at 2 or 4 or 5 percent.[8] Viner's discussion of the nineteenth-century controversy is succinct:

The currency school tended also to minimize or to deny the importance of bank credit in other forms than notes as a factor affecting prices, or as in the case of Torrens, to claim that the fluctuations in the deposits were governed closely by the fluctuations in the note issues. They had a hankering also for a simple automatic rule, and could find none suitable for governing the general credit operations of the Bank. They also had laissez faire objections to extending legislative control of the banking system any further than seemed absolutely necessary.[9]

The problem is that "money" is an elusive construct, difficult to pin down and to fix in some desired quantity for the economy. As a historical generalization, it can be said that every time the authorities stabilize or control some quantity of money M, either in absolute volume or growing along a predetermined trend line, in moments of euphoria more will be produced. Or if the definition of money is fixed in terms of particular liquid assets, and the euphoria happens to "monetize" credit in new ways that are excluded from the definition, the amount of money defined in the old way will not grow, but its velocity will increase (velocity being defined either as total spending or national income—whichever one chooses—divided by the money supply). Modern monetarists have difficulty in deciding whether they should define money as M_1, currency plus demand deposits adjusted; M_2, equal to M_1 plus time deposits; M_3, consisting of M_2 plus highly liquid government securities; or some other designation. I am told that some analysts have gone as high as M_7. My contention is that the process is endless: fix any M_i and the market will create new forms of money in periods of boom to get around the limit and create the necessity to fix a new variable M_j.

The Radcliffe Commission in Britain in 1959 claimed that in a developed economy there is "an indefinitely wide range of financial institutions," and "many highly liquid assets which are close substitutes for money, as good to hold, and only inferior when the actual moment for a payment arrives." The Commission did not use the concept of velocity of money because it "could not find any reason for supposing, or any experience in monetary history indicating, that there is any limit to the velocity of circulation."[10] What interested the Commission most was the suggestion that an attempt be made to substitute for the traditional control of the money supply a complex of controls of that wide range of financial institutions:

Such a prospect would be unwelcome except as a last resort, not mainly because of its administrative burdens, but because the further growth of new financial institutions would allow the situation continually to slip out from under the grip of the authorities.[11]

It is useless to debate what items should be included in "money," as economists have done for much more than a century:

In common parlance, *bank currency* means *circulating bank notes* —"paper money." Yet, it would seem that some writers include under the same head, checks and *promissory notes*, if not also loans and deposits. (Italics in original.)[12]

The matter was neatly put by John Stuart Mill:

The purchasing power of an individual at any moment is not measured by the money actually in his pocket, whether we mean by money the metals, or include bank notes. It consists, first, of the money in his possession; secondly, of the money at his banker's, and all other money due him and payable on demand; thirdly of whatever credit he happens to possess.[13]

There are problems in going from the purchasing power of the individual to that of a country, since credit for one individual may or may not subtract from that available to others, depending upon banking institutions on the one hand, and euphoria on the other. On credit, the novelists perhaps deserve a say:

Beautiful credit! The foundation of modern society. Who shall say this is not the age of mutual trust, of unlimited reliance on human promises? That is a peculiar condition of modern society which enables a whole country to instantly recognize point and meaning to the familiar newspaper anecdote, which puts into the speculator in lands and mines this remark: "I wasn't worth a cent two years ago, and now I owe two million dollars."[14]

It would be tiresome to support these generalizations by going through the historical development of close money substitutes that monetize credit. Out of a long list we shall deal only with bills of exchange, call money, and the gold-exchange standard. But the analysis could apply equally well to bank notes, bank deposits, clearinghouses, specialized banks (e.g., banques d'affaires, *Maklerbanken*, or *Baubanken*), trust companies, negotiable CDs, the Eurocurrency market, installment credit, credit cards, NOW accounts, and so on.

Bills of Exchange

Bank notes, representing promises to pay on demand, and bills of exchange, consisting of claims for payment in the future made by a seller of goods on the buyer, were initially developed because of an inelastic supply of coin.* Bills of exchange

---

* Alfred Marshall noted that paper money was used in China 2,000 years before his writing and the apt term "flying money" was given there to bills of exchange 1,000 years ago. See Appendix E, "Notes on the Development of Banking, with Special Reference to English Experience," in *Money, Credit and Commerce* (1923; New York: Augustus M. Kelley, 1965), p. 305n.

were frequently discounted with banks and converted into bank notes or coin (not deposits until the nineteenth century). They were often used in payment directly. The drawer passed it on, and so did the recipient. "The bill was now money." Even if some of the parties to it should be men of doubtful credit, says Ashton, it would still circulate.[15] In the first half of the nineteenth century, some bills for as little as £10 circulated with fifty or sixty names on them. Payment habits differed. Bank notes were disliked in Lancashire, and the money supply there around the turn of the nineteenth century consisted of coin and bills of exchange.[16] Bank of England note circulation declined by £9 million from 1852 to 1857, a period of expansion. Deposits of five banks in London rose from £17.7 million to £40 million. The average volume of bills of exchange in circulation, however, expanded over the same period from £66 million to £200 million, according to the contemporary estimates of Newmarch.[17]

Bills of exchange were not necessarily drawn each time a consignment of goods took place, covering the exact amount of the transaction. In 1763, in Sweden, Carlos and Claes Grill bills on Lindegren in London could not be identified with particular shipments, which were often made in rapid succession, but were drawn when the firm needed money, generally for remittances to creditors.[18] This would seem to be the evolution of accommodation paper, in which the credit of a house or individual is gradually separated from that of particular transactions. In the end, the accommodation bill was nothing more than an I.O.U. or promissory note. Real-bill partisans, like H. Parker Willis of Columbia University and his teacher J. Laurence Laughlin of Chicago, were firmly opposed to "accommodation paper" and regarded commercial bills based on trade as self-liquidating.* In a period of falling

---

* For an early example of such attitudes, see the hypothetical discussion of the board of directors at a New York bank in the 1850s by James S. Gibbons, *The Banks of New York, Their Dealers, the Clearing House, and the Panic of 1857* (New York: D. Appleton, 1859), p. 50.

prices, however, the merits of the "virtuous" bill drawn by the seller on a buyer are exaggerated. The buyer may be unable to move the goods at a profit, and hence unable to meet his obligation.[19] Of much greater interest is the ratio of the debt to the debtor's wealth.

The bill of credit, as Franklin said, is

> found very convenient in Business; because a great Sum is more easily counted in them, lighter in Carriage, concealed in less Room, and therefore safer in Travelling or Laying Up, and on many other Accounts they are very much valued. The Banks are the General Cashiers of all Gentlemen, Merchants and Great Traders. . . . This gives Bills a Credit; so that in *England* they are never less valuable than Money, and in *Venice* and *Amsterdam* they are generally more so. . . .[20]

The suggestion that in England bills were "never less valuable than Money" is somewhat optimistic, as we shall see, but the efficiency of bills when they were as good as money is clear. During the first half of the nineteenth century there was a continuous debate as to whether bills of exchange were "money," "means of payment," or "purchasing power," but all members of the Currency School agreed that only bank notes need be controlled, and not bills of exchange or bank deposits.[21]

A director is pleading the loan application of a Mr. Black, "rich beyond a contingency," who wants to build a new house on Fifth Avenue for $60,000 and to spend $40,000 to furnish it, and proposes expanding his firm's discount line at the bank by the whole amount. Another director objects:

> "Mr. President, my notion is, that we have no right to discount any thing at the Board but a *bona fide* commercial note that will be paid when due. And on top of that the indorser must be able to take it up himself, if the drawer should fail or die. Don't you see that we are discounting this paper to pay for Mr. Black's house and furniture, just for his single enjoyment? This isn't commercial paper, sir! It's accommodation paper in the true sense."

Gibbons's book, with chapters on the various tasks in a bank, is a mid-nineteenth-century precursor to Martin Mayer's *The Bankers* (New York: Ballantine Book, 1974).

The problem arises where the ratio of the debt represented by the bill to the debtor's wealth gets out of hand, as may happen in periods of euphoria. Drawing of bills in chains is evidently infectious. Described by Adam Smith as a normal business practice, it can easily be overdone.[22] A draws on B, B on C, C on D, and so on; all increase the amount of credit available for use. The vice of the accommodation or finance bill, according to Hawtrey, is its "use for construction of fixed capital when the necessary supply of bona-fide long-run savings cannot be obtained from the investment market." He claims the system was particularly abused in the London crisis of 1866 and the New York crisis of 1907.[23] We have already noted that the spectacular failure of the DeNeufvilles in 1763, which produced panic in Hamburg, Berlin, and (to a lesser extent) London as well as Amsterdam, was the result of the unraveling of a particularly impressive chain of discounts. If one house fails, the chain collapses and may bring down good names, those with a reasonable ratio of debt to capital, as well as bad. With accommodation bills, traders with limited capital of their own are able to acquire the use, at least temporarily of large volumes of borrowed funds, a use they may try to stretch into longer term. Sir Francis Baring knew of clerks not worth £100 who were allowed discounts of £5,000 to £10,000. This was about 1808, during the period of suspension of the gold standard, when the lack of a need to watch the exchanges played an active role in the "phrenzy of speculation," and incidentally instructed the Currency School.[24] In 1857, John Ball, a London accountant, reported knowing firms with capital of under £10,000 and obligations of £900,000, and claimed it was a fair illustration.[25] In Hamburg during the same boom, Schäffle reported on a man with a capital of £100 and £400,000 worth of acceptances outstanding.[26] These ratios, if accurate, represent a tremendous jump from the mid-eighteenth century, when many firms, according to Wirth, speculated for ten to twenty times their real capital during the boom of 1763. (He added, however, that many participated in this dangerous undertaking on pure credit, without any capital at all.)[27]

When they were abused, finance or accommodation bills gave rise to excessive credit expansion. At all stages, fictitious names were introduced into the chain from time to time, to improve the appearance of creditworthiness. From time to time, also, such bills were written for odd amounts, to suggest an underlying commercial transaction. And when this was done, claims were sometimes made (e.g., by German banks drawing on Dutch banks after the halt in American lending) that the banks abroad knew it was finance paper disguised as commercial bills.[28]

It has been held, on occasion, that the movement from bills of exchange to a system wherein international money consisted almost entirely of deposits markedly changed the world of finance. The late Harry Johnson, for example, wrote me in 1976, when we were debating privately the significance of the role of the lender of last resort, that there may have been a justification for such a lender in a world of bills of exchange, but not in the modern period, when international finance is largely conducted through foreign deposits. Schumpeter claimed that the Bank of England could work on a very small margin of reserves because of the mass of foreign short-term claims in bills, estimated by Hartly Withers in 1909 at £150–£200 million.[29] We shall postpone discussion of this issue until later. There is no obvious a priori basis for these assertions.

Call Money

For call money, take the crashes of 1882 and 1929. The crash of 1882 in France is not well known, and had limited repercussions outside the country. However, as described in a superb book by Jean Bouvier, it was a classic mania and panic, financed by call money or money lent to brokers by bankers "on call", that is for one day (in French, *reports*).[30]

The Union Générale was a bank started by one Eugene Bontoux, an engineer who had worked with Rothschild and then left to initiate rival operations in Austria, Serbia, and southeastern Europe. An early Union Générale, begun in 1875, did badly. Bontoux started his in Paris in 1878 as France was entering a boom based on railroads, banks, and the Suez Canal. The boom peaked in December 1881; crash came in January 1882. Bouvier's interest lies in whether Bontoux, a Catholic, failed of his own mistakes or was done in by a conspiracy of establishment Jewish and Protestant bankers, resisting an intruder. The subject lies outside our purview, but for the record, Bouvier issues a Scottish verdict of "not proven."

Bontoux's Union Générale was capitalized at 25 million francs, increased in the spring of 1879 to 50 million, and a second time in January 1881 to 100 million; a third increase, planned for January 1882, would have raised the capital to 150 million. The initial capital was only one-fourth paid in.* With each increase in capital, a premium was required above the 500 francs par, to be paid into the reserves of the bank to take account of the rise of the stock in the market. These

---

* After the bank's dissolution, the French prosecutor of Bontoux wrote that there had been grave irregularities in the issuance of the shares and in the increases in capital. Subscriptions to the capital had been made by the bank both in its own name and in the names of fictitious client subscribers. A rival bank, the Banque de Lyon et de la Loire, formed in April 1881 with a capital of 25 million francs (raised to 50 million in November), and with one-quarter of its capital theoretically paid in, was similarly a bubble. Of 50,000 shares originally issued, more than half had not paid amounts due, and the bank had less than half of the 6.5 million francs of capital claimed at the outset.

The Union Générale also bought its own securities in the open market, and, as we shall see, loaned money to others to buy them. (See Jean Bouvier, *Le Krach de l'Union Générale, 1878–1885* [Paris: Presses universitaires de France, 1960], pp. 123, 164–65, 167.)

premiums were 20, 175, and 250 francs, respectively. Shares
were registered in the names of individuals rather than payable to bearer, because of the three-quarters of par value still
owed on them, but this did not prevent roughly half of the
200,000 original shares from floating in the trading market.

Both in Paris and in Lyons, trading in securities was conducted through fortnightly settlements. A purchaser would
pay 10 percent down, borrow 90 percent from an *agent de
change*, or broker, who in turn borrowed from the market for
reports. Money was invested in *reports* by banks, by special
caisses (funds created especially by banks and other investors
for this outlet), and by individuals. A bank and *caisse*, moreover, could favor brokers who specialized in trading in a
particular stock. Thus, banks such as the Union Générale and
the Banque de Lyon et de la Loire—not to mention three or
four even less successful, if less spectacular, banks, created
during the boom—could support their own stock indirectly.
When the market was steady, speculators made gains and
losses, and brokers would typically pay out or receive very
little net, assuming that speculators were working on roughly
the same margin, e.g., 10 percent. In a rising market, however,
more funds were needed to pay off realized profits. These
often were reinvested in the market, but if they were not
reinvested, the market needed more capital. Assume a speculator bought a share at 100, paying 10 down and borrowing
90. If he sold at 110 and took out his 20 francs, 11 of this
would come from the new speculator, and 9 had to be new
reports. As the market rose, therefore, the call-money rate
(*taux des reports*) had to rise to attract new money. In Paris
during this period it went from 4–5 percent at the end of 1880
to 8–10 percent in the spring of 1881, reaching a peak of
10–12 percent in the autumn of 1881.[31]

When the market turned down, fresh money also was required, this time from the speculator. If he bought a share
at 100, for 10 down and 90 in *reports*, and it then fell to 90,

he had to produce 9 more francs to be even with the 10 percent requirement. If he had been fully leveraged earlier, and lacked the 9 francs extra, he was sold out. If the price dropped below 90, the broker, bank, or individual that had loaned to him lost money. The stock of the Union Générale went from 1,250 francs in March 1881 to a peak of 3,040 on December 14, as the mania gathered speed in the autumn. Thereafter followed a period of distress, with quotations at 2,950 on January 10, 1882, and 2,800 on January 16. On January 19 it fell to 1,300. Brokers lacked 18 million francs on that day, as speculators could not produce the cash needed to meet requirements, and were 33 million short when it came to the month-end liquidation on January 31.[32]

The Banque de Lyon et de la Loire had a more spectacular collapse: from a peak of 1,765 francs on December 17, 1881, to 1,550 on December 28, when it was supporting its own stock, to 1,040 on January 4, 650 on January 10, and finally 400 on January 19, the day after it closed its doors.[33] The signal for the collapse of the Banque de Lyon et de la Loire was the victory of Bontoux over Savary in getting the right to found a Banque de Crédit Maritime at Trieste, announced January 4, 1882. Like the success of the South Sea Company in destroying its rival Billingsley, with his bubbles in York Buildings and Welsh copper, the coup boomeranged.[34] People in trouble on Banque de Lyon et de la Loire sold off Union Générale. The combination of highly geared speculation and a credit mechanism resting on bank and personal credit recycled through call loans spread collapse among banks, *caisses*, brokers, individuals, and businesses in a matter of days. Business, it should be noted, was adversely affected in advance of the stock market collapse, as in 1929, not because of a change in the money supply but because at the peak of the fever the business world of Lyons turned to speculate in Union Générale: "silk merchants, cloth manufacturers, industrialists, tradesmen, dry-goods merchants, grocers, butchers, people with fixed incomes, janitors, shoemakers."[35] "A lot of capital was diverted from regular business to be invested in the stock market, either in securities or in call money."[36]

Readers familiar with the stock market crash of 1929 will recognize in the foregoing account a host of points of similarity: preoccupation with speculation and a decline in business as the stock market approached its apex; the role of brokers' loans by banks and by individuals, which provided the basis for driving securities prices way up, and letting them fall way down, without significant changes in the money supply. There was a major difference in that new banks were not created on any large scale in 1928 and 1929 to act as both objects and instruments of speculation. One similarity of interest may be observed, however. As the stock market reached its height, call loans of "all others," as opposed to New York banks and banks outside New York, went up from just under $2 billion at the end of 1926 to $3,885,000,000 on December 31, 1928, and $6,640,000,000 on October 4, 1929. Meanwhile, brokers' loans of New York banks declined from $1,640,000,-000 at their height at the end of 1928 to $1,095,000,000 on October 4, 1929.[37] With the crash, "all others" and banks outside New York, took call funds out of the market. They were fearful that the Stock Exchange might be closed as it had been in 1873, which would have frozen their hitherto liquid day-to-day loans.[38] At this stage, New York banks maintained and even slightly increased their brokers' loans in a declining market, presumably to help arrest the decline. Similarly, in 1882, one consortium of Paris banks, headed by the Banque de Paris et des Pays-Bas (*Parisbas*) advanced 18 million francs in five credits to the Union Générale directly, while another group, headed by the Rothschild house, loaned 80 million francs to the company of brokers to get them through the end-of-January settlement, and to give them and their clients time to work out arrangements.[39] In both crises there were many bankruptcies of brokers, clients, and (in

1882) banks and their *caisses*. The central money-market banks eased the adjustment, but in Paris in 1882 they stopped well short of saving the Union Générale.

The Gold-Exchange Standard

Our third illustration of the virtually infinite set of possibilities for expanding credit on a fixed money base is international in character. It is the gold-exchange standard, or the system of adding to international central-bank reserves with a fixed world gold stock by counting in them not only gold holdings but also holdings of foreign exchange against countries that adhere to the gold standard. The system was long thought to have been a post–World War I development, based on the recommendations of the Genoa Conference of 1922 and of the Gold Delegation of the League of Nations, and pushed hard by Governor Montagu Norman of the Bank of England, who sought to expand world holdings of the pound sterling as relief for the British balance of payments. However, the gold-exchange standard has recently been shown to have flourished before the war.[40] It seems likely that the boom in world lending of 1913–14, which ended in war rather than in a panic or crash, was financed by increasing world holdings of sterling, francs, and marks.

Just as bank notes and bills of exchange are more efficient monies than coin, so foreign balances dominate bullion under stable conditions, being easier to use in transactions, free of the need for transport, safeguarding, and assay, and directly useful without conversion into national money. Unpleasant remarks have been made about the gold-exchange standard, notably by Triffin[41] and Rueff.[42] It has been called "absurd," a "swindle," "exploitative," and so on. Clearly, a gold-exchange standard does lend itself to credit expansion, like bank notes, bills of exchange, call money, credit cards, negotiable certificates of deposit, etc. A country can borrow reserves by selling bonds in a foreign market such as London or New York, and then holding the resulting sterling or dollars as part of its central-bank reserves. If London (or New York, as the case many be) does not regard the increase in the liquid claims owed by it to the foreign long-term borrower as a reason for contracting its own credit superstructure, this financial intermediation, like all others, permits expansion of credit, despite the adoption of a Currency School rule of a fixed money supply, or basing the world monetary system on gold.

It must be borne in mind, however, that international lending on the gold standard may have the same unstable character as the gold-exchange standard. Before countries borrowed foreign balances as reserves for domestic monetary expansion, they borrowed gold. Jeffry Williamson has observed that during the nineteenth century, the United States borrowed in Britain during upswings, not only to acquire real capital in the form of imports, but also to enlarge the gold base of the American banking system. Our understanding of the role of gold in international lending, as derived from Frank W. Taussig and his students who worked on the transfer problem, was faulty. Gold not only performed an instrumental role in helping with the transfer of real goods and services; to a considerable extent it was the object of borrowing, and enabled the borrower to expand its credit without inducing contraction in the lender.[43]

Instability of Credit and the Great Depression

The notion that speculation leading to manias and crashes rests on an inherent instability of credit is an old one. Alvin Hansen, writing on business cycles, treats it at length in a general survey of "early concepts," and in a chapter on mid-nineteenth century economists—John Stuart Mill, John Mills, and Alfred Marshall—entitled "Confidence and Credit."[44] In his judgment, these views are obsolete because they neglect the investment and savings decisions of large firms. Perhaps. But theories which attach importance to the instability of credit persist well into the twentieth century. Hawtrey is a classic economist in this vein, and so is A. C. Pigou, whose book *Industrial Fluctuations* (1927) has a chapter dealing with panics.[45] Neglect of the instability of credit began by and large with the depression of the 1930s, with the Currency and Banking schools converted into monetarists and Keynesians.

The monetarist view of the Great Depression is set out in a monumental work by Milton Friedman and Anna Schwartz who maintain that the depression was the result of mistakes in monetary policy made by the Federal Reserve System. For the most part, they focus on the decline in the money supply from August 1929 to March 1933. Whenever the question turns on the start of the depression, the point is made that the money supply did not increase in the years 1928 to 1929, or that it fell 2.6 percent from August 1929 to October 1930, when it should have increased. Friedman and Schwartz contend that the stock market crash of October 1929 had little or nothing to do with the intensity of the decline in output, and that the depression was the consequence of domestic policies in the United States, having only a tangential connection with international capital movements, exchange rates, or deflation abroad.[46] This monetarist view of the depression has held sway in the United States ever since the appearance of the Friedman and Schwartz book.[47]

A recent study by Peter Temin takes issue with Friedman and Schwartz from a Keynesian point of view.[48] He asks whether the decline in spending resulted from a decline in the money supply or the other way round, and he tries to decide the question on the basis of sophisticated econometrics. Much of the argument runs in terms of how much consumption deviated from what one might have forecast it to be, giving rise to a technical debate about what consumption depended upon in the U.S. economy of the 1920s, and what relationships among consumption, income, wealth, and similar variables one should specify in forecasting a "normal" trend in consumption. Further argument involves the behavior of the rate of interest: if the change in money precedes the change in spending, one would expect the interest rate to rise, whereas if spending declines in advance, the rate of interest falls. As it happened, interest rates declined sharply after the 1929 crash, except for instruments like second-grade bonds, which measure not the rate of interest but confidence.[49] Still another argument turns on "real" as against nominal balances, i.e., money stocks deflated by the price level, representing real purchasing power. Most monetary analysis deals with the money supply over time on a deflated basis, rather than in nominal amounts, i.e., with real instead of nominal balances. Temin concludes that real balances did not decline.[50] On his showing, they went up between 1929 and 1931 by varying amounts ranging from 1 to 18 percent, depending upon whether one chooses M_1 or M_2 and a wholesale or consumer price index. Annual averages further dampen the movement; on the basis of monthly figures, and averaging M_1 and M_2 expressed as percentages or relatives of a base year and of the two price indexes, the money supply not only did not decline but actually increased 5 percent between August 1929 and August 1931, if we use the same month to minimize seasonal influences. Temin concludes there is no evidence that money caused the depression between the stock market crash and the British departure from the gold standard in September 1931. By implication, autonomous changes in consumption or investment were responsible.

This may dispose of Friedman and Schwartz, but it fails to explain the depression. One of Temin's students has helped by giving an increased role to the stock market crash. The decline in the market reduced nominal wealth, which together with income explains consumption.[51] This amounts to shifting emphasis from income to wealth in the consumption function.

The difficulty with all these lines of reasoning, however, is the speed with which the collapse of production took place, and the fact that it began well before the stock market crash. Industrial production fell from 127 in June to 122 in September, 117 in October, 106 in November, and 99 in December. Specifically, automobile production declined from 660,000 units in March 1929 to 440,000 in August, 416,000 in September, 319,000 in October, 169,500 in November, and 92,500 in December. No quantity theory of money or autonomous shift in spending, with or without a decline in the stock market, can account for these precipitous movements. They require an old-fashioned theory of the instability of the credit system. As the stock market moved toward its apex, call money rose from $6.4 billion at the end of December 1928 to $8.5 billion in early October. Funds were diverted from consumption and production. Moreover, first New York banks and then outside banks held back in lending to the stock market and elsewhere. When the crash came, the credit system suddenly froze. Lending on imports, for example, seems to have come to a complete stop, with a precipitous decline in the prices of import commodities from September to October, and an overall decline in the value of imports from $400 million to $300 million between September and December 1929.

The monetarist-Keynesian debate leaves little if any room for instability of credit and fragility of the banking system, or impacts on production and prices when the credit system becomes paralyzed through loans rendered bad by falling prices—all of which go far, in my judgment, to explain what happened in the early stages of the 1929 depression. As already noted, this is an old view, held by many economists prior to 1940, that has unaccountably slipped into disrepute during the Keynesian revolution and the monetarist counter-revolution. A notable up-to-date exception is Hyman Minsky.[52]

An earlier one was Henry Simons, the Chicago economist who thought the Great Depression was caused by changes in business confidence, leading through an unstable credit system to changes in liquidity and effects on the money supply. Friedman, who admires Simons, does not agree. He does not believe that the credit system is unstable; his causation runs the other way, starting with the money supply.[53]

Henry Simons's views were set forth in his *Economic Policy for a Free Society*,[54] written after World War II under the strong influence of the depression of the 1930s. As summarized by Friedman, his policy recommendations called for a 100 percent currency reserve against bank deposits, to prevent changes in deposits arising from changes in public willingness to hold currency, and a vigorous effort to stamp out elasticity of credit elsewhere in the system. This would involve restrictions on open-book credit and installment loans, as well as limitation of government debt to non-interest-bearing money at one end of the spectrum and very long-term debt (ideally, perpetual obligations) at the other. Simons advocated a system in which all financial wealth would be held in equity form, with no fixed money contracts, so that no institution that was not a bank could create effective money substitutes. He was concerned about the speculative temper of the community and the ease with which short-term nonbank borrowing and lending made society vulnerable to changes in business confidence.*

Friedman's liberal propensity to let the market decide opposed Simons's recommendations which called for limiting the character of money and financial assets. Friedman favors variety and diversity in money and capital, as in all other markets, and believes it a sign of the ingenuity and efficiency of the free market that financial intermediaries develop to

---

* For a modern statement of the Simons position, see the letter to the *New York Times* of November 7, 1977, under the title "Banking: Our 'Underregulated Creators of Money,'" by Professor Albert G. Hart of Columbia University.

reconcile the needs of borrowers and lenders.[55] He is content to dismiss Simons's prescriptions on this score because he is confident that control of the money supply suffices to prevent major business cycles, and that instability of the credit mechanism is not to be feared—contentions on which this chapter is meant to cast doubt. It is easy to agree with Friedman's skepticism about Simons's positive proposals: however desirable (and there is grave doubt on this score, along the lines Friedman has indicated), they are surely inoperable. For the state to forbid firms and individuals to lend and borrow in fixed money terms is utopian. But Simons's diagnosis of the tendency of the system toward unstable short-term borrowing and repayment is right on target.

The Rate of Interest

In a later chapter we shall discuss the role of the rate of interest in crisis. Here the question is whether it can restrain the instability of credit, slow down speculation, keeping it short of dangerous extension. If the monetary authorities fix some proxy for the money supply, or for liquidity, or if they work directly on the rate of interest itself (for present purposes there is no need to choose among these instrumental variables), can the upswing and decline of the crisis be greatly moderated or eliminated entirely?

I see no a priori way to answer the question of whether a central-bank policy of holding the money supply constant, limiting the liquidity of the money market, or raising the discount rate at the first sign of euphoric speculation would prevent mania leading to crisis, or correct it after it got under way. Moreover, economics cannot conduct carefully controlled experiments. Nor can appeals to history settle the issue conclusively, since they are open to the objection that if the course of action had been somewhat altered, the outcome would have been different. Nevertheless, the weight of the historical evidence strongly favors the case that while monetary policy might have moderated booms leading to bust, it would not have eliminated them all.

The Bank of England was severely attacked for blindness to the approaching crisis in 1839 and for failure to raise interest rates sooner. The general view that it had been dilatory is said, in fact, to have been the proximate cause of the Bank Act of 1844.[56] In the 1850s, the glut of gold reduced interest rates for the years 1852 and 1853. Thereafter the money market became continuously tighter, as the monetarists would have wished, though not tight enough to ward off the severe crisis of 1857.[57] Bill creation kept on rising as the discount rate rose, and declined as it fell, rather than responding to policy changes in the opposite direction, and speculation based on bill creation seems to have been uninhibited by rising discount rates.[58] One Charles Jellico in a paper in 1856 proposed that Bank rate should vary as a function of the Bank of England reserve, to enable the public to have a clear idea of what to expect—a suggestion which Elmer Wood claims shows no grasp of Bank of England transactions.[59] In 1863 and 1864 the Bank twice raised the interest rate to 9 percent. It perhaps delayed but did not prevent the 1866 crash, which is regarded by Juglar as not independent but a violent and inevitable completion of 1864. Liquidation was completed in France in 1864; there were two shakeouts in Britain that year, but the main deflation was delayed.[60] In 1869 the National Bank of Austria-Hungary raised interest rates at the end of July. Its action was too late: a crash in the fall of 1869 came anyhow, a pale imitation of the Great Crash of 1873 in the same city.[61] The bank raised its discount rate again in 1872. At 5 percent for exchange and 6 percent for Lombard loans at the time of the last increase in March 1873, the rate was too low, according to Wirth.[62] In similar fashion, with the same timing and the same absence of result (unless it precipitated the crisis), the Federal Reserve Bank of New York raised its discount rate from 5 to 6 percent on August 9, 1929.

In 1873 the Bank of England, changing its discount rate twenty-four times, had managed to avoid the financial crises which seized Austria and Germany in May and the United States in September. In November the rate was raised to 9 percent to prevent the Germans from drawing out the remaining sterling accumulation left over from the Franco-Prussian indemnity.[63] Whether this represented successful fine-tuning against the possibility of crisis, or merely increasing sensitivity to short-term capital movements, the secondary sources do not make clear.

In the panic of 1907, the preparatory expansion had involved lending in New York by outside banks in historically unknown amounts, along with heavy borrowing by New York in London on accommodation paper—a combination of two of the methods of expansion discussed earlier, if one equates out-of-town banks lending in New York to the gold-exchange standard. (The basis for doing so, of course, is that interbank deposits serve as reserves for the owner of the assets, but not necessarily as a one-for-one claim against reserves of the bank receiving the deposit.) Lacking a central bank, New York could take no discretionary action in interest rates. In London, gold exports as a result of American borrowing led to advances in Bank rate in October 1906, followed by the Bank of England's advice to the market that further acceptance of American finance bills was a menace to stability and unwelcome.[64] This slowed down the boom but failed to prevent the "rich man's panic" of March 1907 and the full-scale panic of October.

It is hard to know what to conclude from this. If central bankers were omniscient and omnipotent, they might be able to use central bank weapons to stabilize the credit system; they could then correct the instability implicit in the infinite expansibility and total collapsibility of credit. But "there are no positive limitations to the expansion of individual credit."[65]

And with financial intermediation at the national and international levels, the same holds true of banking institutions.

Central banking arose to impose control on the instability of credit. The development of central banking from private banking, which is concerned to make money, is a remarkable achievement. By 1825, division of labor had been agreed upon: private bankers of London and the provinces financed the boom, the Bank of England financed the crisis.[66] In the United States, which was without a central bank after 1837, the major banks in New York were in a bind between their roles as profit seekers, which made them contributors to the instability of credit, and as possessors of country deposits against whose instability they had to guard. The short run warred with the long run, the private good with the public. No one chose the New York banks to act responsibly, and it was not clear that it was to their advantage to do so. The problem is a general one in politics, business, the academy, the family, everywhere.

CHAPTER 5

The Emergence of Swindles

Excursion into swindles and other white-collar crimes perhaps takes us away from economic analysis of manias, panics, and the role of the lender of last resort. Nevertheless, it is inescapable. Commercial and financial crises are intimately bound up with transactions that overstep the confines of law and morality, shadowy though those confines be. The propensities to swindle and be swindled run parallel to the propensity to speculate during a boom. Crash and panic, with their motto of *sauve qui peut*, induce still more to cheat in order to save themselves. And the signal for panic is often the revelation of some swindle, theft, embezzlement, or fraud.

As in other aspects of financial crises, the treatment here is qualitative. This time the excuse is better: statistics on swindling are incomplete. Cases that come to light may be only some ill-defined part of the iceberg.

More and more, swindling and the loosely related question of bankruptcy are finding their way into theoretical economics. Some of it takes the name of the archetypal swindler, Charles (Carlo) Ponzi. "Ponzi finance," for example, is defined by Minsky as a type of financial activity engaged in when interest charges of a business unit exceed cash flows from operations.[1]

Another theorist notes that a borrower who has some control over the price in the market in which he issues his own personal debt will want to play the "Ponzi game of financing," i.e., the repayment of debt with the issuance of new debt.[2] This theorist, Martin Hellwig, makes a distinction between commodity markets and money and capital markets, on the ground that a speculator trading in commodities does not have to worry about the risk of bankruptcy, whereas operators in money and financial markets do. This goes too far. When commodity prices fall sharply, loans with commodity collateral leave deficiency judgments against defaulting debtors, who may or may not be able to discharge them. Moreover, swindling in commodities is not unknown, as proved by the McKesson Robbins scandal of the late 1930s, when warehouse receipts used as collateral proved to have been forged, by Billie Sol Estes, the Texas plunger, or by the American Express salad oil incident of the 1960s, when "tanks of salad oil" were filled, except for the top, with water.[3]

We distinguish swindles from ordinary robbery and corruption. Daniel Defoe thought the stock-jobber cheat 10,000 times worse than the highwayman, because he robbed people he knew and ran no physical "risque."[4]* Within the field of white-collar crime, swindles should be distinguished from bribery, whether of government officials by business or of the employees of one business by those of another. The class of illegal and/or immoral transactions in which we are interested involves both misrepresentation and the violation of an ex-

---

* The miser Père Grandet reserved the same opprobrium for the bankrupt: "To fail . . . is to commit theft which the law, unfortunately, takes under its protection. . . . A highway robber is better than a bankrupt: the one attacks you and you can defend yourself, he risks his own life; but the other. . . ." See Honoré de Balzac, *Eugénie Grandet*, trans. K. W. Wormeley (Boston: Roberts, 1891), p. 115. In his *Balzac, les réalités économiques et sociales dans la Comédie Humaine* (Paris: Colin, 1961), Jean Hervé Donnard has a chapter called "Crises, Fraudes et Faillites," followed by one titled "Spéculation" (pt. 2, sec. 1, chaps. 2, 3), underlining the connections between speculation, crises, frauds, and bankruptcies.

plicit or implicit trust. Trust runs not between man and God, or between man and the state, but between particular groups.

Corruption has been discussed historically in a series of articles by Jacob van Klavaren.[5] Much of his interest attaches to corruption as a market transaction, as a way to get things done which are profitable but forbidden, as in black markets, or simply dishonest, such as the looting of India by Clive or Hastings. On the other hand, van Klaveren also discusses the systematic embezzlement from the Royal African Company and the East India Company by insiders who skimmed off profits due to stockholders through contracts with companies they themselves controlled. In a similar manner, the Credit Mobilier in the United States in 1873 diverted profits from Union Pacific stockholders to the inside group run by Oakes Ames, a congressman from Massachusetts, and his Congressional and business cronies. Drew, Fisk, and Gould milked the Erie Railroad in similar fashion.[6]

In this book our interest is mainly in financial markets, in the swindling of stockholders by directors; of investors by securities promoters, including brokers, investment bankers, and underwriters; of firms by employees; and in the case of fictitious names on bills of exchange, of some future, as yet anonymous, recipient of the bill by the drawer.

The line separating moral from immoral acts is a wavery one, which happily has become more distinct with time. Modernity is distinguished from backwardness in many respects, as Gerschenkron has brilliantly shown;[7] one dimension is morality. In early stages of development, codes provided for honor and trust only within the family. In these circumstances, nepotism was efficient, since a stranger had virtually a license to steal. In 1720 a firm could buy a man's services, but not his loyalty; to be a clerk was an invitation to start a new and competitive business at a time when embezzlement and fraudulent conversion were not regarded as crimes.[8] Lines between business and theft, commerce and piracy, were inexact.[9] Hammond notes that it was not until 1799 that the borrowing of bank funds by officials was definitively ruled illegal,[10] although the 1720 House of Commons investigation of the South Sea bubble did rule that the directors of the South Sea Company, having been guilty of a breach of trust in lending money of the Company on its own stock, should make good investor losses out of their own estates.[11]

A financial journalist writing a preface to the fictionalized biography of Ponzi draws a parallel between 1920 and the 1970s, and suggests that swindles are a product of inflation, when the cost of living pinches family budgets and leads heads of households to take risks to add to income.[12] A somewhat different view holds that destabilizing speculation in the absence of "avoidable ignorance" is gambling, which provides utility to the people who indulge it, even when they know they are likely to lose.[13] It is not clear whether swindles should be included in the category "avoidable ignorance." Cynics may share the belief of W. C. Fields that "You can't cheat an honest man" and that victims of swindles have mainly themselves to blame. *Mundus vult decipi—ergo decipitatur*—the world wants to be deceived, let it therefore be deceived.[14] In the view of psychiatry, I am told, swindler and victim are bound together in a symbiotic, love-hate relationship that both find satisfaction in and depend on.

Fraud and the Cycle

We believe that swindling is demand-determined, following Keynes' law that demand determines its own supply, rather than Say's law that supply creates its own demand. In a boom, fortunes are made, individuals wax greedy, and swindlers come forward to exploit that greed. The position is occasionally expressed elsewhere that sheep to be shorn abound, and need only the emergence of effective swindlers to offer themselves as sacrifices: "There's a sucker born every minute." In

Little Dorrit, Ferdinand Barnacle of the Circumlocution Office
tells Arthur Clennam, who had hoped that exposure of Mr.
Merdle's swindles would serve as a warning to dupes, that
"the next man who has as large a capacity and as genuine a
taste for swindling will succeed as well."*

Greed not only creates suckers to be swindled by profes-
sionals but also pushes some of the amateurs over the line
into fraud, embezzlement, defalcation, and similar misfeasance. The demise of Overend, Gurney and Company, the
well-established "Corner House," after the original partners
had retired and the firm had gone public, was brought about
by a pleasure-loving gallant inside the firm who had appointed
an outsider as adviser for £5,000 a year, paid in advance and
returned to the insider. D. W. Chapman, the insider, kept
ten horses and entertained lavishly at Prince's Gate, Hyde
Park. His outside adviser, Edward Watkins Edwards, a former
accountant, recommended all sorts of new activities to be
added to the bread-and-butter discount business: speculation
in grain, production of iron, shipbuilding, shipping, railroad
finance. The firm became "partners in every sort of lock-up
and speculative business," and Edwards drew commissions on
them all. By the end of 1860 the firm was earning £200,000
a year on its discount business, but losing £500,000 a year
net.[15] The bubble was pricked in part by the failure of an
unrelated firm of railway contractors, Watson, Overend and

---

* Dickens' realism, which is brilliant on thieves, workhouses, and
debtors' prisons, does not extend to swindling, in which Trollope, Balzac,
and Zola far surpass him. He continuously mocks Mr. Merdle, "a
name of worldwide repute." His "immense" undertakings "bring him
in such vast sums of money that they are regarded as national benefits
. . . a man of this time . . . the name of the age," but Dickens never
says exactly what he did or what produced his downfall. (Dickens's
distaste for swindling is implicit in Mr. Merdle's name, as may be
understood by those who know French.) In *The Way We Live Now*,
Trollope describes in detail not only Mr. Melmotte's swindles in pro-
moting stock in the Salt Lake City to Vera Cruz railroad, but also his
forgeries, which came from inability to get enough cash to maintain
the value of his stock while he lived well. *Little Dorrit* was inspired by
the 1847 railroad mania, but the manias in it are asserted rather than
described.

Company.[16] (Similarly, it was said that after the fall of the Creditanstalt in Vienna in May 1931, there was a run on German banks by investor-speculators who did not know the difference between Austria and Germany.)

From the world of fiction—in this case, *Melmouth réconcilié*, by Honoré de Balzac—the comparable figure to Chapman is Castanier, a bank cashier, whose mistress, Madame Aquilinia de la Garde, has expensive tastes in silver, linen, crystal, and rugs, passions that prove his undoing. For a time he survives by issuing promissory notes. At the point of no return, when he finally calculates his debts, he might be saved by leaving Mme. de la Garde, but he cannot give her up. Finally, because of the impossibility of continuing his financial maneuvers, given the growth of his debts and the enormity of the interest due, it becomes necessary for him to fail. Even now he prefers fraud to honest bankruptcy and dips into the bank's till.[17]

Let us grant that swindling grows with prosperity. It increases further in financial distress from a taut credit system and prices that stop rising and begin to decline. Ponzi resisted the suggestions of his associates, who in their turn swindled him, that he should take the money and run.[18] Others do not resist. The London banker Henry Fauntleroy forged to keep his bank solvent and was executed for it in 1824. John Sadlier forged conveyances of estates in order to raise money on them. These men served as models for Augustus Melmotte, the swindler of Trollope's *The Way We Live Now*, who forges both a conveyance and a deed when his Mexican railroad stock declines in the market and no more can be sold to raise cash.[19] John Blunt of the South Sea Company, Bontoux of the Union Générale, Jacob Wasserman of the *Darmstäder und Nationalbank* (Danatbank), and the directors of the Creditanstalt all tried to support their stock by buying it in the open market when it slipped, in order to sell more later. Note that a bank buying its own stock rapidly weakens its ratios of cash and capital to deposits, as cash and capital in the open market both shrink while deposits remain unchanged in the short run. Even the Bank of England loaned on the collateral of its own stock once, in 1720. Clapham notes that it did not penetrate into the far wilder and "absolutely dishonest" finance of the South Sea Company.[20]

When the swindle or embezzlement is revealed, distress is increased, often precipitating crash and panic. In 1772, Alexander Fordyce absconded from London to the Continent, leaving his associates to meet obligations—if they could, which they could not—of £550,000, largely in dubious acceptances of the Ayr Bank. Fordyce had personally been short of East India stock, which had risen briefly, but long enough to wipe him out.[21] On August 24, 1857, a cashier in the New York office of the Ohio Life Insurance and Trust Company was revealed to have embezzled almost all the assets of that highly reputed enterprise to sustain his stock market operations, a revelation which ignited a series of failures reverberating to Liverpool, London, Paris, Hamburg, and Stockholm.[22] In September 1929 the Hatry empire collapsed in London. It consisted of a series of investment trusts and operating companies in photographic supplies, cameras, slot machines, and small loans, all of which Clarence Hatry was trying to parlay into a larger operation in steel. He was caught using fraudulent collateral in an attempt to borrow £8 million to buy United Steel, and his failure led to tightening of the British money market, withdrawal of call loans from the New York market, a topping out of the stock market, and the October crash.

Bubbles and Swindles

Bubbles may or may not be swindles. The Mississippi bubble was not a swindle; the South Sea bubble was. But bubble or swindle, it generally starts out with an apparently legitimate or at least legal purpose. In the Mississippi bubble, this was the *Compagnie d'Occident*, to which the Law system added the farming of national taxes and the *Banque*. While John Law owned about one-third of the Place Vendôme, plus other real estate in Paris, and had at least a dozen magnificent rural estates, his operations amounted not so much to a swindle as a mistake, based on two fallacies: (1) that stocks and bonds were money, and (2) that issuing more money as demand increased was not inflationary, a mistake of the Banking School generally.[23] In the South Sea bubble, the monopoly of trade in the South Atlantic was purely incidental—although this view does not go undisputed.[24] Very quickly, consolidation of British government debt overwhelmed the South Atlantic trade aspects of the enterprise, and stock-jobbing overwhelmed government debt shortly thereafter. John Blunt and his insiders deliberately sought to make profits on stock, issued to themselves against loans secured by the stock itself, i.e., free. As capital gains were drawn off, they were converted into estates, for which Blunt had six contracts to buy at the time of the collapse, a man named Surman four on which he owed £100,000. In order to pay out profits, the South Sea Company needed both to raise more capital and to have the price of its stock moving continuously upward. And it needed both increases at an accelerating rate, as in a chain letter or a Ponzi scheme.

Ponzi himself promised to pay 50 percent interest for the use of deposits for 45 days, based on a plan to arbitrage foreign exchange between actual depreciated exchange rates at which foreign currencies—and with them, International Postal Union coupons—could be bought abroad in 1920, and the higher fixed rates at which these coupons could be redeemed for U.S. stamps in the United States. The calculations were purely window dressing. Ponzi took in $7.9 million and had only $61 worth of stamps and postal coupons on the premises when he was arrested on a hot day in Boston in

August, 200 years to the month after the collapse of the South Sea bubble.[25]

History has given less immortality to certain of Ponzi's forerunners. Consider, for example, the former Munich actress Spitzeder, who paid 20 percent a year to Bavarian farmers to milk them of 3 million gulden, for which she and her helpers drew a long jail sentence at the end of 1872; and Placht, a dismissed officer, who borrowed the pennies of 1,600 widows and orphans at 40 percent a year to play the stock market unsuccessfully, costing him in the end six years of incarceration.[26]

As a boom progresses and greed mounts, excuses become thinner, more nearly gossamer bubbles. In 1720 and again in 1847 (two occasions when lists were compiled), such swindles were numerous, although they have been embroidered with hoaxes perpetrated by and on later historians.[27] In 1720, for example, there was one proposal for carrying on an undertaking of great advantage which would in due time be revealed. The perpetrator charged two guineas a share and made off with £2,000, keeping his secret intact by failing to attend a meeting with the investors.[28] Another scheme was for the "nitvender," or selling of nothing.[29] A project of modest current interest offers a premature example of women's liberation:

A proposal by several ladies and others to make, print and stain calicos in England and also fine linnen as fine as any Holland to be made of British flax. . . . They were resolved as one man [*sic*] to admit no man but will themselves subscribe to a joint-stock to carry on said trade.[30]

In later periods, stock promotions continued to have little connection with reality, as historians and novelists alike point out. "Many companies were founded without undertaking operations, railroads without way or traffic."[31] "Construction companies grew like mushrooms. Instead of building, many of them speculated in building sites."[32] "Limehouse and

Rotherihite bridge. . . . It was not at all necessary for them that the bridge should ever be built; that, probably, was out of the question. . . . But if a committee of the House of Commons could be got to say that it ought to be built, they might safely calculate on selling out at a large profit."[33]

Financial distress leads to fraud, so that the burden of losses can be dumped on others. If the market goes decisively the wrong way, for example, bucket-shop operators abscond. When new cash subscriptions failed to meet profits paid out to greedy insiders, Blunt dishonorably borrowed the cash of the South Sea Company for himself.[34] In 1861, Bleichröder characterized Bethel Henry Strousberg as "clever; but his manner of undertaking new ventures in order to mend old holes is dangerous, and if he should encounter a [sudden] obstacle his whole structure may collapse and under its ruins bury millions of gullible shareholders."[35] Bleichröder was right. It did. Another German financier, the Hamburg banker Gustav Goddefroy, lost heavily in railroad and mining shares in 1873 and then bled his overseas trading company white to support his position in the stock market.[36]

These incurable optimists, who know they are going to win the first time, but lose, frequently try again, often doubling their bets and enlarging their risks by operations of dubious morality or evident illegality. Nearer to our day, at a time when U.S. banks were allowed to underwrite securities, there are the examples of Albert Wiggins of the Chase Bank and Charles Mitchell of National City, who continued to sell Chilean and Peruvian bonds at the old prices, after they had heard by cable from those governments that they had stopped paying interest.[37] Horace understood the position, if Sprague quotes and translates him accurately: "Make money; make it honestly if you can; at all events, make money."[38] Equally cynical is Jonathan Swift over the South Sea bubble:

> Get money, money still
> And then let virtu follow, if she will.[39]

On this topic, Balzac has the last word: "The most virtuous merchants tell you with the most candid air this word of the most unrestrained immorality: 'One gets out of a bad affair as one can.' "[40]

Noble Gamblers

The literature abounds in condemnations of noble gamblers and insiders, who might have been thought to regard financial obligations as debts of honor, but seem to be better at promising than at paying their subscriptions.[41] The Austrian nobility was worse than the Junkers, who at least ostensibly disdained money. Edmund Lasker maintained that "when the dilettantes enter, they make it even worse than the professional swindlers."[42] Daigremont in Zola's *L'Argent* sends Saccard to the Marquis de Bohain to help launch his Banque Universelle: "If he wins, he pockets it; if he loses, he does not pay. That is known, People are resigned to it."[43] Again in novels and in real life, nobles seek seats on boards of directors. Wirth enumerates Austrian princes, Landgrafs, counts, barons, Freiherren, and other nobles on the boards of railroads, banks, and other industrial firms "for which they have no capacity."[44] To control the accounts of the Banque Universelle, Saccard appoints a *sieur* Rousseau and a *sieur* Lavignière, the first completely subservient to the second, who is tall, blond, very polite, approving always, devoured by ambition to come on the board.[45] *L'Argent* is a *roman à clef* deriving from Eugene Bontoux and the Union Générale, whose subscribers included the Pretender, royalists, notables, and country squires.[46] In Britain, the *Economist* in October 1848 included the nobility and aristocracy at the head of a list of dishonor:

Present prostration and dejection is [*sic*] but a necessary retribution for the folly, the avarice, the insufferable arrogance, the headlong, desperate and unprincipled gambling and jobbing which disgraced nobility and aristocracy, polluted senators and senate houses, and traders of all kinds.[47]

Rosenberg claims that while the Austrian and French aristocracy led the other estates in pursuit of the golden calf, Berlin bureaucrats successfully opposed a similar movement in Prussia, noting an abortive attempt by Mevissen to get some counts on the board of a 50 million thaler bank. Junkers speculated in spirits and land products, he admits, but shied away from urban undertakings.[48] Perhaps this was so in 1857, though there is evidence to the contrary. In the following decade, the perception of money as evil had weakened. Railroad finance, both inside Germany and in Strousberg's maneuvers in Rumania, was tinged with scandal, reaching up to the peaks of the aristocracy and virtually into the Prussian court itself.[49]

Venal Journalism

Speculation was helped, and on occasion handicapped, by the press. Much of it was for sale, some was critical, some both. Daniel Defoe excoriated stockbrokers in November 1719, when the South Sea bubble was at 120, yet turned around to defend it at the peak of 1,000 in August 1720.[50] He expressed his "just contempt" for people who claimed he wrote for the Royal African Company, stating he had sold his stock; but a modern critic concludes that he either continued to hold the stock or was hired by the Company to attack individual traders who competed with the monopoly.[51] A century later, responsible journalism had grown up in Britain, but the press was still in an underdeveloped stage in France. In 1837 a journalist wrote: "Give me 30,000 francs of advertising and I will take responsibility for placing all the shares of the worst

possible company that it is possible to imagine."[52] Laffitte
financed newspapers.[53] Charles Savary of the Banque de
Lyon et de la Loire had 500 journalists singing the exaggerated
praises of his operations, using releases, largely paid for, as if
they were stories created by the journal's staff.[54] Journals
often sought favor with banks, the stock exchange, and the
public by whipping up the speculative fever.[55] Bleichröder
was cautious in avoiding speculation and outright misrepresentation, but he owned general and financial newspapers and
used journalists. On one occasion in 1890–91 he financed a
trip to Mexico for one Paul Lindau, who wrote thirty-four
articles and a book on the country without mentioning his
connection with Bleichröder, who was then engaged in the
sale of Mexican bonds on the Berlin market.[56] A critical press
developed slowly during the nineteenth century on the
Continent.

In the 1890s in the United States, on the other hand, a
financier close to the line was pursued by the press, and
lived in fear of it, if we can believe Theodore Dreiser's
fictionalized biography of Charles Tyson Yerkes, the Chicago
streetcar tycoon who operated along, and sometimes over, the
knife-edge that lies between legitimate and illegitimate operations. The consequence was the need for favorable publicity,
which Yerkes sought and won through his gift of an observa-
tory to the newly formed University of Chicago. The
well-publicized gift restored his credit at a low point and
enabled him to sell his streetcar bonds in Europe.[57] In the
end, however, the press drove him from Chicago.[58]

Dubious Practices

The forms of financial felony are legion. In addition to outright stealing, misrepresentation, and lying, there are many
practices close to the line: diversion of funds from the stated

use to another, paying dividends out of capital or borrowing, dealing in company stock on inside knowledge, selling securities without full disclosure of new knowledge, using company funds for noncompetitive purchases from insider interests, taking orders but not executing them, altering the company's books . . . one could go on. A remarkable man in the 1846 railway mania managed to do most of them.

George Hudson, who at one time was chairman of four railways, mistakenly believed he was above the law which applied to his less powerful competitors. His accounts were muddled, and there is a possibility he did not understand that he had appropriated shares or funds belonging to the York and North Midland railway. As a private individual he made contracts with various companies of which he was an officer, in direct violation of the Companies Clauses Consolidation Act. He raised the dividend of the Eastern Counties railway from 2 to 6 percent just before making up the accounts, and then altered the accounts to justify the payments. Dividends of the York and North Midland were paid out of capital. He defended his course of action against similar accusations in the case of the Yorkshire, Newcastle and Berwick by noting that he had personally advanced funds to the railway to extend its network. The risk was his, and he was entitled to the advantages which ultimately accrued to himself and the other guaranteeing parties. Lewin, from whose book *The Railway Mania and Its Aftermath* this account is taken, points out that Hudson's embarking on his own authority on transactions which he honestly deemed advantageous to the company, but which were nevertheless of doubtful legality, ended a career of great brilliance and benefit to the British railway network. Hudson was the greatest figure in the railway world of his day, and no man since has amassed such power.[59]

A much less interesting and imposing character in the United States during the next decade was Robert Schuyler, grandson of the Revolutionary General Philip Schuyler. Robert Schuyler was president of the New York and New

Haven, the New York and Harlem, and (for a time) the Illinois Central roalroads. Called the "genteel swindler" by one author, he absconded to Europe in 1854 with almost $2 million in cash obtained from fraudulently selling New York and New Haven stock and keeping the proceeds. Van Vleck suggests that the crisis of 1857 in the United States was precipitated by English withdrawals of capital following the publication of the news of Schuyler's defalcation. Not so— in fact, quite the contrary. Schuyler had resigned from the presidency of the Illinois Central in 1853, but his fraud perpetrated on the New York and New Haven led to a mass sale of Illinois Central stock and bonds by ignorant investors. The stock fell drastically, and the bonds went from close to par to sixty-two by August 1855. This was the opportunity the British investors were looking for. They bought heavily. By February 1856 the bonds were back to ninety. Over 40,000 shares of the stock were held in Europe, and all but one-seventh of the $12 million in bonds.[60] As always, the question of whether foreigners buy or sell a security turns not on how the news strikes them, but how they react compared to domestic investors. Schuyler can be connected with a panic in September 1854, if one can call it that, but not with 1857.[61]

The decade of the 1920s in the United States has been called "the greatest era of crooked high finance the world has ever known."[62] Notorious swindlers of the period include Harold Russell Snyder, for whom stealing seemed the only way to extricate himself from the fix the stock market crash had put him in; Arthur H. Montgomery, who paid the sincerest form of flattery to Ponzi by organizing a foreign-exchange investment scheme that would make 400 percent in sixty days, of which he would keep nearly everything; and Charles V. Bob, who sought and obtained favorable publicity by a $100,000 gift to the Byrd Antarctic Polar Expedition and won the right to call the admiral "Dick," which presumably helped promote his aviation stocks that enjoyed a boomlet after Lindberg's 1927 flight to Paris.[63]

Swindling techniques vary. Frauds that made use of the mails (a practice outlawed in 1889) were proselytizing by telephone, messenger, and even radio in the 1920s. But the basic principle of selling the same horse twice, or more, has not changed much. Try this pitch by a conniving promoter in Mark Twain's and Charles Dudley Warner's *The Gilded Age*:

We'll buy the lands on long time, backed by the notes of good men; and then mortgage them for money to get the railroad well on. Then get the towns on the line to issue their bonds for stock, and sell their bonds for enough to complete the road and partly stock it, especially if we mortgage each section as we complete it. We can then sell the rest of the stock on the prospect of the road through an improved country, and also sell the lands at a big advance. All we want is a few thousands to start the surveys and arrange the things through the legislature. . . .[64]

The Temptation of Banks

It would be comforting to think that illicit practices have declined over the last 250 years, as journalism, for example, has become less open to prostitution, more responsible, more ready to expose malfeasance. It is difficult to believe so. As has been noted, there are no firm statistics on which to base a judgment. One takes little comfort in the fact that Martin Mayer's *The Bankers* does not dwell on safeguards against defalcation in the same way that J. S. Gibbons did in 1859: "There is perhaps no record of a bank fraud extant of which the perpetrator was not honest yesterday."[65] Gibbons added, with emphasis, "It will occur to the reader that there is one peculiar feature running through the whole system; and that is *the apprehension of fraud*."[66]

Recent experience offers ample evidence that what Gibbons said in 1859 is still true today, at least in part. Observe, for example, the case of Investors Overseas Services, not sold in the United States because of Securities and Exchange Commission regulations. IOS was thought to be a safe haven for European money escaping from withholding taxes and seeking action in the stock market. But the "plungers" of IOS proved to be looters. When Bernard Cornfeld went to prison for his role in the operation, Robert Vesco took over; he is said to have looted the residue of more than $200 million. The First National City Bank branch in Brussels, the Banque de Bruxelles in the same city, Franklin National in New York, Herstatt Bank of Cologne, and Lloyds Bank in Ticino all suffered large losses, fatal to Franklin and Herstatt, in unauthorized foreign-exchange speculation by employees. The losses of Credit Suisse in Chiasso came from speculations through a Liechtenstein subsidiary with illegally exported Italian capital on which an 8 percent return had been guaranteed. The exact nature of the fraud is unclear from newspaper accounts, but it would appear that the guaranteed dividend was paid out of capital. The small, private LeClerc bank in Geneva failed, according to newspaper reports, when large sums of depositors' money were tied up in real estate promotions by one of the partners. The more something changes, the more it remains the same.

The Wages of Sin

What happens when a swindler is found out? Charles Blunt, the brother of John Blunt and himself an insider in the South Sea Company, in early September 1720 cut his throat "upon some discontent," as contemporary newspapers put it; Charles Bouchard, the retired manager of LeClerc, was found dead in Lac Léman, an apparent suicide, in May 1977. Psychiatry holds that suicide in these circumstances comes from an intolerable loss of self-esteem, stemming from the realization of the irrationality of past behavior. It is now understood that the picture of stockbrokers jumping from Wall Street windows in October 1929 as they faced bankruptcy is a myth.[67] Nevertheless, the response does occur: there were Ivar Kreuger in March 1932;[68] Denfert-Rochereau of the *Comptoir d'Escompte*, who had financed the unsuccessful corner of the copper syndicate in 1888 and was also involved in difficult negotiations with czarist Russia about a conversion issue of bonds; Eli Black of United Brands in February 1975. In fiction, Mr. Merdle cut his throat in a public bath with a tortoiseshell penknife in Dickens's *Little Dorrit*, and Augustus Melmotte in Trollope's *The Way We Live Now* took prussic acid at his club.

Suicide is one form of exit. Flight is another. The prize case is Robert Knight, who doctored the books of the South Sea Company and then escaped to the Continent, there to make another fortune in Paris after breaking out of an Antwerp jail.[69] Robert Vesco fled to Costa Rica. Charles Savary, who swindled the Banque de Lyon et de la Loire, died in Canada. Eugene Bontoux returned to France after five years of self-imposed exile to take advantage of a loophole in French law that held that prison terms not begun within five years of sentencing had to be dropped.[70] The analogue roughly a century earlier was Arend Joseph, whose failure in January 1763 initiated the financial distress which culminated in the bankruptcy of the brothers de Neufville on July 25, touching off the panic of the same year. Arend Joseph departed Amsterdam with 600,000 guilders in a coach-and-six for the free city of Kruilenburg in Holland, where he was immune from further process. He left behind in Amsterdam debts of 1 million guilders.[71]

What is the appropriate punishment for financial swindling, a white-collar crime? As an economist, I am not qualified to discuss such an issue. However, I cannot forebear from calling attention to one punishment suggested, or at least mentioned, three times. At the time of the South Sea bubble, one member

of the House of Commons, Molesworth, in a speech which
Carswell says was thought absurd at the time, considered
that Parliament should declare the directors of the South Sea
Company guilty of parricide and subject them to the ancient
Roman punishment for that transgression—to be sewn into
sacks, each with a monkey and a snake, and drowned.[72] The
suggestion is echoed in Dreiser's novel *The Titan*. Here the
punishment consists of strangling first, then being sewn into
a sack, without company, and thrown into the Bosphorus,
a punishment reserved for cheating girl friends.[73] In the *House
of All Nations*, written a quarter of a century later, a character
suggests that old sultans used to punish a faithless wife by
tying her into a sack with two wildcats and sinking her in the
Bosphorus.[74] Whatever the details, it sounds excessive, despite
modern concern that white-collar crime is let off lightly.

Whether the transgressor is punished in one way or another,
or lives out his days in indulgent luxury, is no concern of this
work. What matters to us is the revelation of the swindle,
fraud, or defalcation. This makes known to the world that
things have not been as they should have been, that it is time
to stop and see how they truly are. The making known of
malfeasance, whether by the arrest or surrender of the mis-
creant, or by one of those other forms of confession, flight,
or suicide, is important as a signal that the euphoria has been
overdone. The stage of overtrading may well come to an end.
The curtain rises on revulsion, and perhaps discredit.

CHAPTER 6

The Critical Stage

Warnings

Can financial crisis be avoided by timely warning? Milton Friedman has said that if the government knows more than the speculators, the appropriate solution is for government to make the knowledge available by publishing either the information or its forecast.[1] Harry Johnson echoes this view in the statement that if the government knows something that speculators do not know, it can calm speculative fears by making that knowledge public.[2] This is another a priori position which finds little support in the historical record. A word to the wise may be sufficient, but then it may not.

The record in this case starts about 1825. Many writers have taken the Bubble Act of June 1720 as a warning by Robert Walpole and King George II against speculation.[3] But the object of that legislation, as Carswell points out, was to repress competitors of the South Sea Company, the other bubbles and swindles that were draining off cash subscriptions which the South Sea Company itself needed.[4] Not repealed until the nineteenth century, and in fact strengthened in 1749, the

Bubble Act made swindles and starting a legitimate business both difficult.

Beginning in the nineteenth century, warnings in the course of speculative booms came frequently, with authority, but to little avail. In the spring of 1825, Prime Minister Canning, the chancellor of the exchequer, Lord Liverpool, Sir Francis Baring, and W. R. McCulloch in *The Scotsman* all warned against excesses of speculation. Not only did it do no good, it actually contributed to the crisis. In the crash and panic of December 1825, Lord Liverpool, who nine months earlier had specifically stated that the government would bring no relief to speculators,[5] felt committed not to come to the rescue. In May 1836, roughly a year before the crisis of 1837 in Britain, J. Poulett Thompson, president of the Board of Trade, excoriated the prevalent spirit of speculation, which differed from that of 1825, he said, only insofar as people were throwing their money away on domestic rather than foreign schemes.[6] In the fall of that year, as the gambling spirit crossed the channel, Belgian and French authorities also made futile attempts to repress speculation, including forbidding the quotation of notes and shares of corporations. Speculation had gone beyond the narrow framework of the Bourse, it was said, and was catching up nonprofessionals, such as rentiers and little people, including even "women and foreigners." Chambers of Commerce at Liège, Vervier, and Antwerp condemned stock-market speculation and warned against incorporation. The Belgian king went so far as to refuse a charter to a proposed bank, the Mutualité Industrielle. Investment did slow down, but Lévy-Leboyer states that this was the result of a decline in business rather than a response to the administration and business establishment.[7] Again in July 1839, Lamartine in the French Chamber of Deputies spoke against speculation, objecting especially to guarantees of railroad securities.[8]

The only suggestion that official condemnation of speculation may have been effective comes from a French observer, commenting on the 1857 crisis. In March 1856 the minister of the interior brought legal action against certain swindlers. Emperor Napoleon III congratulated O. de Vallée, the author of a book, *Les Manieurs d'argent*, dealing sternly with dubious financial practices. The Senate passed laws. The Bank of France raised the discount rate to 10 percent. Napoleon III published a letter in *Le Moniteur* on December 11, stating his decision not to use means that are employed only when catastrophes beyond human anticipation occur. According to d'Ormesson, the fever fell and the memory of the 1857 crisis reflects a certain glory on French commerce.[9] Not all observers agree: Rosenberg specifically says that the warnings and action came too late.[10]

Restriction by the Austrian National Bank in 1869 produced a "great crash" which proved to be only a mini-crash by the standard of four years later. It did not help.[11] Neither did the warnings and revelations of Eduard Lasker, who in February 1873 exposed in the Diet, of which he was a member, the scandalous interconnections between the Prussian government, especially the Commerce Ministry, and railroad concessionaires.[12] This was perhaps too late. More timely were warnings issued by the *Economist* in 1888 against commitments in Argentine land bonds (*cedulas*). In April the *Economist* said that "the bonds . . . might . . . become a very inadequate security. Just at present all real estate at the River Plate commands inflated prices, but the occurrence of financial difficulties might easily render them unsaleable."[13] Then, in May: "A collapse of the 'boom' in real estate, which is easily conceivable, would be sure to severely depress the value of the cedulas."[14] However timely, the warnings were ineffective.

More memorable is the Cassandra-like utterance of Paul Warburg, a partner of Kuhn, Loeb & Co. and the father, along with others, of the Federal Reserve System. In February 1929 he followed Governor Roy Young, then chairman of the Federal Reserve Board, in warning publicly that the New York market was too high and showed symptoms reminiscent of the 1907 panic. The market paused briefly in acknowledgment and moved higher.*

One problem with warnings, of course, is embodied in the fable of the boy who cried "Wolf." Economic forecasters may know the direction of a move in business conditions, prices, and credit, but their capacity to foretell its precise timing is limited. Roger Babson did badly in the 1929 depression by being right too soon: he got his clients out of the market in 1928. In warning the market, or in providing it with information that it ought to have, one must first get the bemused speculators to pay attention, and then time the announcement soon enough to do good but late enough to be credible and heeded. Neither task is easy. In fact, like moral suasion, body-English, jawboning, and asking the congregation to do as the preacher says rather than as he does, attempting to convince speculators of the errors of their ways through talk is generally futile.

Financial Distress

Distress has at least two meanings: a state of suffering on the one hand, and a hazardous situation on the other. Commercial distress reflects the first definition, financial distress principally the second. In common usage, commercial distress implies that there has been a sharp decline in prices and business activity, and that many mercantile and industrial firms are bankrupt. Financial distress for a single firm means that its earning power has fallen far enough to create a non-trivial probability that it will be unable to pay interest and principal on its debt, with consequent deterioration in its

---

* During his term as Federal Reserve Board chairman, Arthur F. Burns insisted that too many loans had been made by banks to developing countries. That warning may or may not prove to have been effective.

credit standing.[15] Financial distress for an economy also has a prospective rather than an actual significance, and implies financial adjustments or disturbances ahead. It is a lull before a possible storm, rather than the havoc in its wake.

Like overtrading, discussed in Chapter 2, distress is an imprecise term. It is nonetheless widely used in discussions of financial crises. Other words used to describe the interval between the end of euphoria and the onset of what classic writers called revulsion and discredit (in our terms, crash or panic) are "uneasiness," "apprehension," "tension," "stringency," "pressure," "uncertainty," "ominous conditions," "fragility." More colorful expressions include "an ugly drop in the market"[16] or a "thundery atmosphere."[17] A French writer notes the "presentiment of disaster."[18] A German metaphor speaks of the "bow being so bent in the fall of 1782 that it threatened to snap."[19]

While distress may be an objective condition for the single corporation, it cannot be so regarded for an economy at large. In retrospect, one may often observe how markets became tense when certain magnitudes diverged from normal settings: reserve ratios of a central bank, the ratio of debt to capital or wealth of a large number of firms or individuals, the ratio of external debt service to exports, and the like. There may be contemporary awareness of the approach of some limit, such as the note-issue limit of the Bank of England under the Bank Act of 1844, the $100 million gold minimum requirement of the U.S. Treasury in 1893, the ceiling on advances by the Bank of France to the French Treasury in 1924, the gold-reserve ratio of the Reichsbank under the Dawes plan in June 1931, or the free gold available to the Federal Reserve System prior to the passage of the Glass-Steagall Act in February 1932. Limits excite, as one chancellor of the exchequer noted in 1857:

Now when you impose a limit, there is no question that the existence of that limit, provided it makes itself felt at a time of crisis, must increase the alarm. People feel at the moment that a peril presses on them, they begin to calculate how much remains of that fund to which they look for assistance in times of commercial difficulty, and in whatever way you fix the limit; whether by Act of Parliament, or, as Mr. Thomas Tooke [a leader of the Banking School] proposed, by a sort of usage, or, as in France, by the discretion of the Government acting on the Bank of France, there is no doubt that in moments of crisis the limit must aggravate the alarm.[20]

Overshooting of the limit may have psychological rather than objective significance. In March 1924, although sophisticated bankers knew that a small increase in the French monetary supply would not be dangerous, the public had come to regard the ceiling on Bank of France advances to the Treasury as an index to economic health. As one minister put it, Frenchmen were close to the limits of elasticity of confidence in their own currency.[21]

Causes of distress are difficult to disentangle from symptoms, but they include demands on the capital market for cash when cash is tight, sharply rising interest rates in some or all of the capital market, balance-of-payments deficits, rising bankruptcies, the end of price increases in commodities, securities, land, buildings, or whatever else may have been the object of speculation. These developments may all be interrelated, symptoms that the credit mechanism has been stretched taut, beyond normal limits.

In the nineteenth century, financial distress was magnified by the system of requiring only partial payment for securities issues and relying on subsequent calls. In 1825 and 1847 in Britain, and in 1882 in France, calls for successive payments (needed by issuers of securities as capital expenditures progressed) often found securities purchasers embarrassed. They had counted on selling the security at a profit before the next installment was due. Tooke describes this embarrassment in 1825 as acute because the call for cash payment was immediate and pressing, while prospects for earnings were remote and uncertain.[22] Financial distress developed in January 1847, when railroad calls amounted to £6.5 million in a single month.[23]

The chain-letter aspect of securities issues began to be revealed in the South Sea Company in June, July, and August 1720, with repeated attempts to raise cash through new issues of stock. In a single year (1881) 125 new issues with a market value of 5 billion francs were sold in Paris, at a time when annual savings were estimated at 2 billion.[24] Nor was this an era when private companies were going public in large numbers, as in 1887–90 in Britain or 1928–29 in the United States, when private ownership could be exchanged for public stock without the need for fresh savings.

The end of a period of rising prices leads to distress if investors or speculators have become used to rising prices and the paper profits implicit in them. Of course, it is difficult—many would say impossible—to distinguish in advance a pause in a continued upward movement from a topping out that presages downturn. Uncertainty on this score is itself a cause of distress. A more powerful cause of distress occurs when, after a period in which credit has been stretched in an effort to make capital gains, such gains are no longer available, even on paper. Then creditworthiness declines and a fixed line of credit suddenly becomes dangerously high.

Distress may arise from external drains—bad harvests requiring imports, tight money abroad that attracts domestic funds, a return of foreign capital to its usual habitat. In these cases, tautness of credit arises less from expansion of the system's liabilities than from reduction in its cash base. The capital outflow may be only potential. The London money market experienced distress in 1872, when the Reichsbank acquired substantial sterling claims that could be converted into gold, as a consequence of the Franco-Prussian indemnity; and again in the years after 1925 when, as a result of capital outflows and franc undervaluation, the accumulation of sterling balances by the French poised a sword of Damocles over the pound in the threat of conversions into gold. The essence of financial distress is loss of confidence. What comes next—slow recovery of belief in the future as various aspects of the economy are corrected, or collapse of prices, panic, runs on banks, a rush to get out of illiquid assets and into money?

The issue is concisely posed by James S. Gibbons:

Bank officers are not always insensible to alarm when respectable merchants, failing in their best endeavors, are driven into a corner and assume an air of desperation. They know the danger that hangs over the market. Credit is prodigiously extended; the public excitement is wrought up to a high pitch of apprehension, and there need be but a single failure of a "great house" to explode the "mighty bubble." Who knows that it is a bubble? Who knows that the highest point of pressure is not reached today, and that tomorrow the waters will not begin to subside? And then gradually things fall into their old channels, confidence revives and it is proved that there was no bubble to burst after all.[25]

How Long Does Distress Last?

If there is no panic—as there was not in France in 1866, and in Britain in 1873 and 1907—financial distress may gradually subside. In the United States we have in recent years had near panics over Penn Central, the Herstatt and Franklin National bank failures, and New York City, not to mention distress about the developing-country loans of the major money-market banks. But there has been no panic.

When financial distress *is* followed by crash or panic, there is no standard interval. It may be a matter of weeks or of years. John Law's system peaked in December 1719 and collapsed in May 1720. In the South Sea bubble of 1720, the lunatic note sounded clearly at the end of April, the ugly drop in the market occurred in August, and collapse came in the first days of September.* In 1763 distress developed in March, with the actual crisis precipitated by the failure of DeNeuf-ville in Amsterdam in July. In 1772 the Bank of England applied brakes by raising the discount rate early in the year; the Ayr Bank cut back operations in May, but too late. Fordyce absconded on June 10, precipitating panic in Britain on June 22; the consequent distress in Amsterdam lasted until the failure of Clifford & Co. in December.

Timing of crises from 1789 to 1815 was dominated by particular apocalyptic events, such as the guillotining of Louis XVI in January 1793, the landing of Frenchmen at Fish-guard in February 1797, and the penetration of the Continental blockade in 1799. Distress on these occasions was limited; panic was virtually immediate. In 1809–10, on the other hand, the setback arose from a tightening of the Continental block-ade, in addition to an indigestible excess of exports to Brazil. Pressure mounted, slowly from the middle of 1809, then more rapidly from mid-1810 to the climax of bankruptcies in Janu-ary 1811.

It is tedious to go through the list one by one, but a few points may be made. Calls for further payments on railroad subscriptions in January 1847 set the background of tension against which speculation in grain peaked in May, collapsed in August, and led to panic in November. The crisis of 1866 can be thought of as the delayed result of the 1864 collapse of cotton prices, which had brought panic to France in that year. Britain had two "critical moments" in 1864, one in January—the real crisis, related to the prospective collapse in cotton prices—and another in the last quarter. This, at least, is one French view.[26] British treatment of the period tends to look more to speculative expansion, especially affecting discount houses and stretching back to 1863, plus a series of firms resembling the Credit-Mobilier. For example, W. T. C. King writes that one Albert Gottheimer appeared as Albert

* The connections between these and the rolling of crises from one market to another are discussed in the following chapter.

Grant to float the imposing Credit Foncier and Mobilier of
England, which ultimately achieved a paid-up, or rather called-
up, capital of £1 million.[27] The conversion of Overend,
Gurney & Co. to a public company in July 1865, at the peak
of the boom and "dividend race," led to a 100 percent
premium on the stock in October, causing the Bank of England to raise its discount rate from 3 to 7 percent; the crash
did not occur until May 1866. On the parochial British view,
distress lasted from October to May, and intensely from the
January 1866 failure of Watson, Overend and Co. On the
French showing, the period of distress covered almost two and
one-half years.

In the United States, with few exceptions, periods of
stringency, crisis, and panic occurred in the autumn when
western banks drew large sums of money from the East to
pay for shipments of cereals.[28] Sprague notes that the crisis
of 1873 came in September because of the early harvest, adding that the outbreak of a crisis invariably came as a surprise
to the business community and that the crisis of 1873 was no
exception.[29] There is a contradiction here. Heavy movements
of funds caused distress on a seasonal basis, whereas the statement that crises were always a surprise suggests the absence
of distress. In the 1873 case, "excessive tightness" of money
from September 1872 to May 1873, which caused the railroads
to turn from issuing bonds to borrowing on short term, could
have been seen as a sign of distress against which seasonal
tightness precipitated the crash.[30] Thus, the surprise of the
business community is doubly curious.

Distress may be continuous or may oscillate in a rhythm of
its own. The crash of the Union Générale in January 1882 was
preceded by three separate tense periods in July, October,
and December 1881.[31] The panic of October 1907, known to
be coming (but the exact timing of which Sprague holds was
not foreseeable), was preceded by a "rich man's panic" in
March, when Union Pacific stock, the security most widely
used as collateral for finance-bill operations, dropped 50

points.* Markets recovered from this blow, as from a failure of New York City bonds in June (when only $2 million was tendered for an offering of $29 million worth of 4 percent bonds), from the collapse of the copper market in July, and from the $29 million fine levied against the Standard Oil Company for antitrust law violations in August—only to succumb to the failure of the Knickerbocker Trust Company in October.[32]

Onset of a Crisis

Students of logic will recall the discussion of the damp squib thrown by A to land at B's feet, by B to C, C to D, and so on, only to explode after Y threw it in Z's face. Who is to blame? A, *causa remota*? Or Y, *causa proxima*? *Causa remota* of the crisis is speculation and extended credit; *causa proxima* is some incident which snaps the confidence of the system, makes people think of the dangers of failure, and leads them to move from commodities, stocks, real estate, bills of exchange, promissory notes, foreign exchange—whatever it may be—back into cash. In itself, *causa proxima* may be trivial: a bankruptcy, a suicide, a flight, a revelation, a refusal of credit to some borrower, some change of view which leads a significant actor to unload. Prices fall. Expectations are reversed. The movement picks up speed. To the extent that speculators are leveraged with borrowed money, the decline in prices leads to further calls on them for margin or cash, and

---

* Christina Stead may be referring to this episode in *The House of All Nations* (New York: Simon & Schuster, 1938) when she has one of her characters, Stewart, say: "My first job. By jove we had fun. At one time they had a short position in Union Pacific which exceeded the floating supply. Were they ruined? Not that time. They came to terms with them . . . they had to, otherwise a world panic would have resulted."

to further liquidation. As prices fall further, bank loans turn sour, and one or more mercantile houses, banks, discount houses, or brokerages fail. The credit system itself appears shaky, and the race for liquidity is on.

It is seldom possible to identify the original sellers, nor is it useful to blame them. Conspiracy theories abound. One can single out bear speculators like Joseph P. Kennedy, Sr., or Bernard Baruch in 1929; the Protestant-Jewish cartel which allegedly did in Eugene Bontoux in 1882; or Thomas Guy, who liquidated £54,000 of South Sea stock over six weeks between April and June 1720, never selling more than £1,000 at a time, and founding the fortune used to endow Guv's Hospital in London, "the best memorial of the Bubble."[33]

One could go on, but to no purpose. Someone sells. Occasionally it is a foreigner. In 1847, for example, it was the French (according to one S. Saunders, quoted by Evans) who bought up surplus wheat and sent it to England in June and July to the extent of 70,000 quarters, which were allegedly forced upon the market at prices much below the current rates, driving the price down from 96 to 56 shillings and bringing a large number of houses connected with the corn trade to bankruptcy.[34] The story is not persuasive. The price of wheat had risen from 46s. in August 1846 to 93s. (or 96s. or 105s. or 110s., depending on the source) in May 1847, because of violent storms which ruined the crop and because of the potato disease in Ireland and on the Continent. The price broke in July 1847 with the coming of fine weather and the prospect of a good crop. Imports of wheat and flour rose from 2.3 million quarters in 1846 to 4.4 million in 1847, aided, to be sure, by repeal of the Corn Laws;[35] 70,000 quarters is a trivial proportion of this sum. France had a problem on its hands: it had the shortest crop in wheat in 100 years in 1846 (along with the potato crop failure), and then the largest crop in 100 years in 1847. But the condition was general, and British wheat speculation had been excessive.

There is also a suggestion that German sellers of Argentine

bonds contributed to the Baring crisis of 1890. It is true that German investors stopped subscribing to Argentine loans in 1888, whether because of general uneasiness,[36] because they disapproved of the instability in the Argentine exchange rate,[37] or because of the domestic boom which led them equally to get out of Russian bonds.* German sales contributed to distress rather than to crisis, since they loaded British investors with a higher proportion of the £200 million in bonds issued by Argentina. In November 1888 a £3.5 million offering of the Buenos Ayres Drainage and Waterworks Company failed, and Baring felt obliged to lend to Argentina through acceptance credits. Falling raw materials prices in 1890 made it impossible for the Argentine government to meet these credits as they came due. The Baring crisis of November 1890, after two years of distress, was the proximate result of a Bank of England warning to Baring Brothers to limit the level of its acceptances (which stood at £30 million in the summer of 1890), of the crisis in New York in October, and of the maturing of £4 million of acceptances in November at a time when Baring could no longer sell securities left on its hands from underwriting or borrow further on short term.

Pure information may precipitate a crash, as when the Paris-Lyons-Marseilles railroad was revealed to cost 300 million francs instead of the 200 million envisaged.[38] *Causa remota*, much more important, was the adverse balance of payments from heavy imports of railroad materials, and especially the crop failure of 1846 followed by the glut of 1847. The Granger movement helped precipitate the collapse

---

* Part of the reason why Germany sold off Russian bonds was political, as was the basis for German buying of Italian bonds. The French bought Russian bonds and sold Italian. But Germany did float a Mexican loan of £10.5 million in 1888, so one cannot make the case that the domestic boom in Germany required capital which in non-political circumstances would have gone abroad. See Fritz Stern, *Gold and Iron: Bismarck, Bleichröder and the Building of the German Empire* (London: Allen & Unwin, 1977), pp. 427, 433, 442. Mr. Stern has kindly told me that there is nothing in the Bleichröder correspondence which bears on German selling of Argentine securities.

in the United States in 1873. The Grangers, who in some ways resembled the environmentalists of today, started in the late 1860s and early 1870s as activists for legislation which would control intrastate transportation by prohibiting discriminatory charges, establishing regulatory commissions, and even setting maximum rates.[39] With railroad securities oversold on credit—including a number of "superfluous and ridiculous" enterprises like the Rockford, Rock Island and St. Louis line, sold at par and destined to decline to 6 cents on the dollar—the prospect of local control put an end to optimism and gave a start to liquidation.

For accidental detonators, incidents that prevented a nascent crisis from subsiding by itself, observe a historical parallel in ships sunk at sea. In 1799, with interest rates at 12 and 14 percent and the price of sugar 35 percent below the peak before the convoy had broken through the blockade, British merchants attempting to assist in the Amsterdam crisis sought to provide cash, i.e. coin. The sum of £1 million sterling was sent in the frigate *Lutine,* destined for Texel, where her arrival was awaited with eagerness. Unhappily she sank in a storm off the Dutch coast, dashing all hopes of alleviating the crisis.[40] The historic analogue occurred roughly sixty years later, when the crisis of 1857 in New York was brewing. On September 15, amid news of extreme stringency in Philadelphia, Cincinnati, and Chicago, came word that the steamer *Central America,* bound from Panama to New York with $2 million in gold, presumably from California, was unreported and overdue. Two days later it was learned that she had gone down, uninsured, with heavy loss of life and cargo.[41] In such circumstances, men think that the Lord has turned against them.

Accident may thus precipitate crisis, but so may action designed to prevent it, or action by the authorities taken in pursuit of other objectives. (We return to this subject later in discussing the role of the lender of last resort.) The matter was put well by H. S. Foxwell apropos the crisis of 1808–9:

To refuse accommodation altogether is always held to be dangerous. To make personal reference is invidious, especially for a
National Bank. It is just possible that the Bank might have resorted
to the expedient used in 1795–96, I mean the granting of *pro rate*
discounts. . . . [In seeking to contract the circulation] it must have
put severe pressure on the market and risked the creation of a
panic. . . . The Bank was responsible for the solvency of this
crowd of small, ill-managed institutions [country banks], but dared
not call them to account, on peril of provoking a general collapse
of credit.[42]

The suggestion of *pro rata* discounts is dubious (see below),
and the statement that the Bank of England was responsible
for the country banks' solvency is debatable to monetarists.
Nevertheless, the dilemma is neatly posed. Not to apply
discipline will let the credit market get still further out of
hand; to apply it may prick the bubble and induce collapse.

One aspect of the problem is lags. Raising the discount rate
in the face of an external drain reducing cash in the system
may work well to induce a return flow. A Bank of England
discount rate of 10 percent can "draw gold from the moon,"
in the folklore of the City, but how long does it take to produce that result? The issue was a matter of some debate between the Banking and Currency schools on the question of
the Bank Act of 1844 and the need either for its suspension
or for a lender of last resort. In 1825 and 1836, speculation
in boom turned the exchange adverse, leading to financial
stringency. On one interpretation, the boom broke before the
Bank of England belatedly raised the interest rate in an effort
to reduce its liabilities; thus, a combination of tight money and
declining prices produced the crisis, forcing the Bank to
reverse course and to lower interest rates and lend.[43] The
Banking School believed that the change of Bank rate, rather
than the topping of the boom, checked the drain of specie
and produced a return flow practically instantly. The Currency
School, on the other hand, had two wings. One took the
view just stated; a second, represented by Lord Overstone,

thought there would be lags in the operation of Bank rate, requiring some lender of last resort to fill the gap.[44]

Even after the Bank of England had learned how to use Bank rate better than in the 1820s and 1830s, there were still crises, and in some cases crashes and panics. Hawtrey points to a lag at the level of commercial banks and internal drains, based on backlogs:

Bankers may take proper steps, but panic because they work slowly: They may have really checked the fundamental danger of the position . . . stopped the stress of new orders . . . and yet the demand for fresh credits and the drain of cash may go on undiminished. The consequence may be a state of panic among the bankers, who, unaware of the cause of the apparent ineffectiveness of the measures they have taken [the working off of the backlog of old orders] despair of saving themselves from failure, call in existing loans regardless of the embarrassment of debtors, and precipitate a series of bankruptcies among their customers and themselves.

The fact is that there is no golden rule for keeping the extension of credits within bounds. . . .[45]

Apart from lags and mistakes of discount policy, the authorities may precipitate panic by brusque action in early stages of distress. In the summer of 1836, with credit extended in acceptances drawn by American houses on British joint-stock banks, the Bank of England refused to discount any bills bearing the name of a joint-stock bank, and specifically instructed its Liverpool agent not to rediscount any paper of the three so-called "W banks" (Wiggins, Wildes, and Wilson) among the seven American banks in Britain, an action that "seemed vindictive"[46] and led immediately to panic.[47] As it turned out, the Bank of England had to reverse its policies. It had long conferences with the "W banks" in October, extended them lines of discount in the first quarter of 1837, but failed to prevent their failure in June of that year. The Bank's instinct was right: to frustrate the extension of dangerous credit. But credit is a delicate thing. Expectations can quickly be altered. Something, sometimes almost nothing, causes a shadow to fall on credit, reverses expectations, and the rush for liquidity is on.

Crashes and Panics

A crash is a collapse of the prices of assets, or perhaps the failure of an important firm or bank. A panic, "a sudden fright without cause," from the god Pan, may occur in asset markets, or involve a rush from less to more liquid assets. Financial crisis may involve one or both, and in any order. The collapse of South Sea stock and the Sword Blade Bank almost brought down the Bank of England. The 1929 crash and panic in the New York stock market spread liquidation to other asset markets, such as commodities, and seized up credit to strike a hard blow at output. But it did not lead to a money-market panic, as revealed in sharp increases in interest rates, or to runs on banks, probably because of the effective action of the New York Federal Reserve in pumping funds into the market.[48] In 1893, lack of confidence in the ability of the United States to maintain the gold standard under pressure from the silver interests led from money-market pressure and ultimately panic to bank failures, and through them to pressure on securities markets.[49]

The system is one of positive feedback. A fall in prices reduces the value of collateral and induces banks to call loans or refuse new ones, causing mercantile houses to sell commodities, households to sell securities, industry to postpone borrowing, and prices to fall still further. Further decline in collateral leads to more liquidation. If firms fail, bank loans go bad, and then banks fail. As banks fail, depositors withdraw their money (this was particularly true in the days before deposit

insurance). Deposit withdrawals require more loans to be
called, more securities to be sold. Merchant houses, industrial
firms, investors, banks in need of ready cash—all sell off their
worst securities if they can, their best if they have to. Firms,
corporations, and households known to be in trouble may be
carried on the books for a time, in the expectation or hope that
prices will pick up again and float the frail bark of credit off
the bottom. Examiners may *in extremis* look the other way as
banks value loans and securities at cost rather than market
value, extend loans due, or add to loans of embarrassed
borrowers to enable them to pay current interest. But when
bankruptcy occurs, the nettle of bad loans must be grasped.
Prices, solvency, liquidity, and the demand for cash—in
German *Bargeld*, in French *numéraire*—are interrelated. Not
only banking institutions, as Sprague states, but households,
firms, and banks are "very similar to a row of bricks, the fall
of one endangering the stability of the rest."[50] The metaphor
is a cliché, but nonetheless apposite.

At the height of the panic, money is said to be unavailable.
Descriptions are frequently exaggerated, not least about 1825:

Bankers in Lombard Street called on the Governor [of the Bank
of England] on Sunday [after the panic of country banks had
reached Pole, Thornton & Co. on December 12] to warn that if
such a house, drawn on by 47 country banks, were allowed to
stop, a run would take place on every bank in London.
It was allowed to stop. A panic seized upon the public, such
as had never been witnessed before: everybody begging for money
—money—but money was hardly on any condition to be had.
"It was not the character of the security," observes the *Times*,
"that was considered: but the impossibility of producing money
at all.[51]

This was the occasion when the failure of seventy-three banks
brought Britain, according to Huskisson, within twenty-four
hours of barter, whatever that statement may imply.[52] "It
was, as the Duke said of Waterloo, 'a damned nice thing—the
nearest run thing you ever saw in your life.' "[53] Barter was
avoided by exchanging silver for gold with the Bank of France,

and by the luck of the Bank of England in finding, just as it ran out of £5 and £10 notes (which were all it then issued), a block of £1 notes left in the vault from 1797. With government approval these were issued on December 17 and "worked wonders."[54]

In 1857, New York Central stock went from 93 to 61, Reading from 96 to 36.[55] The price of pork fell from $24 a barrel to $13; flour, from $10 to $5 or $6.[56] Interest rates in September went from 15 to 24 percent, as 150 banks in Pennsylvania, Maryland, Rhode Island, and Virginia failed in the last four days of the month. The panic reached a peak in October, when 1,415 banks in the United States failed and interest rates went to 60–100 percent per annum.[57] This, of course, was for monies borrowed for a few days.

Very high rates of interest, such as 4 percent a day, have sometimes been quoted for a particular kind of loan, as for call money in 1884, when commercial discounts continued at 4.5 to 5 percent a year for first-class endorsed paper;[58] or 5 percent a day at the peak, as a premium for cash at the onset of the panic of 1907.[59] Perhaps the apogee of the liquidity squeeze was recorded in 1907, when one bank paid $48 per $1,000 for the cash gate receipts of the Harvard-Yale football game.[60]

Will the storm subside, the flood crest and fall? We come to this question ultimately. Before that, we note, first, how boom and crash spread from one country to another and, second, the steps taken locally and internationally to halt panic and reverse the damage it does.

CHAPTER 7

International Propagation

Allocating the Blame for Crisis

A widespread historical pastime is fixing blame for a crisis geographically. President Hoover, for example, insisted that Europe was responsible for the 1929 depression. He was prepared to admit some fault in the United States, especially stock market speculation, and to blame the world as a whole for overproduction in wheat, rubber, coffee, sugar, silver, zinc, and to some extent cotton. Primarily, however, the fault belonged to Europe, its cartels, and to "European statesmen [who] did not have the courage to face these issues."[1] Friedman and Schwartz, on the other hand, observe that while the gold-exchange standard rendered the international financial system vulnerable, the crisis originated in the United States. The initial climactic event—the stock market crash—was American, and the series of developments which started the stock of money downward in late 1930 was predominantly domestic.[2]

Earlier, in 1837, President Jackson divided the honors for that year's crisis equally between Britain and the United States:

It would seem impossible for sincere inquirers after the truth to resist the conviction that the causes of the revulsion in both countries have been substantially the same. Two nations, the most commercial in the world, enjoying but recently the highest degree of apparent prosperity, are suddenly, without any great national calamity, arrested in that career, and plunged into embarrassment and distress. In both countries have we witnessed the same redundancy of paper money, and other facilities of credit, the same spirit of speculation, the same partial success, the same difficulties and reverses, and, at length, the same overwhelming catastrophe.[3]

The 1837 crisis brings forth a similar verdict from a modern economist which can be regarded as general: although observers twenty years after the event called the panics of 1836–37 the "American panics," on the ground that they originated in and were confined to houses trading with the United States,[4] Matthews calls it "futile to try to draw any hard-and-fast line assigning to either country causal primacy in the cycle as a whole or in its individual phases."[5]

Friedman and Schwartz again are inclined to blame the United States for the recession of 1920–21, citing the evidence of gold movements.[6] Another observer disagrees:

How was [the early postwar fall in economic activity] brought about? . . . I think the answer must be: It was a deliberate policy inaugurated by the two economically dominating countries, the U.K. and the U.S.A. It is impossible to give priority to any of them. The earliest official statement of the policy was undoubtedly made by England. On the other hand, causally USA's policy must have the greater weight. . . .[7]

Some few crises are purely national—the gold agio crisis in the United States in 1869, the City of Glasgow Bank in 1878, the Union Générale in France in 1882. In the half century before World War I, Canadian financial crises were fairly frequent, coming in 1879, 1887, and 1908, but seemed only loosely related to main financial currents that bound Western Europe, Scandinavia, and the United States together.[8] In these instances, the issue of geographical causality does not arise. In international crises, one or more countries may be left out of the circuit from time to time for evident reasons: France in 1873, because it had undergone severe deflation in 1871 and 1872 in the effort to transfer the Franco-Prussian indemnity; or the United States in 1847, before its railroad boom had gotten under way and when the country was unaffected by European potato disease or by the tumultuous European wheat situation. Moreover, the relationships of some areas to the major storm centers are obscure in particular cases: e.g., Cologne to the London-Paris crisis in 1848, or Italy to the crises of 1866 and 1907. For the most part, however, crises built up in international financial structures will ricochet from country to country. Time and again, observers like Juglar,[9] Mitchell,[10] and Morgenstern[11] have observed that financial crises tend to be international, either running parallel from country to country or spreading by one means or another from the centers where they originate to other countries. Interest in the international propagation of cycles arises because of the possible need for one or more international lenders of last resort, a subject broached in Chapter 10.

Transmission Mechanisms

Boom, distress, and panic are transmitted through a variety of connections between national economies: psychological infection, rising and falling prices of commodities and securities, short-term capital movements, interest rates, the rise and fall of world commodity inventories. These connections, moreover, can take various forms, and may be interrelated in various ways. We offer a few paragraphs of analysis, then proceed to historical illustration.

Boom and panic in one country seem to induce boom and panic in others, often through the purely psychological channels discussed in Chapter 3. Just as one huge bubble breeds others in a country, so a host of bubbles in a financial market seems to inspire the production of others in other countries. Panics also travel through psychological conduits.

Commodity connections may or may not involve changes in commodity trade. When the price of cotton soars in the 1830s in one country, it does so in all, and when it declines, as after 1864, it does so worldwide. A decline in the price of a given commodity—especially a widely traded item like wheat or cotton—may produce bankruptcies and bank failures at long distances from the source of the original change in demand or supply, depending upon the vulnerability of markets, related in turn to the leverage of speculators.

The same holds true for securities. Internationally traded securities rise and fall worldwide, but domestic securities may also do so in synchronous fashion, without being traded, through the psychological connection or through impacts on interest rates transmitted through short-term capital movements.

On the monetary side, there may be increases and decreases in the real money supply, owing to discoveries of new or exhaustion of old gold and silver mines, or changes in credit and prices with a steady supply. In addition, international financial expansion can take place through the gold-exchange standard, as discussed in Chapter 4, or through other forms of intermediation such as the Eurocurrency market. A given country may inflate, and its boom may be transmitted abroad through capital outflows; these may or may not, in the short run, bring domestic inflation to an end. Capital movements may respond to real causes, such as war, revolution, new markets, innovations, and the like, or to changes of policy (monetary, fiscal, etc.), or to disequilibrium exchange rates.

For interrelations, consider the connections between exchange appreciation and deflation, or exchange depreciation and inflation, relating exchange rates to prices, through which they can be connected with bankruptcies, bank suspensions, and changes in the money supply. Friedman and Schwartz state, for example, "It would be difficult indeed to attribute the sequence of bank failures [in the United States] to any major current influence from abroad."[12] I find it easy. Depreciation of the Argentine, Uruguayan, Australian, and New Zealand currencies in early 1930 helped push down wheat prices in the United States.* Falling prices of grain were communicated to corn and other feeds, sowing bankruptcies among farmers, as well as failures among banks in farm communities, particularly in 1930 in Missouri, Indiana, Illinois, Iowa, Arkansas, and North Carolina.[13]

Alternatively, a boom not paralleled abroad can be fed by capital inflows which increase credit base. The bubble is pricked when foreigners' expectations change, leading to an external drain, tight credit, and the need to liquidate holdings.

In short, the connections among national booms and panics are many and intricate. They can perhaps best be examined in context.

South Sea and Mississippi Bubbles

Åkerman calls the crisis of 1720 the first international crisis because the speculation of 1717–20 in France and England had its echo in the cities of the Netherlands and northern Italy, along with Hamburg. (In an earlier passage he suggests that what I would call the fifteen *standard* international cycles begin with 1825.)[14] The South Sea and Mississippi bubbles were connected in a number of ways. As early as 1717, British investors were following events in the Rue de Quincampoix in Paris, where trading took place on John Law's banks and companies. By May 1719 the British ambassador in Paris, a man named Stair, had letters from friends and relatives in Scotland begging him to buy stock for them in the Compagnie des Indes. Thirty thousand foreigners, including British nobility, poured into Paris to subscribe in person. In May, Am-

---

* In a world of inflation it would have raised them in the depreciating countries, as we discovered after 1971; in a world poised on the brink of deflation, it lowers them in the appreciating country.

bassador Stair urged his government to do something to
compete with John Law and slow down the capital inflow into
Paris from Britain. As Law's system peaked in December
1719, some speculators, like the Duke of Chandos, sold South
Sea bubble and bought Mississippi.[15]

While Britishers bought Mississippi in Paris, many Conti-
nentals bought South Sea in London. Sir Theodore Janssen
had a long list of subscribers from Geneva, Paris, Amsterdam,
and the Hague. Lambert's list of French names included the
banker Martin, who, as already noted, subscribed £500 with
the remark: "When the rest of the world are mad, we must
imitate them in some measure." When the early birds liquidated in July, the Canton of Berne, which had speculated with
£200,000 of public funds, sold out for a profit of £2 million.[16]

Amsterdam stood between Paris and London. It apparently
did well. The Dutch were said to have sold their Mississippi
Compagnie des Indes at the right psychological moment, and
lost little in the crash. In April 1720, a bit prematurely perhaps, David Leeuw liquidated his South Sea stock and bought
Bank of England and East India Company. By the end of that
month, the Dutch banker Crellius observed coolly that Exchange Alley ressembled "nothing so much as if all the Luna-
tics had escaped out of the Madhouse at once."[17] In June and
July there were twelve-hour relays by ship between Britain
and Amsterdam, and on July 16 some eighty Jews, Presby-
terians, and Anabaptists, speculators from Exchange Alley,
were off for Holland and Hamburg to mend their fortunes by
speculating in Continental insurance stocks.[18] By autumn,
London and the Continent were demonstrating oneness in
disaster. Samuel Bernard, a French banker, was sent to London
to sell South Sea stock against gold, to be brought back to
France in revulsion against Law's system. Dutch banks "short-
ened sail, recalling advances, refusing further credit, selling
stocks held as collateral."[19] The pound sterling exchange rate
in Amsterdam, which had risen from 35-4 (guilders to the
pound) to 36-1 when the first increase in South Sea stock took

place in April and "France, Holland and to some extent Denmark, Spain and Portugal" were buying, fell to 33-11 on September 1, as "foreigners lost their taste for English securities." At the height of the panic it recovered to 35-2.[20]

1763–1819

The crisis of 1763 involved mainly Holland, Hamburg, Prussia, and Scandinavia, with repercussions on, and help from, London. France was not involved; the Seven Years War had been directed against her. George Chalmers, a perceptive contemporary observer, claimed that speculation in land in the United States was a factor in the crisis, but the statement is not supported in other writing on the period.[21] Amsterdam had been the entrepôt center for the payment of money to British allies, and the Dutch had been expanding credit both by investing in British government stock and in *Wisselruitij* (chains of accommodation bills), by which especially the De-Neufvilles had built a giddy edifice on a tiny base, with bills drawn on merchant houses in Stockholm, Hamburg, Bremen, Leipzig, Altona, Lübeck, Copenhagen, and St. Petersburg. In addition to the accommodation paper, there circulated in Amsterdam bills drawn with the security of goods shipped. When prices of commodities fell after the war—especially sugar, so far as I can determine, presumably as a result of shipments being resumed from the French West Indies—prices fell, and the bills could not be paid.[22] Hamburg was said to have warned Amsterdam houses that they would suspend payment unless support was furnished to the DeNeufvilles. In one account, the letter arrived too late.[23] Another states merely that a plan to save the firm failed because its reputation was too bad.[24] In the long run, the DeNeufvilles would have been able to pay out 70 percent of their obligations, but they settled with creditors for 60 percent before that became known. In the end, the Hamburg creditors had to wait thirty-six years, to 1799, to collect even this much.[25] The coup de grace occurred when King Frederick II of Prussia, who had debased the silver currency in 1759 to help fight the war, decided to recall the old currency and have a new one minted in Amsterdam, on the basis of credits drawn on Dutch bankers.[26] Withdrawing the old coinage before issuing new put deflationary pressure on credit in the system.

London, as we shall see subsequently, came to the rescue of Amsterdam and, in so doing, took over a considerable portion of Dutch trade and finance with Scandinavia and Russia. Very much against his will, King Frederick had to assist Berlin merchants caught in the crisis through having their bills protested.[27] Swedish houses complained early in the fall of 1762 that bills they drew were protested and not paid in Amsterdam, while remittances sent to cover the bills were retained. Whether Amsterdam tried to save itself by selling off its British securities is debatable. Wilson claims Amsterdam communicated the crisis to London in this fashion; Carter insists she cannot find evidence of sales in the transfer books.[28]

One could go on. The 1772 crisis spread from Scotland and London to Amsterdam, and thence to Stockholm and St. Petersburg. Heavy outflows of specie from Paris to London fed the canal and country-bank mania during the Reign of Terror in 1792, which peaked with the guillotining of Louis XVI in January 1793; this stream of precious metal reversed itself in 1797, when monetary order had been more or less restored under the Consulate after the Assignats. There was the Hamburg-Liverpool crisis of 1799, associated with breaking the Continental blockade. Next we reach what one might expect to be a highly localized British crisis in 1810, when British exporters first overdid sales to Brazil and then were cut off from their Baltic outlets by blockade. But this crisis, too, found echoes in Hamburg and New York.

The international aspects of the crises of 1816 and 1819 can also be summed up in a few words. The prospect of ending the war in 1814 led to heavy British sales of manufactures to the Continent. Smart calls this an exporting frenzy that soon broke like the South Sea and Mississippi bubbles. When prices collapsed, the goods were sent on to North America, resulting in the tariff of 1816 in the United States. This was deep depression without panic or even crisis.[29] In 1818 and 1819 there were panics on both sides of the Atlantic; these were doubtless connected, but the exact nature of the interrelations is not obvious. The 1819 crisis in Britain followed the collapse of commodities speculation in 1818, the discredit and distress "originating clearly in great previous overtrading."[30] The year 1819 was marked by the resumption of specie payments and by the Peterloo massacre, when protesting Manchester workers and their families were charged by cavalry, with at least eight protestors killed; Smart called it a "disastrous year."[31] In America, the Second Bank of the United States precipitated panic by having its branches call on state banks to redeem large balances and notes held by the Second Bank. The purpose was to assemble $4 million in specie to repay the borrowing undertaken in Europe in 1803 to effect the Louisiana purchase.[32] But the Second Bank itself was a bubble, having been reestablished in 1817 after dissolution in 1811. It was run by greedy and corrupt directors who accepted promissory notes in payment of stock, registered stock in different names to get around the law limiting concentration of ownership, voted loans on the security of bank stock, permitted other loans without collateral, and allowed accounts to be overdrawn. Hammond observes that the sober pace of eighteenth-century business had given way to a democratic passion to get rich quick, and men imbued with this passion and unscrupulousness had seized control of the Second Bank.[33] Perhaps in this sense the crisis was international.

1825–1896

The 1825 crisis involved Britain and South America, although there was a distinct spillover to Paris that was stretched out until panic struck there in January 1828. With the panic in London in December 1825, Continental sales halted. This had impact on banks in Paris, Lyons, Leipzig, and Vienna, and obliged Italy and other markets which depended on these centers to reduce their purchases. Distress from burdensome stocks in the textile-producing area of Alsace was general; firms were low on cash, but sustained themselves by circulating 9 to 10 million francs, or perhaps as much as 15 to 16 million francs, in promissory notes. When this edifice was toppled in December 1827 by Parisian banks' refusal to renew the Alsatian paper, the London crisis resulting from overtrading in South American stocks had arrived on the Continent.[34]

Åkerman calls the crises of 1825 and 1836 Anglo-American, in contrast to the one in 1847, which was Anglo-French.[35] But 1825 was not non-French, as has just been shown, and the first two were Anglo-American in different ways: the 1825 crisis was Anglo–South American, the 1836 crisis Anglo-U.S. In addition, the situation in 1836 was far more complex than in 1825.

As noted earlier, President Jackson considered that responsibility for the 1836–39 crisis should be divided equally between Britain and the United States, and Matthews thought it futile to assign causal primacy. Monetary expansion in the two countries was vastly different. Wildcat banking aided by silver imports had started in the United States, while new joint-stock banks had been created in Britain since the new legislation of 1826 and 1833. British speculation was in cotton, cotton textiles, and railroads; American speculation in cotton and land, especially land capable of producing cotton. Moreover, Anglo-American houses in England financed British exports to the United States. For this reason, as well as the link in cotton, the two markets could be regarded as joined.

The crisis was by no means a purely Anglo-U.S. affair. Hawtrey states that it broke out in England in 1836 and 1837, spread to the United States, and then in May 1838, when England was quietly recuperating, erupted in Belgium, France, and Germany to spread back again to England and the United States in 1839.[36] This is a bit too simple. The crisis in the United States also affected France and Germany directly through the decline in the volume of imports, through price declines, and through a series of financial connections. Lyons felt the loss of outlets for silk immediately. American purchases were important to the success of the fairs at Frankfurt and Leipzig. American commission houses in Paris, which financed their purchases largely in London, and the American banker Samuel Welles, who did likewise, were threatened with failure as early as the spring of 1837.[37] The Maison Hottinguer, a French bank, helped Nicholas Biddle of the Bank of the United States underwrite the corner in cotton, which strangled cotton spinners in Manchester, Rouen, and Alsace in the summer and fall of 1838, before the collapse of the corner in November of that year, broken by Anglo-French boycott.[38] Moreover, as we shall see in Chapter 10, the Bank of France came to the rescue of the Bank of England. By the 1830s, then, the financial world had complex transatlantic interrelations in trade, commodity prices, and capital flows, not only between Britain and the United States but also including France in intimate connection with both.

In 1847, as noted in the previous chapter, distress developed in London in January with railroad calls, and the crisis itself came late in the summer. It was Anglo-French, as Åkerman stated, but had echoes in British-Indian trade, in Amsterdam and the Low Countries, and to a certain extent in Germany and even New York. Some sense of the spread of the crisis can be gained from the record of bankruptcies collected by Evans. Unhappily, these are by number rather than by volume of assets of failed banks and firms, which would give a better idea of their importance. The data are likely to be more complete for Britain than for other countries, from which Evans purports to give only the "principal foreign failures," doubtless seen mainly with British eyes. Despite its deficiencies, which are serious, a table constructed of the

Reported Failures in the Crisis of 1847–48, by Cities
(number of failures)

City	1847					1848								
	Aug.	Sept.	Oct.	Nov.	Dec.	Jan.	Feb.	Mar.	Apr.	May	June	July	Aug.	Oct.-Dec.
London	11	19	21	25	7	3	7	3	1	8	2	1	1	1
Liverpool	5	4	28	10	4	3	3						1	
Manchester		6	11	8	1				1					
Glasgow	2	4	6	9	7	6				1				
Other U.K.	2	4	16	7	7	2		1	1					1
Calcutta					1	11	5	1	1	2				1
Other British Empire											1	2	1	4
Paris		1				2	1	14	2					
Le Havre				1		1	1	5	2					
Marseilles		1			1	1		2	13					
Other France			2			1		1		1	1			
Amsterdam				3	1	1		14	4		1			
Other Low Countries	1		1	4				4		1	1			
Hamburg	1			2		1			7	4	3	1		
Frankfurt					3	1			1					
Berlin								3	4	1				
Other Germany		2			1		1		6					
Italy		3		7	1									
Other Europe		1	3	3	2	1	1		1	1				
New York		1	3	3	1				1	5				4
Other U.S.														7
Elsewhere	1				1					2	1			2

SOURCE: Derived from names of firms and banks listed by D. Morier Evans, *The Commercial Crisis, 1847–48* (1849; reprint ed., New York: Augustus M. Kelley, 1969), pp. 69, 74, 91–92, 103–4, 105–6, 112–13, 118–20, 123, 127.

monthly failures gives a useful impression of how the shock wave of a crisis spreads. The British crisis is seen to have almost died away, except for London, when revolution in France and Germany produced the reactions of March and April 1848, which are probably underrecorded in Evans' data.

An item of some interest is the failure of the A. Schaaff-hausen bank of Cologne on March 29, 1848 (not April, as recorded by Evans), which played a role in the development of German banking. In seeking to save the situation, the Prussian government allowed the bank to be converted into a joint-stock company, contrary to a standing policy of opposition to credit expansion; this precedent paved the way for the substantial expansion of German banks in the 1850s, with important consequences for German growth.[39] Since Cologne had been a Hanseatic city, one would have expected the bank to be tied into the merchant-banking network of London-Antwerp-Hamburg-Bremen-Le Havre-Marseilles featured so prominently by Evans. The only non-German mention I can find of Cologne, however, is the inclusion of the name of the Schaaffhausen bank in this list. A local source claims that Cologne was at the crossroads of trade among Holland, Brabant, France, and eastern and upper Germany, and that the city suffered many bankruptcies as a consequence of the British crisis of 1825. He admits, however, that apart from some financing of leather imports from Latin America, most banking finance was local and undertaken for heavy industry. Johann Wolter and Abraham Schaaffhausen got their start as leather merchants, purchasing Latin American hides from Spain first through Amsterdam and then directly. Abraham, the son, was a merchant, commission agent, forwarder, and banker with international connections. The trouble in 1848, however, came largely from financing real-estate speculation in the city. Almost one quarter of the portfolio of the bank consisted of owned land and loans to a single builder, together amounting to 1.6 million thalers, compared to the bank's capital of 1.5 million. As social unrest built up and depositors sought cash, the bank first took on a Dutch partner and then received help from the Prussian Bank's branch in Cologne, the same bank's branch in Münster, the Prussian Seehandlung (another state financial agency), and the Prussian lottery. Permission for A. Schaaffhausen to convert into A. Schaaffhausen'schen Bankverein may have been related to the fact that joint-stock banks were forbidden to invest in building sites and all other forms of speculation.[40]

The boom leading up to the panic of 1857 was worldwide and is surely overexplained. Gold discoveries in California (1849) and Australia (1851) led to export spurts to those countries, and enlarged the credit base of Europe and the United States. It would have done so to a greater extent had it not been for the fact that India was exporting far more than it was importing, and beginning to receive, along with the United States, the capital flow from Britain that had been discouraged from investing on the Continent by the revolutions of 1848. This balance-of-payments surplus was taken in silver, replaced in Europe by newly-mined gold. Both Europe and the United States had railroad and banking booms. Expansion also came from joint-stock banks in Britain and Germany, and from the Crédit Mobilier, Crédit Foncier, and Crédit Agricole in France, which loaned strongly to trade and industry. Scandinavia in particular had been stimulated by the boom in trade generated by the repeal of the British Corn Laws, timber duties, and Navigation Acts.[41] Bad harvests and the Crimean War, which cut off Russian exports, raised the price of grain for farmers worldwide. These were, in fact, the golden years for British farmers, despite the repeal of the Corn Laws in 1846. After the war, grain prices sank as Russian supplies came back to the market, and railroad building was seen to have been overdone. The dominoes started their collapse in Ohio—or, rather, the New York branch of an Ohio bank—and fell in New York, Ohio, Pennsylvania, Maryland, Rhode Island, and Virginia, and then in Liverpool, London, Paris, Hamburg, Oslo, and Stockholm.

Evans' data on bankruptcies for 1857 are even sketchier than those for 1847 and do not permit us to trace the path of destruction in the same fashion. It is possible, furthermore, to go back of the failure of Ohio Life and Trust Company and observe British withdrawals from the United States as interest rates tightened at home.

What is striking is the concentrated nature of the crisis from the Ohio Life revelation on August 24, to suspension of the Bank Act in London on November 12, through Hamburg's loan from Austria (the Silberzug) on December 10. Clapham observes that it broke out almost at the same moment in the United States, England, and Central Europe, and was felt in South America, South Africa, and the Far East.[42] Rosenberg calls it "the first *worldwide* crisis" (my emphasis). The chamber of commerce of Elberfeld asserted: "The world is a unit; industry and trade have made it so."[43]

As we have seen, 1866 really belongs to an extended crisis stretching from 1864 to 1866. Åkerman says that it parallels the 1857 crisis insofar as it follows the Civil War, as 1857 followed the Crimean War, and as the collapse of cotton in 1866 paralleled that of wheat a decade earlier.[44] The inclusion of 1864 eliminates a general view that the crisis was strictly British.[45] That view was never very persuasive. It is true that the United States played little or no significant role. The timing of the panic on Black Friday, May 11, 1866, was intimately tied to the Prussian-Austrian war, largely through stock market collapses attributable to rumors of war and the actuality, and through these to the *corso forzoso* of May 1, 1866, when the Italian government suspended convertibility of the lira into gold, and in return for this privilege borrowed 250 million lire from the national bank.[46] Like the Overend, Gurney collapse, the *corso forzoso* had been triggered by an internal run on notes against gold, stimulated by capital withdrawals toward Paris, which in turn had suffered from foreign security liquidation. The London market was shaky in mid-April because of rumors of war. The Berlin bourse panicked on May 2 with mobilization, and again on May 12 when war actually broke out. The Prussian Bank raised its discount rate to 9 percent on May 11. The panic in London that same day was part of a general rush for liquidity against a vulnerable company at a time of acute financial distress. Alfred André, a Parisian banker with major interests in Egypt, spent "an exhausting week" in London looking after the interests of his firm at the time of the Overend, Gurney crisis. He returned to Paris May 17, having concluded that the finance companies were ruined and that business was paralyzed in Italy, Prussia, Austria, and Russia, with France standing up pretty well, but only momentarily.[47] It is impossible on such a showing to conclude that 1866 was exclusively a British affair. This is not to jump to the other extreme and argue, as does an East German Marxist, that the crisis in Germany was not connected with the Prussian-Austrian war but was deeply bound up in overproduction and/or underconsumption, arising from bourgeois inability to control the contradictions between capitalist productive proportions and productive powers, whatever all that may signify.[48]

I see no connection between the U.S. gold crisis of September 1869 and the Austrian crisis of the same month, although there may be one. Both national currencies were floating. Both countries had had investment booms following wars, though the devastation from the conflicts was of very different magnitudes. Wirth prefaces his brief discussion of the "great crash of 1866," which preceded the real great crash of 1873, by some remarks about German and Austrian investments in the United States, the invasion of European markets by U.S. goods, and the extension of shipping and banking connections across the Atlantic.[49] Since he does not mention the U.S. gold crisis, however, it seems unlikely that he is suggesting a connection. Accounts of the 1869 gold crisis in the United States equally ignore Austria.[50] A possible link may run through wheat, the greenback price of which Jay Gould and Jim Fisk were trying to raise when they bid up the gold premium (discount in dollars). The difficulties following the September 1869 "crash" were concentrated in Hungary, which of course is a wheat-growing country.[51] It would be bizarre if the two episodes were connected yet produced no visible effects elsewhere. The only hint I can find of direct connection is a statement by Gould that, according to his studies, the United States could sell wheat to England in competition with the low-priced labor and water transportation from the Mediterranean with the gold agio at 45, but with gold below 40 it could not.[52] It is hard to convert a competitive situation in wheat into complementary financial vulnerability. The decline in the gold agio in the United States in September should have assisted, rather than harmed, Hungarian economic prospects.

The 1873 story is sufficiently familiar not to require laying out in detail: the Franco-Prussian indemnity, paid one-tenth in gold in 1871, led to substantial speculation in Germany that spilled over into Austria. German acquisition of £90 million from the indemnity endangered stability in Britain, because of the threat of conversion into gold. France deflated to pay the indemnity and remain outside the inflation in Europe. The only mystery is the connection, once more, between the collapse in May 1873 in Austria and Germany, after some months of distress, and that in the United States in September. Apparently the connection lay through German investments in American railroads, for Germany first supported speculation in railroads and western lands, then cut it off by bringing investment to an abrupt halt. McCartney states that 1873 is generally accepted as the first *significant* (my emphasis) international crisis: it erupted in Austria and Germany in May, spread to Italy, Holland, and Belgium, leapt the Atlantic in September, and then crossed back again to involve England, France, and Russia. A second panic indeed hit Vienna on November 1, but was short-lived.[53] In his table of international stock exchange panics, Morgenstern records "clear evidence of transmission throughout the year, extended to Amsterdam and Zurich."[54] In the fall of 1875, Baron Carl

Meyer von Rothschild, writing to Gerson von Bleichröder and commenting on the low state of stock market prices everywhere, noted that "the whole world has become a city."[55] An issue that must be postponed is whether the failure in 1873 to arrest the panic quickly, as occurred in London in 1847, 1857, and 1866, had anything to do with the protracted nature of the depression that followed.

There ensued a series of less intimately related failures and panics: the City of Glasgow in 1878, Union Générale in 1882, and New York stock market in 1884; the European-wide stock market panics in 1887 over the threat of war between Russia and Turkey; the copper corner in 1888 in Paris, with the failure of the *Comptoir d'Escompte*; and the Baring crisis of 1890, Panama scandal of 1892, New York panic of 1893, and so on. These require less attention here because their propagation have been studied in detail by Morgenstern.[56] The 1890 Baring crisis, for example, produced not panic in New York but financial stringency, as British investors sold good U.S. stocks to carry bad Latin American loans.[57] There is also the view that the financial crisis in New York in October 1890 precipitated the Baring Brothers collapse in November by producing a number of failures in London, thereby making it more difficult for Baring to continue in a period of acute distress.

1907

Morgenstern's table does not cover Italy, for which we have the benefit of a monograph on the crisis of 1907 illustrating with clarity and significant detail the interactions between collapse abroad and at home.[58] Italy had participated in the upswing of the first years of the century. Speculation fed by credit had been rife. There were fictitious ventures, and a steel trust that used funds borrowed for real investment to speculate in its own securities, paying high dividends out of borrowings to stimulate speculator interest. Distress set in as early as May 1905, with the collapse of many new companies. A second relapse occurred on the Genoa stock market in October 1906. By April and May 1907 foreign lending from Paris and London had slowed down, and the distress became more acute.

The Società Bancaria Italiana was a mushroom bank that had started in 1898 with capital of 4 million lire; that capital was raised to 5 million in 1899, 9 million in 1900, 20 million in 1904, 30 million in 1905, and 50 million in March 1906, with new people and old (often troubled) banks acquired at each stage.[59] It so lacked central direction that the Milan office did not know the risks that had been assumed by the branch in Genoa.[60] In particular, the bank was deeply involved in advances on securities (*riporti*). Governor Stringher of the Banca d'Italia was worried about it because of its poor loans and heavy borrowing from the central bank as early as December 1906.

When the market tightened up, as Paris and London cut off credit to Italy and to the United States in the spring of 1907, the upstart, marginal bank was doomed. Direct connections between Turin-Milan-Genoa and New York were limited, but Italian centers were connected to Paris, New York mainly to London, and Paris and London to each other. Bonelli asserts that when Paris cleared the decks of its London securities, and Paris and London both stopped lending, the colonial countries of the world found themselves suddenly deprived of capital, obliged to halt ongoing investment projects, and compelled to cut back output and employment, with consequent downward pressure on demand and on prices. The analogy between Italy in 1907 and a colonial territory is striking, and so is the model foreshadowing the dire consequences of the 1928 halt in foreign lending by the United States. Incidentally, Bonelli asserts that the consequence of the Parisian cutoff of loans for Italy would have been much more serious had it not been for the deus ex machina of emigrant remittances, largely from the United States.[61] Here was a direct connection across the Atlantic, largely New York to Naples.

This account focuses on the narrow direct connections. It contrasts with that of a contemporary observer, a New York banker named Frank Vanderlip, in a paper called "The Panic as a World Phenomenon." The basic causes of the panic, Vanderlip found, were the Boer War, the Russo-Japanese War, and the San Francisco earthquake. But after such a grandiose beginning, he settled down to a discussion of overtrading by newly formed trust companies and the need for an expansive currency.[62]

Once again the narrative runs the risk of ennui, and on this account we abstain from describing the international aspects of all crises except 1929. In 1914 foreign holders dumped securities in foreign markets. In 1920–21, despite what Friedman and Schwartz say about the origin of the crisis in the United States, the fact is that a boom based on a scramble to replace inventories exhausted by war (and, in Britain, on roseate prospects of taking over German export markets) collapsed simultaneously everywhere. The recession of 1937 was strictly a U.S. phenomenon, based on a cobweb in inventory accumulation. The year 1974 saw the levying of a $50 billion annual tax on oil by the Organization of Petroleum Exporting Countries, with the proceeds largely hoarded and no offsetting expansion of investment anywhere.

The International Ramifications of 1929

I have dealt with the 1929 depression in part in Chapter 4 and elsewhere, and may be excused if the present account of its international aspects is succinct.[63] As Hoover stated, some part of the real cause of the depression was expansion of production outside of Europe during World War I, expansion which proved excessive at 1925 prices when European production recovered after that year. In addition, there were the

financial complications of reparations and war debts; badly
set exchange rates, especially for the pound and the French
franc, which piled up French claims in London; and recycling
of German reparations after the Dawes Plan by American
private lending to German corporations and public bodies.
Some blame attaches to the reduction of interest rates in New
York in the summer of 1927 to assist the British in maintaining the pound, when U.S. domestic purposes might better have
been served by restraint. When the New York stock market
took off in March 1928 and especially after June, foreign
lending came to a halt. For a time, Germany and the periphery
of states in Latin America and Australia shifted to borrowing
at short term. In the face of a reduced inflow of capital,
Germany deflated her economy to transfer reparations abroad.
Argentina, Australia, Uruguay, and Brazil found their balances
of payments turning sharply adverse. Unable to fund their
accumulations of short-term indebtedness, or to borrow more,
these countries saw their exchange rates begin to depreciate
shortly after the stock market crash of October 1929, as the
prices of wheat, coffee, rubber, sugar, silk, cotton, etc., fell
sharply. Prices and business in the United States were strongly
affected by the liquidity seizure, as noted in Chapter 4. An
open-market program undertaken by the Federal Reserve
Bank of New York on its own initiative, over the protest of
the Federal Reserve Board in Washington, alleviated the credit
squeeze by the first of the year, although at a lower level of
output and prices.

The first half of 1930 witnessed a comeback in international
lending, to such an extent that April-June 1930 recorded the
peak of U.S. lending for any quarter between the wars. However, the lowered level of prices and the loss of confidence in
Germany, especially after the National Socialist gains in the
September 1930 elections, meant that the world as a whole
remained in distress. Banks in Central Europe, largely Austria
and Germany, tried to improve their positions by bidding up
their prices of their own stock. Two private banks, the Banque

Adam and the Banque Oustric, failed in Paris, the latter un-
leashing a scandal that implicated three government officials
and led to the fall of the government. The deflationary Laval
government came in early in 1931. And then the rolling
deflation started: the Credit Anstalt in Austria in May, the
Danatbank in July, the German standstill agreement of July,
a series of withdrawals from Britain in August, culminating
in the depreciation of sterling in September. At this stage the
gold bloc of France, Belgium, the Netherlands, and Switzerland started converting dollars into gold, exerting pressure
on bank reserves in the United States. Japan went off gold
in December 1931. Deflation in the United States came from
appreciation of the currency (i.e., the depreciation of the
pound sterling and the sterling area as a whole), and from the
reduction of bank reserves. In February 1932 the Glass-
Steagall act made it possible to reflate on the monetary side
through open-market operations, but it was far too late. Bank
failures continued to spread in a positive-feedback process of
falling prices, bankruptcies, and bank failures. Bottom was
reached only with the general Bank Holiday of 1933, and the
depreciation of the dollar in the spring of that year.

In view of this history, I find it impossible to understand
the view that the 1929 depression was of domestic origin
in the U.S.

CHAPTER 8

Letting It Burn Out, and Other Devices

Assume plethora, speculation, panic, as in the epigraph from Walter Bagehot. What then? The management of crises will occupy the next three chapters. This, the first, will consider initially the possibility that the best remedy for panic is to leave it alone, letting it run its course. We then discuss a variety of assorted expedients that have been used in the real world, short of issuing new money through a lender of last resort. The two chapters that follow consider the role of the lender of last resort, first domestically in Chapter 9, then internationally in Chapter 10.

No Management

Most monetarists and quite a few nonmonetarists take the view that the evil of panic will work its own cure, the fire can be left to burn itself out.[1] "Cool if not very imaginative heads in the Bank [of England] parlour thought it in the nature of panics to exhaust themselves."[2] Lord Overstone maintained that support of the financial system in crisis is not really necessary, as the resources of the system are so great that, even in times of the utmost stringency, large loans are to be had by those offering a sufficient rate of interest.[3] My colleague Rudiger Dornbusch has adopted the same position in informal discussion, taking great pleasure in pointing to an incident in 1847 when a rise in the private rate of discount to 10 and 12 percent in London stopped the flow of gold to the United States and even resulted in the sending of a small sloop to overtake a ship that had already sailed for America, getting it to turn around and unload £100,000 in gold.[4]

There is, of course, much truth in this contention, and some danger in coming to the rescue of the market to halt a panic too soon, too frequently, too predictably, or even on occasion at all. We shall address the dilemmas of a lender of last resort in the next chapter. Here we consider historically, not a priori as the theorists do, whether the lender of last resort can always be dispensed with altogether.

The notion that a panic should be allowed to pursue its course is perhaps compounded of two strains. One strain takes a certain amount of pleasure or *Schadenfreude* in the trouble visited upon the market, as retribution for excesses of the past; this somewhat Puritanical or Fundamentalist standpoint rather welcomes hellfire as the just deserts of others. The others sees panic as a thunderstorm "in a mephitic and unhealthy tropical atmosphere," clearing the air. "It purified the commercial and financial elements, and tended to restore vitality and health, alike conducive to regular trade, sound progress and permanent prosperity."[5] The most powerful statement of this position I have found comes from Herbert Hoover, as he characterizes, without approval, the view of Andrew Mellon:

The "leave-it-alone liquidationists" headed by Secretary of the Treasury Mellon . . . felt that government must keep its hands off and let the slump liquidate itself. Mr. Mellon had only one formula: "Liquidate labor, liquidate stocks, liquidate the farmers, liquidate real estate." He insisted that, when the people get an inflationary brainstorm, the only way to get it out of their blood is to let it collapse. He held that even panic was not altogether a bad thing. He said: "It will purge the rottenness out of the system. High costs of living and high living will come down. People will work harder, live a more moral life. Values will be adjusted, and enterprising people will pick up the wrecks from less competent people."[6]

The opposing view concedes that it is desirable to purge the system of bubbles and mania investment, but that a deflationary panic runs the risk of spreading and wiping out sound investments which may not be able to obtain the loans necessary to ensure survival.

The evidence of high rates of interest charged for liquidity, adverted to earlier (page 115), is not significant, especially when these rates are expressed as a percentage per annum when they are really premiums for liquidity for one, two, or at most a few days. The real question is whether funds are available at these rates, whether the market is cleared by rationing (not market-clearing prices), and whether the quantity allowed is zero. There is considerable testimony from various crises to suggest that borrowing in panic is difficult and sometimes impossible:

> *1763:* After first Arend Joseph and then DeNeufville failed in 1763, and panic broke out on July 25, a succinct, not very informative or convincing report says: "Panic: even on securities and on goods, no money was to be had."[7]

> *1825:* "A panic seized upon the public, such as had never been witnessed before: everybody begging for money—money—but money was hardly on any condition to be had. 'It was not the character of the security,' observes the *Times.* 'that was considered, but the impossibility of producing money at all.' "[8]

> *1847:* Interrogation of Thomas Tooke before the Select Committee on the Commercial Crisis of 1847:

Question 5421: "For several days, if not some weeks, the Bank of England was the only establishment that was discounting?" Answer: "Yes."

Question 5472: "The Governor of the Bank of England said he could not sell £1 million of stock [English government bonds] in the week after October 14, if there had been no letter. Do you think possible?" Answer: "No, perfectly impossible, taking the word impossible to signify with the exception of such a reduction in price as could not be contemplated."[9]

1847: Evidence of Mr. Glyn:

Question: "Are you aware that it was the opinion of the Bank broker that a very large sum might have been sold without materially affecting the prices of Consols [English perpetual bonds]?" Answer: "I was not aware that the Bank broker had stated that. I should say, from what I saw at the time, that a sale of a million or two million, which were the figures talked of, would have been almost impossible without knocking down the funds to such a price as would have created a further panic."

Mr. Browne, M.P., did not think such sales could have been effected, unless at a great sacrifice, adding that "if the panic had been equal to what we might suppose it might have been, under such circumstances, I doubt whether they could have been sold at all."[10]

1857: "At one stage during the crisis it was impossible to negotiate paper at all, the charge under the most favorable circumstances being 12 and 15 percent."[11]

A letter from Liverpool: "Bills of exchange of the first Quality in themselves, and to which this and other Banks were willing to add their Endorsement, were absolutely inconvertible into Cash, and it is my Belief that many Houses, who were not merely solvent but able to pay 40s and 60s to the Pound, must have stopped had not the Government letter been issued."[12]

"Commercial confidence in Hamburg is entirely at an

end. Bills of only three or four of the first houses are
negotiable at the highest rate of interest. . . . A government bond advance of 15 million marks banco failed to
help. The panic was so great that government bonds
could not be discounted, and on no security whatsoever
would capitalists part with their money. . . . When it was
known on December 12 that assistance would help all,
the panic ceased. Government bonds which had not been
discountable at 15 percent on the first of the month were
readily taken at 2 and 3 percent."[13]

1866: "The Bank court raised the discount rate to 9 percent and intimated that loans on Government securities
were available at 10 percent. Before that announcement
it was impossible to sell either Consols or Exchequer
bills. Jobbers in other securities refused to deal."[14]

1873: "The National Trust Company of New York had
eight hundred thousand dollars worth of government
securities in its vaults, but not a dollar could be borrowed
on them; and it suspended."[15]

1883: "The growing demand for money finally led to a
money famine. Time loans were unobtainable, call loans
were 72 percent in June, 72 percent on July 28th, 51 percent on August 4. First-class commercial paper was
quoted 8 to 12 percent nominal, with a very small amount
of money available."[16]

The evidence is by no means unambiguous, qualified as it is
in the case of selling government bonds by such remarks as
"with the exception of such a reduction in price [i.e., increase
in the rate of interest] as could not be contemplated." Moreover, there is occasional information on the other side of the
argument, especially in the United States under the national
banking system, in which a lender of last resort was largely
unavailable:

1884: "To add further to the discomfiture of dealers,
money became exceedingly stringent, and at one time

commanded as much as 4 percent for 24 hours use. This
caused a further sacrifice of stocks since few could afford
to pay the high rate asked. The exorbitant charge was, of
course, the direct result of the distrust prevailing, since
there was no actual scarcity. . . . It was to . . . the desire
to realize and obtain cash that the large decline on
Thursday and Friday of nearly 7 percent on United States
Government bonds is to be attributed. There was no loss
in confidence in these, nor was there in good railroad
bonds and stocks.

"One result of the phenomenal and temporary rise in
rates for money was to bring a vast amount of foreign
capital to the market. Some of it was sent here to buy
stocks at their depressed prices, and more to loan on
stocks or on any other good securities at the high rates
of interest. The effect of this was to completely turn the
foreign exchanges which had been running so heavily
against us. . . ."[17]

This, in its turn, is not unambiguous, since the panic seems
to have started before the stage of acute liquidity shortage
had been reached.

Miscellaneous Devices

The dominant argument against the a priori view that panics
can be cured by being left alone is that they almost never *are*
left alone. The authorities feel compelled to intervene. In panic
after panic, crash after crash, crisis after crisis, the authorities
or some "responsible citizens" try to bring the panic to a halt
by one device or another. It is possible that they are unduly
alarmed, and that the position would correct itself without
serious harm. They may be stupid and unable to learn. The
Chicago School of monetarists assumes, in fact, that authori-

ties are universally stupid and the market always intelligent.
In the panics we are examining, this uneven distribution of
intelligence cannot be tested against crisis management because authorities and leading figures in the marketplace both
exert themselves in the same direction: to intervene in one
way or another, in order to halt the spread of falling prices,
bankruptcy, and bank failure. If there is a learning process at
work—and the assumption of rationality requires one—the
learning has taken the form of discovering the desirability
and even the wisdom of a lender of last resort, rather than
relying exclusively on the competitive forces of the market.

History offers a number of occasions when the authorities
were resolved not to intervene, for reasons explored in the
next chapter, but found themselves reluctantly forced to do
so. Lord Liverpool threatened to resign as chancellor of the
exchequer in December 1825 if an issue of Exchequer bills
were provided to rescue the market after he had warned
against excessive speculation six months earlier.[18] Lord
Lidderdale, governor of the Bank of England at the time of
the Baring crisis, refused categorically to accept a "letter of
indemnity" to permit the Bank to exceed its lending limits.[19]
In each instance, face was saved by finding another device to
accomplish the task of averting panic. On numerous other
occasions, including the intervention of Frederick II in the
Berlin aspects of the crisis of 1763,[20] the Bank of England's
refusal to discount for the "W banks,"[21] the U.S. Treasury
decision in 1869,[22] and the rescue of New York in 1975, a
strong moral stand to leave the market to its own devices
was reversed as panic built up.

Stalling

In a run, depositors are in a hurry to get their money.
Banks are in no hurry to pay it out. In the runs on banks
during 1931–33, there were stories current of banks that took

their time to pay off depositors, hoping, like Micawber, for something to turn up. The technique is an ancient one, going back at least to the eighteenth century.

McLeod's *Theory and Practice of Banking* describes how the Bank of England defended itself in September 1720 against a run brought on by its going back on a promise to absorb the bonds of the South Sea Company at £400. To avert failure, the Bank organized its friends in the front of the line and paid them off slowly in light sixpences. These friends brought the cash back through another door: it was deposited, again slowly counted, and then made available for paying out once more. By this means, the story concludes, the run was staved off until the Festival of Michaelmas (September 29). When the holidays were over, so was the run, and the Bank re-opened.[23]

A second story, which may well have the same origin and is likely to be more accurate, has it that it was the Sword Blade Bank, a supporter of the South Sea Company, that resisted attempts on every side to redeem its paper in silver. When the run started on September 19, the bank brought up wagonloads of silver which it proceeded to pay out "slowly in small change." One lucky noteholder is reported to have gone off with £8,000 in shillings and sixpences before the bank closed its doors on Saturday, September 24.[24] The circumstances suggest one story; the dates two. It cannot be the case that the Sword Blade Bank and the Bank of England cooperated, as they were mortal enemies.

The lesson of 1720, whatever its details, was not lost on the Bank of England a quarter century later. The Young Pretender (Charles Edward, grandson of James II) landed in Scotland in July 1745, unfurled his banner in September, invaded England in November, got to Carlisle on November 15, reached Derby on December 4. Panic broke out on Black Friday, December 5, 1745. British consols fell to 45, the lowest price on record, and a run began on the Bank of England. It resisted partly by paying off its notes in sixpences. The time thus gained was used to inscribe London merchants in a proclamation of loyalty and readiness to accept Bank of England notes. The second half of the prescription, collecting pledges of faith in notes, was used again in similar circumstances, when the French landed at Fishguard in 1797. On that occasion, 1,140 signatures of merchants and investors in government stock were collected in a single day.[25] It should perhaps be added that the time gained in 1745 by both the slow payout and the peititon of support was further used to organize the army that defeated the Young Pretender at Culloden in April 1746.

Complete Shutdown

One way to stop panic is to close the market. This was done to the New York Stock Exchange in 1873 and in London and many other cities at the outbreak of war in 1914. On the whole, it is not recommended, since shutdown may drive the panic underground and worsen it. Moreover, short-run and long-run goals are in conflict. Closing the stock market in this panic exacerbates the next, as people dump stocks or pull out call money sooner to avoid getting locked in. The New York Stock Exchange was closed for the first and last time in a panic in September 1873, but a financial editor suggested that fear of closing of the exchange in October 1929 was a factor in the withdrawals of call money by out-of-town banks and "others."[26] The closing of local stock exchanges in Pittsburgh and New Orleans for two months in 1873 presumably had fewer serious consequences, since they traded only local securities, which had brought on their difficulties.[27]

Another means of closing the market is to declare a legal holiday. This was done during the panic of 1907 in Oklahoma, Nevada, Washington, Oregon, and California.[28] The device was the forerunner of the bank holiday which started at a local level in the fall of 1932 and was generalized to the country as a whole on March 3, 1933. A bank holiday closes only the banks, while a legal holiday shuts down all business.

A still less satisfactory device is to suspend the publication of bank statements, as was undertaken in 1873 in the hope that "what you don't know won't hurt you." The technique was designed to hide the large losses of reserves of a few banks, the revelation of which, it was feared, would reduce depositor confidence in these banks still further.[29]

A partial and apparently fully acceptable device in commodity trading is the daily limit which, when reached, automatically closes the market for the day. So far as I can determine, this is relatively new in commodity markets, and has not been applied to securities in times of stress. Nor have I found record of paying off a certain volume of deposits each morning and closing the windows down when that number has been reached.

Time can be gained by moratoriums on payment of all debts, on payments of particular types of obligations, such as bills of exchange having less than two weeks to run—in fact, on the need to declare bankruptcy. The most ubiquitous measure of this sort is the habit of bank examiners in ignoring bad loans in the portfolios of banks as long as they can decently do so. If Real Estate Investment Trusts (REITs), landlords of mortgaged shopping centers, and owners of mothballed 747s are willing to pay interest by adding to a loan, banks are unlikely to raise a question, nor are bank examiners always insistent on taking the conservative and righteous path of pointing with alarm.

Official moratoriums may be less effective than informal ones, however. A moratorium on the settlement of differences in payments due on the 1873 Vienna Stock Exchange lasted a week, from the stock market collapse to May 15. In combination with two rescue committees, a guarantee fund of 20 million gulden was put together by the Austrian National Bank and the solid commercial banks; all these imitations of earlier measures were of little assistance.[30] Another moratorium was noted in Paris after the July Monarchy, when the municipal council decreed that all bills payable in Paris between July 25 and August 15 should be extended ten days. This sterilized the commercial paper in banking portfolios, did nothing to discourage a run by holders of notes demanding coin, and was not helpful.[31]

Clearinghouse Certificates

The major device used in the United States prior to the creation of the Federal Reserve System was the clearinghouse certificate. The clearinghouse was an institution of the 1850s in this country: the New York house was established in 1853, Philadelphia's in 1858, after the panic of 1857. During the panic of 1857, banks failed to cooperate in New York to halt the spread of deflation. The Mercantile Agency of New York took the position that if four or five of the strongest banks had come to the assistance of the Ohio Life and Trust Company, enabling it to meet its obligations, the business and credit of the country would have been preserved.[32] By 1873, through the clearinghouses, banks were ready to go as far as accepting payment on cleared checks in clearinghouse certificates (obligations of the clearinghouse as a whole), rather than demanding currency or bank notes. The advantage of this system was that it reduced the incentive for any bank to try to bid deposits away from its competitors. The system, Sprague insists, had to be accompanied by agreement for pooling of bank reserves; otherwise, a bank with no net drain might be forced to suspend payments after it paid out cash over the counter to its own depositors but received no cash in clearings.[33] In 1873 reserves were pooled. Thereafter they were not, and certificates still helped some, but less.

A further serious drawback of clearinghouse certificates, of course, was that, like scrip, they had only local validity. Thus, they helped maintain domestic payments such as payrolls and retail sales, but they cut down the effective flow of payments between cities. In 1907, sixty out of 160 clearinghouses in the United States adopted clearinghouse certificates to facilitate local payments. Dislocations of the domestic exchanges were no less complete and disturbing, Sprague claims, than on previous occasions. A table giving quotations of New York funds in Boston, Philadelphia, Chicago, St. Louis, Cincinnati, Kansas City, and New Orleans between October 26 and December 15, 1907, shows New York for the most part at a premium or par in other financial centers, but with a range of quotations from a discount of 1.25 percent in Chicago on November 2 to a 7 percent premium in St. Louis on November 26, up from 1.5 percent the previous week.[34] In December 1907, Jacob H. Schiff wrote: "The one lesson we should learn from recent experience is that the issuing of clearinghouse certificates in the different bank centers has also worked considerable harm. It has broken down domestic exchange and paralyzed to a large extent the business of the country."[35]

It is not surprising that the advocates of flexible exchange rates, or of limited regional devices like the European Payments Union, have not hailed the experience under clearinghouse certificates as exemplary of (1) the beauties of local money or (2) the benefits of localized clearing. So far as I know, there is no tendency on anyone's part to regard clearinghouse certificates as anything better than a poor tenthbest. Other devices of the same general character are clearinghouse cheques and certified checks, both of which add to means of payment in circulation without requiring cash.

Banks organized through clearinghouses only after the middle of the nineteenth century. Other groups can organize to mitigate a panic. Consider, for example, the stock market consortium. In October 24, 1907, a bankers' pool headed by J. P. Morgan loaned $25 million at 10 percent in call money in an attempt to stem the collapse of the stock market.[36] Twenty-two years to the day later, on Black Thursday in 1929, Richard Whitney went from post to post on the floor of the exchange, placing bids for stocks in behalf of a syndicate headed once again by J. P. Morgan and Company.[37]

Bank Collaborations

Aside from clearinghouses, banks may collaborate through rescue committees (as in Vienna in May 1873 and earlier), loan funds, funds for guarantees of liabilities, arranged mergers of weak banks and firms, and other devices for having the strong support the weak.* Perhaps three examples will suffice: the role of the Paris banks in the 1828 crisis in Alsace, various devices employed by Hamburg in meeting the difficulties of 1857, and the Baring Brothers loan guarantee fund of 1890.

The Alsatian Crisis of 1828

Three firms in textiles failed in December 1827 at Mulhouse. Without waiting, Paris banks refused all Alsatian paper, and even the Bank of France set itself a limit of 6 million francs, a figure "scarcely the fortune of two Alsatian houses." It then decided against accepting any paper with Mulhouse or Basel endorsements. This precipitated a panic. On January 19, two more Mulhouse merchants failed. On January 22, in Paris, there were rumors of the failure of two Schlumberger firms. The Paris banks sent an emissary, Jacques Laffitte. He arrived in Mulhouse on January 26, offering only to lend 1 million francs on the consignment of merchandise. Before he came, however, two textile men, Nicholas Koechlin and Jean Dollfuss, had left Mulhouse for Paris, followed by two more.

---

* For a discussion of the rescue committee (*Aufhilfsfonds*) in Vienna, see Eduard März, *Österreich Industrie- und Bankpolitik in der Zeit Franz Josephs I: Am Beispiel der k.k. priv. Österreichischen Credit-Anstalt für Handel und Gewerbe* (Vienna: Europa Verlag, 1968), pp. 177–82. März notes (p. 179) that the best account of the crisis is that of Josef Neuwirth, *Bank und Valuta in Österreich. Vol. 2: Die Spekulationskrisis von 1873* (no publishing data given), which I have not seen.

Inventories were being dumped on the market at discounts of 30 to 40 percent. Nine houses failed from January 26 to February 15. It could have been worse, says Lévy-Leboyer. At the last minute a syndicate of twenty-six Paris banks, presided over by J.-C. Davillier, gave a credit of 5 million francs to Koechlin and Dollfuss, who, returning to Alsace on February 3, kept 4 million and distributed 1 million to their colleagues who were willing to offer guarantees. This gesture reestablished confidence, and with 1.3 million francs scraped up in Basel for some others, partly with guarantees of other merchants, confidence was finally restored.[38] Those who qualified for neither the Koechlin-Dollfuss fund nor Basel money failed.[39] It is a cautionary story of "ad hoccery" that reflects little wisdom or credit on the part of the Bank of France or Paris bankers.

The Hamburg Crisis of 1857

The background of the crisis of 1857 in Hamburg should by now be familiar to the reader. Trade had expanded, particularly because of the Crimean War, and credit much more. Hamburg was the all-English city of Germany, but had close relations with the United States in sugar, tobacco, coffee, and cotton, and with Scandinavia. When the deflationary tidal wave swept across the Atlantic, there was no way Hamburg could escape inundation. The panic touched off by Ohio Life on August 24 arrived in Hamburg three months later (following price declines of 30 percent) with the suspension of Winterhoff and Piper, engaged in the American trade.[40] Daily dispatches from the British consulate in Hamburg by date tell the story:

November 21: Some of the leading merchant houses and two banks plan for relief.

November 24: A Discount Guarantee Association (*Garantie-Diskontverein*) is formed, initially with a capital of 10 million marks banco, later raised to 13 million (about £1 million), of which the sum of 1 million marks is to be paid in immediately.

November 23: Two major houses engaged in the London trade fail, and the Discount Guarantee Association grows more cautious in endorsing Hamburg bills.[41] On one authority, the Discount Guarantee Association is exhausted in three days.[42]

November 28: The chamber of commerce and leading merchants induce the Senate to call Parliament (Bürgerschaft) to arrange to issue government bonds in order to lend 50 to 66⅔ percent of the value of hypothecated goods, bonds, and shares to merchants in distress.

December 1: With the suspension of Ullberg and Cremer, ten to twelve houses in the Swedish trade have gone down. The Discount Guarantee Association will not issue any more guarantees. Business is at a standstill.

December 2: A suggestion is made to change the laws of bankruptcy to enable creditors to share in attachments of goods.

December 7: A proposal is made to establish a state bank for discounting good bills to the amount of 30 million marks banco (about £2.4 million). The bank would advance government bills bearing 66⅔ percent interest on mercantile bills of exchange. Parliament rejects this, wanting instead to issue 30 million marks banco of paper currency as legal tender. The Senate rejects this, insisting on clinging to the silver standard.

In the end, a compromise was reached for a State Loan Institute fund of 15 million comprising 5 million marks banco of Hamburg government bonds and 10 million in silver to be borrowed abroad.[43] The story of the silver train (Silberzug) belongs to Chapter 10, as an example of an international lender of last resort.

One observer totaled the sums available for rescue operations to 35 million marks banco: 15 million in the Discount Guarantee Association, 15 million in the State Loan Institute, and 5 million found by the chamber of commerce in ways not made clear. He compares this with 100 million marks banco of protested bills, noting that if merchants speculate with capital equal only to one-sixth the value of their goods, a 17 percent decline in price is sufficient to wipe them out. To the suggestion that the Senate was being 300 years behind the times, he reports with approval the Senate's answer: the merchants had been 300 years ahead of the times in issuing debt. State help in these cases, he insists, merely means assistance to speculation and perpetuation of higher prices at the cost of the consumer, a view that will be developed further in the next chapter and is not unfamiliar today.[44]

Guarantees of Liabilities: The Baring Crisis

The most famous guarantee of liabilities was that worked out by Lord Lidderdale at the time of the Baring crisis. It was not the first in Britain. Already in December 1836, the private bankers Esdaile, Grenfell, Thomas and Company, who served as London agents for seventy-two country banks, had gotten into trouble. It was said that on account of its country banking connection, the firm could not be allowed to fail; moreover, its paper included all the best names in the City. Assets far exceeded liabilities, and the bankers of London were prepared to help with guarantees. The Bank of England led the list with £150,000. Esdailes survived, but only for two years, passing away then, Clapham says, with credit.[45]

As noted earlier, the guarantee was worked out as an alternative to a letter of indemnity permitting suspension of the Bank Act of 1844. The letter was offered by the chancellor of the exchequer, Lord Goschen, to Lord Lidderdale, who was governor of the Bank of England. Lord Lidderdale refused on the ground that "reliance on such letters was the cause of a great deal of bad banking in England."

If he refused to quiet the market by the usual means that had been employed in 1847, 1857, and 1866, Lord Lidderdale was not one to let the market take its medicine. In August 1890 he warned Baring Brothers that the firm would have to moderate its acceptances for its Argentine agent, S. B. Hales. Baring Brothers revealed its acute distress to Lord Lidderdale on Saturday, November 8. Fearful of panic when the condition of Baring was made public, the Bank of England met with the Exchequer on Monday, November 10, turned down the letter of indemnity, and made preparations on two fronts. Its reserves were low, and it was thought that raising Bank rate would rebuild them only slowly. Accordingly, help was sought abroad—a subject for Chapter 10. Second, the Bank formed a committee, headed by Lord Rothschild, to address the question of the large mass of undigested Argentine securities in the market.

As the week wore on, rumors circulated, and Baring bills were increasingly discounted at the Bank of England. By Wednesday, Lidderdale had learned that Baring was solvent in the long run but would need £8–9 million. On Friday, John Daniell, the leading man at Mullens and Co., used by the Bank of England in open-market operations, came to Lidderdale, crying, "Can't you do something, or say something, to relieve people's minds: they have made up their minds that something awful is up, and they are talking of the very highest names—*the very highest!*"[46]

On November 14, Lidderdale met with two cabinet ministers representing the Exchequer, Lords Smith and Salisbury. It was agreed that the government would increase its balance at the Bank immediately. It was also agreed, with more difficulty, that the government would share with the Bank in any losses suffered on Baring Brothers' paper discounted by the Bank between 2 P.M. Friday and 2 P.M. Saturday. On the basis of this agreement, Lidderdale met with eleven private banks, trying to get them to contribute to a fund guaranteeing Baring's liabilities, and obtained the agreement of the State Bank of Russia not to withdraw its £2.4 million deposit at Baring. The private banks as a whole contributed £3,250,000, but this included £1 million from the Bank of England itself (a private bank, but only of sorts), as well as £500,000 each from three leaders, Glyn, Mills & Co., Currie and Co., and Rothschilds. With this start, he obtained that evening the agreement of the five London joint-stock banks to join the guarantee fund for another £3,250,000. On the basis of these assurances, the *Times* of November 15 announced that Baring Brothers would fail but that there would be no loss. The work of the guarantee fund continued on Saturday. For one thing, the joint-stock banks had to hold meetings of directors to approve their subscriptions. This was done by 11 A.M. Then other banks and financial institutions raised the fund from £7.5 million in the morning to £10 million by 4 P.M. (It eventually reached £17 million.) The guarantee fund was taken as a measure of the strength of the London financial system more than the Baring failure was taken as a sign of weakness. Martin's Bank, for one, was in distress over its loans to Baring and Murriettas, another bank involved in Argentina. It joined the guarantee fund for £100,000 on November 18 (Tuesday), too late to afford much help to the Barings, but early enough to demonstrate to the world the strength of Martin.[47] In summarizing the episode, Powell stated: "The Bank is not a single combatant who must fight or retire, but the leader of the most colossal agglomeration of financial power which the world has so far witnessed."[48]

On November 25 a new firm, Baring Brothers and Co., Ltd., was formed as a joint-stock company with a capital of £1 million. The form of the guarantee may be of modest interest.

Guarantee Fund
Bank of England, November, 1890

In consideration of advances which the Bank of England have agreed to make to Messrs. Baring Brothers and Co., to enable them to discharge at maturity their liabilities existing on the night of the 15th of November, 1890, or arising out of business initiated on or prior to the 15th of November, 1890,

We, the undersigned, hereby agree, each individual, firm, or company, for himself or themselves alone, and to the amount only set opposite to his or their names respectively, to make good to the Bank of England any loss which may appear whenever the Bank of England shall determine that the final liquidation of the liabilities of Messrs. Baring Brothers and Co. has been completed so far in the opinion of the Governors as practicable.

All the guarantors shall contribute rateably, and no one individual, firm, or company, shall be called on for his or their contribution without the like call being made on the others.

The maximum period over which the liquidation may extend is three years, commencing the 15th of November, 1890.[49]

Federal Deposit Insurance

The 1890 guarantee was provided privately, post hoc. Since 1934, federal deposit insurance in the United States has prevented bank runs from spreading by providing an *ex ante* guarantee of deposits, limited originally to $10,000 but gradually raised to $40,000. This device was enacted after the greatest banking collapse, probably, that the world has known. What accounts for the reluctance to provide such guarantees earlier?

In the long tradition of United States, free banking, even wildcat banking, was the rule. Anyone could start a bank, and many did. Risks were large, banker turnover rapid. A guarantee of bankers' deposits would have constituted a license to speculate, if not embezzle, and would have removed the major check on banker irresponsibility, the threat of withdrawal of deposits. Deposit guarantees were rejected as conducive to bad banking right down to March 2, 1933, when the Board of Governors of the Federal Reserve was not prepared to recommend such a guarantee, or any other measures, on the eve of the national bank holiday.[50]

There is something to this. The record of the Federal Deposit Insurance Corporation was excellent until about 1970. From the beginning in 1934 through 1970, only one bank with deposits of more than $50 million had failed, and most failures were of minuscule banks with deposits of less than $5 million.

The FDIC had in most cases arranged for takeovers, so that the few depositors with deposits above insured amounts had not been hurt, and the FDIC itself had had to make good few losses.

Since 1970, however, the economic situation has become more disturbed in primary products, especially oil, and there has been speculation in office buildings, shopping centers, resorts, condominiums, and single-dwelling housing. Exchange-rate fluctuations have encouraged bank speculation in foreign exchange. The OPEC price hike has increased the need for borrowing by countries to meet balance-of-payments deficits. The FDIC has a so-called "problem list" of banks that have been in financial difficulties for some time. At the beginning of 1976 there were two banks on the problem list with deposits of more than $1 billion—the number of such banks in the United States on June 30, 1976, was eighty-eight—and by the end of October the problem list included eight banks of more than $1 billion, one of which was considered a "serious problem."[51] The FDIC's view of the matter is perhaps the most comprehensive, but in the winter of 1975–76 the Federal Reserve Board staff had a problem list that included twelve of the fifty largest bank holding companies in the country. On this showing, advance guarantees do not eliminate the necessity for contemplating trouble, although they may moderate trouble enormously when it comes.

Exchequer Bills

One device short of lending money to a firm in trouble is to issue marketable securities to that firm against appropriate collateral. (Of course, as the first part of this chapter indicated, when markets break down, even the most liquid securities may not be readily sold.) The securities may be private or public, both types were part of the complex package put together by Hamburg in 1857. In 1763 and 1799, in an equally

complex and jerry-built system of support, admiralty bills
were an integral feature.[52] The widest development, however,
was the Exchequer bills issued in Britain in 1793, 1799, and
(without enthusiasm) 1811, but sternly rejected in 1825.

The Exchequer bill was widely thought to have been the
idea of Sir John Sinclair, although it may have originated with
the Bank of England. On April 22, 1793, leaders of the City
met with Prime Minister William Pitt at Downing Street to
devise means of combating the crisis arising from the failure
of 100 of the 300 country banks and the calamitous fall of
prices. The next day, eleven of their number met in Mansion
House to formulate a scheme for state assistance. According
to Clapham, there was no clear guide to what ought to be
done. In due course, the idea emerged to have the government
issue £3 million in Exchequer bills, later raised by Parliament
to £5 million, to be issued to merchants on the collateral of
goods deposited in customs houses. An additional feature of
the plan was to issue £5 notes—the previous minimum having
been £10—to economize on the use of cash. The Exchequer
bills were issued not by the Bank of England but by special
commissioners. Some £70,000 worth was immediately sent off
to be administered in Manchester, and an equal amount to
Glasgow. The device worked like a charm, according to
MacPherson. Three hundred and thirty-eight firms applied
for only £3 million of the total amount. A total of £2.2 million
was granted to 228 firms, only two of which subsequently
went bankrupt. Applications for more than £1.2 million were
withdrawn after the panic simmered down.[53]

In 1799 the panic of Hamburg had an echo in Liverpool,
and Exchequer bills again came into play, to a limited extent.
Parliament provided £500,000 in Exchequer bills, used solely
in Liverpool, against goods stored in warehouses worth £2
million.[54]

In 1811 the question arose again. A Select Committee on
the State of Commercial Credit was appointed on March 1,

1811. It included Henry Thornton, Sir John Sinclair, Sir Thomas Baring, and Alexander Baring, among others. The committee's report, completed in a week, recorded the distress of exporters to and importers from the West Indies and South America, as well as the piles of goods bound for the Baltic that had been cut off and stored in London warehouses, and recommended a new issue of Exchequer bills, this time for £6 million. In the House of Commons support was moderate, given the overtrading to Latin America; the opposition, while sympathetic to the distress, was doubtful of the wisdom of bailing out speculators. Huskisson, who later made his mark as the president of the Board of Trade, claimed that the evil came from too easy credit:

Did gentlemen not see that the race of old English merchants, who never could persuade themselves to go beyond their capital, was superseded by a set of mad and extravagant speculators, who never stopped so long as they could get credit, and that persons of notoriously small capital had now eclipsed those of the greatest consequence; so that speculations now took place even in the lowest articles of commerce. . . . If the relief given was used for further speculation, it would only aggravate the evil—and he feared that this might be done—in which case the present measure would go only to add six millions to the circulation and to raise the prices of all our commodities.[55]

Smart, who gives the fullest account of the debate, notes that many criticized the measure, though few were bold enough to deny it. In the end it passed, but few applications were made and only £2 million was advanced. "Not many of those who were in embarrassed circumstances were able to furnish the desired security, and it is difficult to see what remedy there was in being enabled, by advances, to produce more goods when the radical evil was that there was no market for them."[56]

We have seen earlier—twice in fact—that Exchequer bills were sternly rejected as a means of alleviating the crisis of 1825.

Luck: A Tailpiece

Before we turn to the lender of last resort, there is finally Lady Luck, who may work more effectively on individual cases than on national or world financial crises. I have pondered for some time the story told by Wirth of the Brothers Kauffmann in Hamburg, who were failing during the crisis of 1799 when one of the brothers sent his bride a ticket for the Hamburg city lottery, first prize in which was 100,000 marks banco. She bought for herself the same number in another lottery in the Duchy of Mecklenburg, the prize for which was an estate worth 50,000 Prussian thalers (equal to 100,000 marks banco). She won both, and the Brothers Kauffmann, if you believe the tale, were fully rehabilitated.[57] I have not checked the *Reminiscenzen* of Nolte, whoever he may be, from whom Wirth got the story, but remain skeptical.

There was, however, the lost supply of £1 notes left over from the Napoleonic Wars that did save the day in 1825.

CHAPTER 9

The Lender of Last Resort

Over the last quarter of a millennium "The Art of Central Banking," as Hawtrey called it, has evolved the concept of a lender of last resort. The expression comes from the French *dernier ressort*, the legal jurisdiction beyond which it is impossible to take an appeal. But the term has become thoroughly anglicized, and in central-banking English it gives greater emphasis to the responsibilities of the lender than, as in legal French, to the rights of the petitioner or borrower.

The lender of last resort stands ready to halt a run out of real and illiquid financial assets into money, by making more money available. How much? To whom? On what terms? When? These constitute some of the dilemmas of the lender of last resort, after it is determined, first, whether there should be one, and second, who it should be. All these issues derive from the basic dilemma that if the market knows it is to be supported by a lender of last resort, it will feel less (little? no?) responsibility for the effective functioning of money and capital markets during the next boom. The public good of the lender of last resort weakens the private responsibility of "sound" banking. If, however, there is no authority to halt the disintermediation that comes with panics, with forced sales of commodities, securities, and other assets, and a scramble for the limited supply of money, the fallacy of composition takes command. Each participant in the market, in trying to save himself, helps ruin all.

Origin of the Concept

The lender of last resort is a construct not of the mind of the economist but of the practice of the market. Ashton asserts that the Bank of England was already the lender of last resort in the eighteenth century,[1] although this pronouncement does not entirely square with his statement that "long before the rules for the treatment of crises were laid down by economists, it was recognized that the remedy [for a financial crisis] was for the monetary authority (the Bank of England or the government itself) to make an emergency issue of some kind of paper which bankers, merchants and the general public would accept. When this was done the panic was allayed. . . ."[2]

The parenthetical indecision as to whether the central bank or the government was the final monetary authority remains to this day, and qualifies the statement that the Bank of England emerged as the lender of last resort in the 1700s. That practice preceded theory, however, is exactly right. E. V. Morgan maintains that the Bank of England's realization of its responsibility was delayed by the government's action in issuing Exchequer bills in 1793, 1799, and 1811, and that the Bank assumed the role as lender of last resort only gradually during the first half of the nineteenth century "in spite of the opposition of theorists."[3] The same evolutionary process can be seen in the Bank of France. In 1833 the majority of the Conseil Général overrode Hottinguer's idea for a policy on the English model, as well as Odier's plea for an entirely

new policy, and concluded that the major function of the
Bank of France was to defend the French franc. Capital outflows were not to be feared. Money should not be held arti-
ficially low to encourage speculation and intensify crises.
When crises occurred, however, the Bank should feed commercial transactions by providing abundant and cheap discounts to moderate the intensity of the crisis and shorten its
duration.[4]

The role of the lender of last resort was not respectable
among theorists until Bagehot's *Lombard Street* appeared in
1873, and even now continues to be rejected by many. Should
one worry about the present panic or the next boom, the
condition or the principle? "There are times when rules and
precedents cannot be broken; others when they cannot be
adhered to with safety."[5] The dilemma is that breaking the
rule creates a new precedent and a new rule. Lord Overstone,
the distinguished Currency School theorist, strongly opposed
expansion of the money supply in a crisis, but reluctantly
admitted that a panic may require "that power, which all governments must necessarily possess, of exercising special interference in cases of unforeseen emergency and great state
necessity."[6] The paradox is equivalent to the prisoner's
dilemma. Central banks should act one way (lending freely)
to halt the panic, but another (leave the market to its own
devices) to improve the chances of preventing future panics.
Actuality inevitably dominates contingency. Today wins over
tomorrow.

The Banking Act of 1844 represented a victory for the
Currency School, which stood for a fixed supply of money,
over the Banking School, which thought it useful for the
money supply to grow as output and trade grew. Both schools
were thinking of the long rather than the short run, and
neither approved of increasing the money supply as a temporary expedient to meet a crisis. When the Bank Act was being
considered, thought was given to the provision of emergency

powers to suspend its provisions, and the idea was rejected. After 1847 and 1857, when it proved necessary to suspend the act and provide the possibility of issuing more money as a last resort, Parliament conducted inquiries on each occasion as to whether the legislation was deficient. Both inquiries concluded that it was desirable to have no built-in provision for suspending the act, but that suspension had been useful and necessary. To limit precedent-setting, the bill brokers who had been sudden borrowers wanting incalculable advances in 1857 were told not to expect the like again.[7] The principle of having a rule but breaking it if one had to was so widely accepted that after the suspension in 1866 there was no demand for a new investigation.

In the 1850s, Jellico and Chapman had proposed rules for adjusting the discount rate of the Bank of England to the state of its reserves by mathematical formulas written into legislation. Wood criticizes them as having no real grasp of Bank transactions and methods of procedure.[8] Robert Love, chancellor of the exchequer in June 1875, introduced a bill to provide for authorizing a temporary increase in the amount of Bank of England notes in exchange for securities, under certain contingencies, including panic, a Bank rate above 12 percent, and the foreign exchanges favorable. Tabled and given a first reading on June 12, it never received a second reading and was withdrawn in July.[9] Hard-and-fast rules were agreed not to be workable. The *Economist* and Walter Bagehot thought it proper that the Bank of England, and not the banks themselves, should hold the reserves necessary to get the country through a panic. Mr. Hankey, a former governor of the Bank, called this "the most mischievous doctrine ever broached in the monetary or banking world in this country; viz. that it is the proper function of the Bank of England to keep money available at all times to supply the demands of bankers who have rendered their own assets unavailable."[10] The public, however, sided with Bagehot and practice against

Hankey and theory. If one cannot control expansion of credit in boom, one should at least try to halt contraction of credit in crisis.

Who Is the Lender of Last Resort?

We have already seen at some length the indecision in Britain as to whether the Treasury should relieve panics through the issue of Exchequer bills; whether the Bank of England should discount freely at a penalty rate, suspending the limits imposed by the Bank Act of 1844 if need be; or whether other devices, such as a guarantee of the liabilities of particular firms, should be undertaken. It may be optimal to leave the matter in doubt, along with the question of whether, in fact, the marines will come to the rescue, or if they decide to come, will arrive in time. Thus, in Britain, there was no explicit provision for a lender of last resort, and no fixed rule as to who would fill the role if there was one. In 1825 it was not the Exchequer. The job was given resolutely to the reluctant Bank, the acceptance of which was "the sulky answer of driven men."[11] In 1890 it was neither the Bank nor the Treasury but the warmed-over device of guarantees.

In France, as just noted, the Bank of France, created in 1803, had agreed by the 1830s that it had responsibilities in crisis. However, it thought it had other responsibilities as well, such as to ensure monopoly of the bank note circulation, and this permitted it to let the regional banks fail in 1848 and convert them into subsidiaries (*comptoirs*). The provinces had been fearful of Paris, wanting their own regional banks to have the privilege of note issue because of concern that in a crisis Paris would take care of its own needs at the expense of the country. But having acquired a bank, Le Havre, for example, made the mistake of allowing it to become frozen in industrial credits, such as shipyards, and in loans to importers when the price of cotton was falling. In February 1848 the Bank du Havre made a trip to Paris. "The return was not glorious. The Bank of France had been impitiable."[12] It refused to lend on mortgages, saying, "The statutes forbid it, and you have refused to accept a *comptoir*."[13]

Once it had destroyed the nine departmental banks and converted them into branches, the Bank of France set about acting as a lender of last resort. Its statutes required it to discount only three-name paper; the task became one of producing acceptable names. Sixty *comptoirs d'escompte* were established throughout France, as well as a number of *sous-comptoirs* organized by various branches of trade to hold stocks of goods and issue paper against them. With the names of the merchant, the *sous-comptoir*, and a *comptoir*, the Bank of France could discount the paper and relieve the liquidity crisis. After the crisis was over, a number of the *comptoirs* were taken over by bankers, merchants, and industrialists, becoming regular banks. The most famous of them, the Comptoir d'Escompte de Paris, took its place among the leading banks in the country.[14]

The Crédit Mobilier of the Pereire brothers was not saved in 1868; on this occasion, the Bank of France refused to discount its paper. This can be interpreted as the revenge of the establishment on the outsider, the Rothschilds against the Pereires who had once worked for them;[15] as punishment for not conceding the Banque de Savoie note issue to the Bank of France when the Pereires took over the Savoy bank after the region had been ceded to France by Italy in 1860; or as the entirely normal refusal of a lender of last resort to bail out an insolvent institution.[16] Cameron accuses the Bank of France of conducting guerrilla warfare against the Pereire brothers in the interest of a Rothschild-Pereire quarrel going back to the 1830s.[17]

The Bank of France and Paris bankers again did not come

to the rescue of the Union Générale in 1882, but rescued the Comptoir d'Escompte de Paris in 1889. Critics of the Bank of France ascribe the difference in outcome to venality. A less emotional position asserts that a second large bank failure in seven years might have completely destroyed the French banking system, and that on this account Rouvier, the minister of finance, took the necessary measures to have the Bank of France and the Paris banks, under pressure, advance 140 million to the Comptoir d'Escompte.[18] In the Union Générale operation, as was noted in an earlier chapter, the Paris banks withdrew from the speculative activity when it began to peak in August 1881, and advanced 18.1 million francs to the Union Générale after the crash the following January, not to save the bank, but to permit its more orderly liquidation.[19] Led by the Rothschilds and Hottinguer, and including the Comptoir d'Escompte and the Société Generale (but not the Lyons rival of Bontoux, the Crédit Lyonnais), the consortium represented the establishment, in which it was not really necessary to distinguish the Bank of France from the leading private banks (*hautes banques*) and deposit banks.

In Prussia the king was the lender of last resort in 1763. In 1848 various state agencies, including the Prussian Bank, the Seehandlung, and the Prussian lottery vainly tried to help the Cologne bank, A. Schaaffhausen, before it was allowed to reorganize as a joint-stock bank. With no central bank in 1763, 1799, and 1857 (in Hamburg), city government, the chamber of commerce, and the banks—any and all leading agencies—took part.

The experience of the United States is especially pertinent to the questions: Who is the lender of last resort, and how does it or he know it? Under the First and Second Banks of the United States there was some ambiguity, despite the designation of the Bank in each case as a chosen instrument. On various occasions, the Treasury came to the aid of the banks by accepting customs receipts in postdated 30-day notes (1792), by making special deposits of government funds in banks in trouble (1801, 1818, and 1819), and by relaxing the requirement of a commercial bank to pay the Bank of the United States in specie (1801).[20] With the failure to renew the charter of the Second Bank of the United States in 1833, the Treasury was even busier, both before and after passage of the 1845 law requiring the Treasury to keep funds out of the banks. In times of crisis, and in periods of stringency caused by crop movements, the Treasury would pay interest and/or principal on its debt in advance, make deposits in banks despite the law, offer to accept securities other than government bonds as collateral for deposits of government funds, or buy and sell gold and silver. Banks became accustomed to looking to the secretary of the treasury for help in an emergency, and for relieving seasonal tightness. In the fall of 1872, Secretary of the Treasury George S. Boutwell served as a lender of last resort by the possibly illegal method of reissuing retired greenbacks. His successor, William A. Richardson, did the same thing a year later.[21]

The Treasury could absorb money in deposits and pay out surpluses from existing funds, but apart from the greenback period it could not create money. For this reason, it was unsatisfactory as a lender of last resort, unless it had previously accumulated a budget surplus. In 1907, when the till was low, the Treasury issued new bonds—$50 million of Panama Canal bonds, which were eligible for collateral for national bank notes, and $100 million of 3 percent certificates of indebtedness—hoping to entice existing cash and specie out of hoarding. In the end, the day was saved by a capital inflow from Britain of more than $100 million.[22] Moreover, the devices used were ad hoc in the extreme. An analysis of the crisis of 1857 suggests that the federal government was incapable of interfering effectively, and that the public, including the banks, was left without guidance to stem the tide of the crisis.[23] As we shall see, it was worse than that: intervention proved to be too much and too early.

The complex record of interference by the Treasury raises the question of why the market should not have regulated itself, and if so, how. O. M. W. Sprague, the historian of the crises under the National Banking System for the 1910 Aldrich Commission, kept coming back to the notion that the banks should have taken responsibility for seeing that there were enough reserves to meet all needs.[24] Exactly which banks is not always clear, nor exactly why the duty fell to them in the absence of political responsibility embodied in legislation. Noblesse oblige? Duty? It is, in my judgment, worth setting out a number of passages from Sprague to show why a limited number of New York banks had the obligation to behave differently from banks as a whole in order to stabilize the system:

During the period before the crisis of 1873 some 15 of the 50 New York banks held practically all the bankers' deposits acquired by banks in the city, and 7 of them held between 70 and 80 percent of these deposits. These 7 banks were directly responsible for the satisfactory working of the credit machinery of the country (p. 15).

It must always be remembered that in the absence of any important central institution, such as exists in other commercial nations, the associated banks are the last resort in this country, in times of financial extremity, and upon their stability and sound conduct the national prosperity greatly depends (from the New York Clearing House report of November 11, 1873, p. 95).

The fundamental characteristic of our banking system was illustrated [in 1890], that for any extraordinary cash requirements the reserves of the country banks are an unused asset. Evidence was again given which should have brought home to city institutions the heavy responsibility which they have incurred in attracting the reserves of other banks (p. 147).

The New York banks did not normally maintain the large reserves which the responsibilities of their position demanded (p. 153).

. . . there was the possibility that the contraction of loans by outside banks, trust companies and foreign lenders might come together, creating a situation . . . well nigh impossible if in normal times the important clearing house banks failed to exercise great caution and maintain large reserves (p. 230).

The failure of the banks holding the ultimate reserve of the country to live up to the responsibilities of their position is evident in still another direction. While the exact moment of the outbreak of the crisis of 1907 could not be foreseen, the imminence of a period of trade reaction had for many months been so probable the precautionary measures might reasonably have been expected from these banks if not from banks and the public in general (pp. 236–37).

The outside banks feel no responsibility for the course of the market. They will naturally withdraw from it when affairs at home require more of their funds or when they come to distrust its future. It therefore becomes necessary for the local banks to be able at all times to shoulder at least a part of the loans that may be liquidated by outside banks, and also to supply the cash which they thus secure the power to draw away (p. 239).

It is certainly an element of weakness in our central money market that influential credit institutions should have to be dragooned into doing what is after all in their own interest as well as to the general advantage (p. 255).

. . . feeling common among New York bankers that they can- not reasonably be expected to remit funds which are the proceeds of loans made in the New York money market by outside banks and liquidated in an emergency. . . . It should be remembered, however, that responsibilities are incurred in return for the advan- tages which accrue to the New York banks from their peculiar position. London holds its commanding position because it is known that money lent there can be instantly recalled. Similarly, New York is not meeting the obligations of its position as our domestic money center, to say nothing of living up to future international responsibilities, so long as it is unable or unwilling to respond to any demand, however unreasonable, that can law- fully be made upon it for cash (pp. 273–74).

One could extend the quotations, but the point is clear. The market needs a stabilizer. It is unfortunate for the banks to look to the Treasury for help even on seasonal smoothing. Someone must take the responsibility. Sprague did not believe it should be the Treasury. Who then? The biggest and most profitable banks. If that modifies their profitability, too bad. They should be aware of seasonal currency requirements, the prospect that the out-of-town banks may withdraw deposits, the state of the balance of payments. Not all New York banks —just the ones charging interest on out-of-town deposits, or the largest, or those with intimate connections with the stock exchange, or leading members of the New York Clearing House. In the absence of a central bank to take charge, someone had to take over, some group with responsibility.

The leading bankers of New York drew a somewhat different moral, and on the whole a misleading one. They thought that the difficulties arose from lack of elasticity of the money supply, and fell into the trap of the Banking School. This was the real-bills doctrine, the idea that a money supply expanding and contracting on the basis of trade bills, representing goods moving in domestic and foreign trade, could not be inflationary, and would have the necessary elasticity through discounting at banks and rediscounting at a central bank. There could be no doubt about it: "The laws of finance are as well known, and as sure in their operations as the laws of physics."[25] The lesson that Frank Vanderlip, Myron T. Herrick, William Barret Ridgely, George E. Roberts, Isaac N. Seligman, and Jacob H. Schiff drew from the panic of 1907 was that there should be a central bank with an elastic currency.[26]

Some ambiguity as to where responsibility finally lies may be helpful, insofar as it imparts uncertainty to the market and makes it on that account more self-reliant, provided there is not so much uncertainty as to disorient the market. In the British case, it was vaguely understood that there should be no formal provision for a lender of last resort, but that in crisis there should be one. Intuitive politicians in the British government and the intuitive merchant-bankers who ran the Bank of England thought it best to give power to grant relief neither wholly to the Bank nor wholly to the government, but to leave it uncertain.* If the giving of relief were formally within the power of either the Bank or the government, pressure from the public would be difficult to resist.[27]

Within too large a group, responsibility inheres in no one. With a single entity responsible, pressure for action may build up irresistibly. The optimum may be a small number of actors, closely attuned to one another in an oligarchic relation, like-minded, applying strong pressure to keep down the chiselers and free-riders, prepared ultimately to accept responsibility. To give an up-to-date example, tension in 1975 and 1976 among New York City officials, the unions, bankers, the state, and the federal government as to who would be the lender of last resort for New York may have been enough to ensure uncertainty at a high level, and to encourage Yonkers, Buffalo, Boston, Philadelphia, et al. not to slack in their efforts to right themselves; yet action to save New York was finally taken.

For a moving account of a muddle, see Bonelli on the 1907 crisis in Italy. The Società Bancaria Italiana was failing, and pulling down with it a host of small financial, mercantile, and industrial firms. A consortium of the larger banks put together a fund. The Bank of Italy was involved early and deeply, almost getting itself too heavily committed. The Treasury finally came to the rescue, at the insistence of Stringher of the Bank of Italy, paying out interest on the national debt early

* Note Bagehot's characterization of the character of the then members of the court of the Bank of England: "A board of plain, sensible prosperous English merchants; and they have both done and left undone what such a board might be expected to do and not to do. Nobody could expect great attainments in economical science from such a board; laborious study is for the most part foreign to the habits of English merchants" (Walter Bagehot, *Lombard Street: A Description of the Money Market* [1873; reprint ed., London: John Murray, 1917], p. 166). Later he is more critical: "Unluckily . . . directors of the Bank of England were neither acquainted with the right principles, nor were they protected by a judicious routine. They could not be expected themselves to discover such principles. The abstract thinking of the world is never to be expected from people in high places. . . . No doubt when men's own fortunes are at stake, the insight of the trader does somehow anticipate the conclusions of the closet" (p. 169).

and relieving the liquidity crisis. Bonelli sees the episode as one involving inevitably the Bank of Italy and the government, and suggests that this is the sort of thing that happens when the economy works for more than ten years with no one in charge.[28] Part of the difficulty may have lain in the lack of sufficient cohesion among Turin, Genoa, Milan, and Rome. In this case, there seems to have been too much uncertainty, buck-passing, indecision.

A certain amount of uncertainty, but not too much, is useful in building self-reliance in the market. Uncertainty is also inescapable: "looking to the impossibility of foreseeing what the precise character of the circumstances might be," as the House of Commons committee on 1847 said. It was thus "more expedient to leave to those with whom the responsibility of government might rest at the time, to adopt such measures as might appear to them best suited to the emergency."[29] But to get back to the basic question, consider Sir Robert Peel's statement on the Bank Bill in June 4, 1844:

My Confidence is unshaken that we have taken all the Precautions which legislation can prudently take against the Recurrence of a pecuniary Crisis. It may occur in spite of our Precautions; and if it be necessary to assume a grave Responsibility, I dare say Men will be found willing to assume such a Responsibility.[30]

One man who took responsibility got into trouble. George Harrison, then president of the Federal Reserve Bank of New York, opened the discount window wide at the time of the October 1929 stock market crash, and exceeded his instructions from the Board of Governors in Washington by buying $160 million in government bonds on the open market in October and another $210 million in November. The Board of Governors in Washington resented the New York bank because of the earlier high-handed dominance of the system by Benjamin Strong (who died in 1928), and had little compunction in reining in Harrison when he tried to emulate Strong's penchant for filling a power vacuum by strong leadership. Ambiguity as to whether there will be a lender of last resort, and who it will be, may be optimal in a close-knit society. Given the division in experience and outlook between Washington and New York, such ambiguity paralyzed effective action in the 1929 crash.

To Whom on What?

The rule laid down by Bagehot was that loans should be granted to all comers on the basis of sound collateral. One dilemma, of course, is that the soundness of collateral depends on whether the panic is stopped or not. With continued panic —and further falls of prices—securities, bills of exchange, commodities, and the like quickly turn unsound. In this case, it becomes necessary to look at the character of the borrower, something which J. P. Morgan was reported to consider exclusively. Here the dilemma relates to the wry comment that bankers lend money only to those that don't need it.

Central banks typically have rules. Where these cannot be easily broken—as in the Federal Reserve Act of 1913, which did not permit government securities to be held as reserve against Federal Reserve notes and demand deposits, but only gold and negotiable bills of exchange—there is frequently trouble. The Bank of France and the Reichsbank occasionally discounted only on three-name paper. But discretion to reject paper because it is "unsound," or the borrower because of his character, gives the lender of last resort a life-or-death power which may not always be used with complete objectivity. As we have noticed, the literature is filled with accusations of venality on the part of the directors of central banks. Protestant and Jewish directors of the Bank of France were alleged to have punished the Catholic (and worse-off) supporters of the Union Générale in 1882, while saving the insider Comptoir d'Escompte in 1888.[31] In the crisis of 1772, the Bank of England's issuance of new regulations about discounting and refusal to discount doubtful paper were interpreted as an attempt to break the Jewish houses in Amsterdam that had been most involved in the speculation; then there was the Bank's decision to refuse the bills of Scottish banks, and finally to stop discounting altogether, which was probably "a step taken quite deliberately to break up a group of Dutch speculators."[32] Outsiders particularly suffered. The Bank of the United States was allowed to fail in New York in December 1930 by a syndicate of banks, not the Federal Reserve System, amid accusations that the Bank was being punished for its pushy ways.[33]

The rule of discounting for everyone with good paper evolved slowly in Britain. For a time "the invariable practice" was respectable London names on paper with two months to run; but this description of 1793 is accompanied by a statement that while a request from Manchester had been turned down (along with one from Chichester, where refusal helped to bring a house down), £40,000 had been advanced to Liverpool banks. Only in July 1816 did the Bank, breaking a rigid precedent, agree to accept "country securities of undoubted respectability if the firm cannot get enough London names."[34]

The fact is that the Bank of England made advances not only on two-month paper but on a wide range of different types of assets. In 1816 it broke its rule against lending on mortgages, undertaking a "Transaction quite out of the ordinary course of Business" to relieve the distress of the poor people in the Black Country. On the occasion, it resolved to lend only in the old way, "on notes of respectable parties," but a few years later the Bank began a regular mortgage business on the ground that the volume of discounts, and especially the income from discounts, had collapsed—a private rather than a public purpose.[35] At one stage it even made loans on the security of a mortgage on a plantation in the West Indies, which it ultimately was obliged to foreclose,[36] and (in the 1830s) on unimproved land in England. The land was unencumbered by mortgage but belonged to a duke, an indication that collateral and the character (or status) of the borrower were not unrelated. Loans were not made on land in Scotland or Ireland.[37]

With the growth of railroads, Bank of England loans were made on the collateral of railroad debentures. In 1842, as the second railway mania got under way, the Bank voted to make an occasional loan to firms in difficulty and to well-tried firms for development.[38] The Bank of France began lending to a railroad syndicate in 1858; in fact, it was accused of supporting, if not starting, the feverish speculation in railroads.[39] Walter Bagehot thought the Bank of England mistaken for not lending on railroad debentures when it did so on consols and Indian securities, stating that a railway was less liable to unforeseen accidents than the strange Empire of India.[40] But, of course, Indian securities were guaranteed by the Colonial Office, and in effect were British obligations.

Exchequer bills were issued on the collateral of goods, as were admiralty bills in Hamburg. Clapham observes that many of the Bank's advances in 1825 were not actually on goods but rather on personal security;[41] the Bank loaned freely and was not "over-nice." In a few weeks in 1847 the Bank advanced £2.25 million in all sorts of ways, usual and unusual, including the securities of the Company of Copper Miners, through which it involuntarily acquired a copper works.[42]

The rule is that there is no rule. One doesn't lend to insolvent houses, except to avoid the mischief that would occur if the Lord Mayor of London were to go bankrupt (1793),[43] or to maintain for a time a payroll in Newcastle, a town used to banking disasters.[44] The Bank of France had never discounted as much as 4 million francs for anyone but Jacques Laffitte when Samuel Welles, an American banker, applied in 1837; he proved to be exceptional.[45] (Of course, the Laffitte transaction had also been exceptional. It was a political discount.) The Conseil Général could not abandon such an important bank, so it received a line of credit of 15 million francs.[46] In the crisis of 1830 the Bank of France discounted royal and municipal bonds, customs receipts, woodcutting receipts, obligations of the city of Paris, canal bonds repayable by lottery, and lots more.[47] Cartesianism is not proof against crisis.

In the final analysis, the lender of last resort must make decisions. Some are easy, like whether to discount treasury bills. Some are difficult, such as whether to take shaky collateral from shaky banks. The record is full of firms that were refused help, failed, and paid off 20 shillings in the pound, and of banks that were helped in one crisis but went down in the next. The 241-page appendix to Evans' book on the commercial crisis of 1857 is devoted to court records of bankruptcies in Britain between 1849 and 1858. On the whole, it makes doleful reading, but there are some cautionary tales. G. T. Braine, who was refused accommodation by the Bank of England in 1848, paid 20 shillings to the pound and ended up with a surplus double that originally estimated. One also finds petitions in bankruptcy brought by the Bank, as against Cruikshank, Melville and Co., for the unpaid residue of a bill it drew on another bankrupt firm that had paid only 12s., 6d., to the pound.[48]

Even the judgment of history is not always helpful. We have earlier noted that the Bank of England first refused to help the three American "W banks" (Wiggins, Wilsons, and Wildes) in the fall of 1836 and then relented and advanced them credit in March 1837. To Andréadès, the Bank took a bold step and had no occasion to regret its courage.[49] Clapham holds, on the contrary, that the Bank lent most reluctantly, was not surprised when Wilsons and Wiggins failed at the end of May and Wildes thereafter, and that the consequence was "a long a dreary tale of debt lasting 14 years."[50] To Matthews, the Bank of England's aid to the three banks "in the vain hope of avoiding their supending was a matter of faulty judgment, but the principle on which they operated was a sound one."[51]

When and How Much?

"Too little, and too late" is one of the saddest phrases in the lexicon not only of central banking but of all activity. "Too much, too early" is not an evident improvement. Enough at the right moment is better than either. But how much is enough? When is the right time?

Bagehot's rule is to lend freely at a penalty rate. Freely means, of course, only to solvent borrowers and with good collateral, subject to the inevitable exceptions. It means rejecting the expedients that various central banks are tempted to indulge in crises. Early in 1772 the Bank of England tried to apply the brakes to overtrading by selective limitation of discounts, and was criticized for it.[52] In 1797 the Bank began to prorate discounts, and Foxwell thought that might have been undertaken again in 1809.[53] Another technique when a central bank feels it is getting overcommitted is to tighten up on eligibility requirements for collateral, changing the maturity of eligible bills from 95 or 90 to 65 or 60 days, or adding to the number of names required. In May 1783 the Bank of England had discounted so heavily for its own clients that it departed from its regular practice and refused to make advances on subscriptions to government bonds issued that year. Clapham comments that fortunately no public or private catastrophe of the sort that starts a panic occurred that summer, since the Bank had limited its capacity to meet one.[54] This is the behavior of a private bank worried about its own safety, not that of the public bank undergirding the safety of the system.

Suppose the lender of last resort does not lend through a rediscounting mechanism but instead uses open-market operations. How much should it expand the money supply? Were the $160 million in October 1929 and the $210 million additional through November 1929 adequate? In the view of the Federal Reserve Bank of New York, it was not. The bank was operating under a directive from the board permitting it to buy $25 million a week in government bonds. It violated this rule in October by buying the $160 million, went back to it in the first two weeks of November, and on November 12 recommended to the board that the limit of $25 million a week be removed and that the Open Market Investment Committee be authorized to buy $200 million for the system. After considerable negotiation, the board reluctantly approved on November 27, and $155 million was purchased between November 27 and January 1, 1930. By this time, discounts were running off rapidly, interest rates had fallen sharply, and the need for a lender of last resort—to accommodate the liquidation of call loans in the market—was over.[55]

It is not clear to me whether Friedman and Schwartz approve or disapprove of the role of the lender of last resort. They quote Bagehot on not starving a panic, presumably with approval.[56] They assert that the action taken by the Federal Reserve Bank of New York in buying $160 million in October 1929 was "timely and effective," although they are gently skeptical in noting Harrison's claim that the open-market purchases kept the stock exchange open.[57] Friedman, however, is opposed to all discounting, and believes the stock market crash was not a major factor in producing or deepening the depression.[58] This accounts for the view of most monetarists, including the Currency School (apart from Lord Overstone), that there is no need to have a lender of last resort so long as the money supply is maintained constant. I believe, on the other hand, that the 1929 open-market operations were woefully inadequate in the weeks from mid-October to the end of November 1929. They enabled the New York banking system to take over the call loans of out-of-town banks, as Friedman and Schwartz explain, but only at the cost of cutting back credit extended on commodities and current purchases, which drove down prices not only of stocks but also of commodities, houses, and land, thereby unleashing the depression.[59] Admittedly, it would not have gone as far as it did if there had been an international lender of last resort to halt the unraveling of European (and U.S.) credit in the spring of 1931. This subject we come to in the next chapter.

Timing presents a special problem. As the boom mounts to a crescendo, it must be slowed down without precipitating a panic. After a crash has occurred, it is important to wait long enough for the insolvent firms to fail, but not so long as to let the crisis spread to solvent firms needing liquidity— "delaying the death of the strong swimmers," as Clapham puts it.[60] In a speech during the debate on the indemnity bill on December 4, 1857, Disraeli quoted the leader of an unnamed "greatest discount house in Lombard Street" who said that "had it not been for some private information which reached him, to the effect that in case of extreme pressure there would be an interference on the part of the Government, he should at that moment have given up the idea of struggling any further, and [that] it was only on that tacit understanding that he went on with his business."[61] Questions could be raised about the equity of private information and of tacit understandings for insiders but not outsiders. Still, the remark underlines the importance of timing. Whether too soon and too much is worse than too little and too late is difficult to specify.

In 1857 the U.S. Treasury came to the rescue of the market far too early and helped it inflate still further. In 1873 the response was too slow, no steps being taken during the first part of the year.[62] Sprague refers to "the unfortunate delay of the Clearing House," i.e., the slowness of any authority to move in on the 1907 crisis, in which, as in no other crisis since the Civil War, things were allowed to drag on too long.[63]

If, then, one admits the necessity for a lender of last resort after a speculative boom, and believes that it is impossible for restrictive measures to slow down the boom at the optimal rate without precipitating collapse, the lender of last resort faces dilemmas of amount and timing. The dilemmas are more serious with open-market operations than with a system of discounts. In the latter case, Bagehot specified the right amount: all the market will take—through solvent houses offering sound collateral—at a penalty rate. With open-market operations the authorities have more of a decision to make, but Bagehot is surely right not to starve the market. Given a seizure of credit in the system, more is safer than less. The excess can be mopped up later.

As for timing, it is an art. That says nothing—and everything.

CHAPTER 10

The International Lender
of Last Resort

It follows from the international propagation of financial crises, and from the efficacy under certain circumstances of lending in the last resort, that there is room for an international lender of last resort. Economic history indicates a felt need for someone in this role. Moreover, current distress in international lending to developing countries and to the Eastern bloc, not to mention the balance-of-payments troubles of Britain, Italy, and other nations, has raised the question of whether such a need exists today, and if so, how it will be met.

A Historical View of International Crises

It is surprising how little of economic history is concerned with the international dimensions of crises and the need for a lender of last resort. Central-bank history recognizes the distinctions between internal and external drains. An external drain could generally be turned around by raising the discount rate; this would also draw specie from abroad to meet the internal drain, though often there was a dangerous lag before the medicine worked. Where foreigners took raising of the discount rate as a sign not of strength but of weakness, and sold rather than bought the currency, it might be necessary to get more help than the market would make available. The same was true when lags were long and time limited. In such cases, countries, from time to time, but less frequently than they were called upon to meet internal crises, sought help from abroad. The initiative could be anywhere. The central bank might borrow. Local firms holding assets acceptable abroad, whether domestic or foreign, might dispose of them and remit the proceeds across the exchanges. If prices fell far and fast enough, foreigners might pour in to hunt for bargains.

Last-resort lending and borrowing, however, focuses on central banks as the providers of cash. The first central-bank borrowing of which I am aware was the loan contracted by the Bank of England in 1694 for 2 million guilders from the States General in Holland to assist the British Exchequer in remitting funds to the Continent to support its troops and allies during the Nine Years War. It was hardly a loan of last resort.[1]

In the crisis of 1763 the Bank of England and London private bankers came to the rescue of their Dutch correspondents by granting, in distress, credits larger than those previously given in periods of prosperity. Five consignments of gold were shipped in August and two in September. In addition, the Bank of England and other banks delayed presenting bills for payment. Wilson comments that none of this was pure altruism. Instead, it represented a practical policy based on the knowledge that British prosperity was intimately associated with Dutch, and that accentuation of the Dutch crisis would cut off a source of capital for Britain.[2]

As the 1772 crisis reached a peak in January 1773, Anglo-Dutch trade was in the throes of paralysis. Amsterdam was helpless, and only the Bank of England, Wilson says, could rescue the city. On January 10, a Sunday, the Bank threw open its windows and allowed specie to be drawn against presentation of notes and government stocks. Loads of bullion were sent on the first packboat, and one Dutch banker was said to have drawn £500,000. At the same time, the Bank refused to discount doubtful paper, which had the effect of breaking a good many Jewish houses in Amsterdam.[3] In the same crisis, Catherine the Great of Russia was helping her best customers, the British merchants, the first of a number of occasions on which czarist Russia assisted Western Europe in crisis.[4]

The record is bare of international rescue operations through the rest of the eighteenth century and the Napoleonic Wars. In the crisis of 1825 there was a rumor that the Bank of France was trying to add to the Bank of England's difficulties. Clapham insists, however, that this was wide of the mark. He claims France participated in an early example of international financial cooperation by shipping gold to London in exchange for silver.[5] The higher price of gold in England than in France (15.2 to 1, instead of 14⅝ to 1) favored the exchange,[6] but the arrival via the houses of Rothschild of £400,000 (mostly in sovereigns) from France on Monday, December 19, 1825, helped in timely fashion, for after the peak of the run the previous Saturday, Bank of England coffers were virtually bare.

In the extended crisis of 1836–39, the Bank of England sought help from the Bank of France and the city of Hamburg on two occasions in order to maintain its liquidity. On the first of these, it drew bills on Paris for £400,000. In 1838 it arranged for a line of credit, and in 1839 drew on it for £2 million, using the intermediary services of Baring Brothers on the one hand and ten Paris banks on the other. A similar line of credit with Hamburg brought in £900,000 more in gold, an arrangement possibly designed also to help Hamburg, which needed silver.[7] In 1838 the Bank of England, not the usual gold dealers, sent 320,000 sovereigns to America in three ships and 360,000 sovereigns in two more. Clapham calls the operation without precedent, and damaging insofar as it encouraged American bankers to issue more securities in the British market in 1838 and 1839, but he acknowledges that the Bank was wise to recognize the interlocked interests of Britain and the United States.[8]

The Bank of France borrowed 25 million francs from British capitalists in the second half of 1846, according to French sources;[9] a British source states that the sum was borrowed from the Bank of England itself in January 1847.[10] At that point, the emperor of Russia offered to buy 50 million francs of the French 3 percent rente to assist in financing the heavy imports of wheat needed by France (and Britain). England benefited, since the French used half the money to pay off the British advance.[11] Palmer, then governor of the Bank of England, testified before the Select Committee of Parliament that it was preferable to have an understanding with the principal banks in the United States, Hamburg, Amsterdam, and Paris than to ship gold.[12]

Central-bank cooperation was not universally applauded. Viner says the Bank of England in 1836 found itself obliged to appeal to France for help, "no doubt reluctantly," and adds that the necessity was regarded in Britain as rather humiliating, coming at a time when relations between the two countries were not particularly cordial, "especially as it was reported that the followers of M. Thiers were boasting of the generosity of Frenchmen . . . while recommending that under no circumstances should such liberality be repeated in future."[13] Thomas Tooke thought the loan a "discreditable expedient," a "circumstance of almost national humiliation."[14] On the other side of the channel was more than pride. The

Bank of France was criticized by some who thought it irresponsible, seeking to make a profit from the British arrangement rather than aiding those who implored its help on all sides at home.[15]

In the 1850s international cooperation in crisis amounted to less. The Bank of England contemplated joint action with the Bank of France in November 1857, states Clapham, but he does not indicate what the action was and says little beyond the fact that nothing came of it.[16] Perhaps the most interesting operation was the December *Silberzug* in Hamburg. Hamburg, it will be recalled, was on the end of the line of the rolling crisis which swept from New York (and Ohio) to Liverpool and then to the Continent, especially Scandinavia. On December 4 the Hamburg Senate voted a 15 million mark banco fund composed of 5 million in Hamburg bonds and 10 million in silver, to be obtained by borrowing abroad. Then came the task of getting the loan. Appeals for a loan were made to Rothschilds, Baring, and Hambros in London, to Fould in Paris, and to various political and financial bodies in Amsterdam, Copenhagen, Brussels, Berlin, Dresden, and Hanover. The requests were turned down universally. From Fould came this answer: "Your message is not sufficiently clear." From Berlin: "Bruck and the Kaiser are not financially ambitious." On December 8, when every house in Hamburg except Heine's was threatened with bankruptcy, when captains of ships were unwilling to discharge them for fear their freights would not be paid, word came from Vienna that it would take the whole loan. A train bearing the silver (the *Silberzug*) arrived shortly.[17]

From an early account which I can no longer pinpoint, I gained the impression that the train had only to make a triumphal tour of the city to quiet the panic. The details are more pedestrian. The silver was removed from the train, and loans in silver were made to Merck, Godeffroy, and Berenburg, Gossler and Co., among the leading bankers, plus five smaller ones. The panic ceased on December 12, when it was known that there was enough for all. Some firms, like Donner & Co., which had initially been alotted 700,00 marks banco, turned out not to need any when confidence was restored. Böhme, who gives the most detailed account of the crisis, says that for years the episode kept coming up whenever Hamburgers and non-Hamburgers would talk about exchange, and men reading about it could feel their hair standing on end.[18] The political nature of the rescue operation was revealed in British diplomatic dispatches. From Hamburg the British consul noted that it was fortunate for Britain that Austria and not Prussia had brought the aid, since there would then be no pressure on Hamburg to join the Zollverein.[19] From Berlin on December 29 came a dispatch with a translation of Baron Manteuffel's statement to Hamburg, explaining the various reasons Berlin had been unable to help. Lack of ambition gave way to a series of lame explanations which underlined the fact that Berlin had missed an opportunity.[20]

The subsiding of panic in Hamburg relieved distress in Scandinavia for the most part. A positive item of international official aid, however, was a loan on December 18 by the Bank of England on promissory notes of the Norwegian government, in support of overdue bills the Bank held on Norwegian houses.[21]

At the outbreak of the Civil War in November 1860, panic in New York drew specie from Paris and New York. French reluctance to raise the discount rate and the increasing departure of the French gold-silver ratio from the market led France to exchange £2 million in silver for £2 million in gold with the Bank of England. This failed to remedy the situation sufficiently, so that in 1861 the French bought gold in London at a price above the export point. Needing still more, the Bank of France arranged through Rothschild and Baring to draw £2 million of bills on London.[22]

The crisis of 1873 offers no international action, but does

present two items of interest that underline the sensitive political nature of central-bank dealings. In the letter books for 1872–73 the Bank of England refers to and denies a "ridiculous rumor" that it had thought of applying for a loan to the Bank of France. And in the second week of November the governor of the Bank of Prussia—a predecessor of the Reichsbank, which was not established until 1875—wrote a letter to the Bank of England offering a loan in gold now or at any future time. (Clapham comments earlier that Germany was half-drunk with victory and that Berlin had swelled up like Aesop's frog.) The Bank of England politely but curtly declined the offer: "The Bank is not, nor has been in want of such aid and need not avail itself of the arrangement you so kindly suggest." Clapham adds that this suggestion from the nouveau riche could hardly fail to seem impertinent to the governor.[23] The Germans were outsiders.

In 1890, Lord Lidderdale prepared on two fronts for the crisis that would follow the revelation of Baring's position. In addition to the domestic guarantee, he arranged for the Russian government not to draw its £2.4 million deposit from Baring, and for loans of £3 million from the Bank of France and £1.5 million from the State Bank of Russia, both in gold. Lidderdale told the governor of the Bank of France that the ordinary operations of Bank rate would have brought the gold in time, and that there was nothing discreditable in using unusual measures to meet an unusually sudden storm. Nonetheless, Lidderdale and the City were uneasy about asking the French and the Russians for help. Clapham put it this way: "Suppose for some political-financial reason they had been unwilling to oblige?"[24]

The sensitive character of such international assistance prior to World War I is best revealed in the 1906–7 incidents, when much discussion was devoted not to whether the Bank of France helped the Bank of England—which it clearly did— but whether the Bank of England had asked for such help or, if it did not, whether the steps taken by the Bank of France were largely in its own interest. In his account of the Bank of England from 1890 to 1914, Sayers' chapter entitled "Supposed Continental Support of the Bank" concludes that the Bank of England did not ask for help. It is revealing that the question should seem important. The chapter quotes the *Economist* in September 1906 as stating:

Some talk of the Bank of France helping the Bank of England cope with the American demand for gold, . . . but it would not for a minute be supposed that the Bank would really put itself in so humiliating a position merely in order to permit American speculators getting gold here on easy terms.

Again in the fall of 1907, the Bank of France forwarded 80 million francs in gold eagles (American coin) to London. The Bank of France report for 1907 refers to both incidents as its decisions. French journals cite the alleged reason: to relieve the Bank of England of the necessity of raising its discount rate, which implies that the Bank of England requested help. British sources emphasize that there was no announcement on the British side, as there was in 1890, and that the French wanted to hold down the Bank's discount rate. Hartley Withers, financial editor of the *Times*, wrote later:

The determination it [the Bank of England] showed finally compelled the Bank of France to take some share in the international burden, and to send three millions of its gold, not to America but to London, whence it knew it could rely on getting it back. It is commonly supposed the Bank of England asked it to carry out this operation, but this is quite untrue.[25]

An unpublished thesis on the subject is said to take the view that in dealing in sterling bills in London against gold in 1906, 1907, 1909, and 1910, the Bank of France was primarily practicing open-market operations, which were not undertaken in the Paris market until 1938.[26] It is not clear, however, how the exchange of one international asset for another could affect credit conditions within the domestic economy.

London vs. Paris as the World Financial Center

The general view among Anglo-Saxon students of economic
history is that London was the world's financial center from
some date to 1914, and that centers such as Paris, Berlin,
Frankfurt, New York, and Milan were satellites of it. The
starting date is a matter of some question, but so is the
alleged fact.

According to a German observer, "England had a monopoly
of capital exports to 1850. Then France moved in, largely for
gloire, undertaking capital exports in the service of national
policies, expansionary commercial interests, and the opening
of new markets."[27] This view receives some support with
regard to the 1850s. Writing on the panic of 1857, Van
Vleck notes: "Just as France was the political nerve center
of Europe during the first half of the nineteenth century, so
during the years from 1850 to 1857, it was the center from
which fluctuations in the economic cycle radiated."[28]

The center for the economic cycle is not necessarily the
pivot of the financial system. More positive is the statement
that after assisting during 1820–40 in clearing London's world
payments in such places as the Baltic, Russia, China, Latin
America, and the United States, Paris became between 1850
and 1870 the "first place in Europe for foreign exchange."[29]
The position seems overstated. In any case, the situation was
changed by the Franco-Prussian War. According to Bagehot:

Since the Franco-German war, we may be said to keep the European reserves. . . . all great communities have at times to pay
large sums in cash, and of that cash a great store must be kept
somewhere. Formerly there were two such stores in Europe; one
was the Bank of France, and the other the Bank of England. But
since the suspension of specie payments by the Bank of France,
its use as a reservoir of specie is at an end. No one can draw
a cheque on it and be sure of getting gold or silver for that cheque.
Accordingly the whole liability for such international payments

in cash is thrown on the Bank of England . . . all exchange operations are centering more and more in London. Formerly for many
purposes, Paris was a European settling-house, but now it has
ceased to be so. . . . Accordingly London has become the sole
great settling-house in Europe, instead of being formerly one of
two. And this pre-eminence London will probably maintain, for
it is a natural pre-eminence. . . . The pre-eminence of Paris
partly arose from a distribution of political power, which is already
disturbed; but that of London depends on the regular course of
commerce, which is singularly stable and hard to change.[30]

This view would be echoed from across the Atlantic in 1910,
when Sprague explained that the Bank of England raised its
discount rate in 1907 not to check the flow of gold to the
United States but in order to secure payment from other
countries of money due by them to the United States. Since
London was the central money market in the world, it had
to raise its rates to avoid having to finance all the payments
flowing to the United States.[31]

Different views are possible, however. In discussing the
Italian links with the 1907 crisis, Bonelli states flatly that
Paris was the real center for regulating world liquidity.[32] Such
a remark I would ordinarily dismiss as myopia or parochialism,
Italy being connected to London only through Paris. But one
of the most penetrating students of pre–World War I finance
states that "Paris emerges in this study as the *strongest*
[his italics] financial center in the world before 1914, if the
fact that its short-term rate was relatively the lowest is an
indication of strength. This conclusion seems to contradict
the generally held opinion that London was the world's money
center." Morgenstern attempts to reconcile these statements
by distinguishing between Paris' abundance of capital and
London's machinery for setting funds into motion.[33] The distinction seems forced. Each center had its own particular
clients: Italy and Russia for Paris, the United States and the
Empire for Britain. The attraction of the intermediate countries, such as Belgium, Holland, and Germany, was more to
London than to Paris. Moreover, while London pulled capital

from Paris from 1900 to 1909, its lending was worldwide and not channeled to a limited number of connections.

The whole question emphasizes the rivalry between the two countries, as well as the sensitive political nature of international finance.

The Lender of Last Resort After World War I

There was no international lender of last resort in the 1920–21 crisis. Part of the slack was taken up by flexible exchange rates. In a crisis caused by balance-of-payments weakness and capital outflow, the exchange rate depreciates. This raises international prices (i.e., the prices of goods and services which are exported or imported, and those capable of being exported or of competing with imports), and may cure the symptoms of declining prices from a run out of real inventories to money. But a sharp inflationary stimulus may produce another kind of crisis—out of money into goods, leading to hyperinflation. This is what happened in Eastern and Central Europe in 1923, for example,[34] and is reminiscent of the inflation in France under John Law. It is also the scenario of Paul Erdman's thriller *The Crash of '79*, in which the financial crisis is handled by printing massive amounts of currency and letting the dollar float, leading to a run on goods.[35] Gresham's-law instability operates not only between different types of money (gold and silver) and between financial assets and cash, but also between goods and money.

Most governments in Western Europe in the 1920s sought to stabilize their currencies out of fear of hyperinflation, for reasons of tradition—restoring the *status quo ante bellum*— or, as many monetarists would think, because they were stupid in failing to see the merits of the floating-exchange-rate system. In seeking stabilization, they often used stabilization loans, similar in some respects but not identical to loans of last resort. In 1924, for example, the French franc was under strong attack from a variety of sources. First, many foreigners had bought francs as they depreciated in 1919–20. They had large paper losses but hung on, hoping for a comeback. It was claimed that they would sell only in a panic.[36] There was one. They sold. Second, there was foreign professional speculation in Amsterdam, probably related to Vienna.* Finally, there were hundreds of thousands of Frenchmen with liquid assets in francs, watching signals like the legal ceiling on Bank of France advances to the state.

On March 4, 1924, panic broke out. The franc, which had been 98 to the pound sterling on February 17 and 104 on February 28, went to 107 on March 4. The government and the Bank of France met in emergency sessions. J. P. Morgan & Co. was willing to help but imposed certain conditions: the loan, a six-month revolving credit, should be for $100 million, not $50 million, which the bank, represented by Thomas W. Lamont, judged too small. The Bank of France resisted pledging its gold as collateral, yielding finally only when a face-saving formula was found. In turn, the Bank regents, including Rothschild and De Wendel, exacted a conservative financial program from the state. The program was worked out on Sunday, March 9, and within three days the rout of the speculators began. With great difficulty the rate was brought down from 123 francs to the pound to 116. By March 18 it was 84; and by March 24, 78. The Bank of France then intervened to prevent the rate from going higher (fewer francs to the pound) and bought back all the dollars and sterling it had lost in its initial operation. The squeeze against the

* Stephen Schuker contends that it was impossible to determine the involvement, if any, of the German government, which was resisting French attempts to collect reparations by occupying the Ruhr; the Germans had their hands full with their own monetary chaos (*The End of French Predominance in Europe: The Fnancial Crisis of 1924 and the Adoption of the Dawes Plan* [Chapel Hill: University of North Carolina Press, 1976], p. 96).

speculators was successful.[37] Lamont wrote that "there has never been an operation that has given us more satisfaction."[38]

Success was short-lived. In 1926 there was another attack on the franc, with the rate hitting a low of 240 in July 1926. Recovery to 125 was brought about by Poincaré reforms of a conservative sort, intended to reassure the French holders of wealth and induce them to bring their funds back to Paris from London and New York. A stabilization loan was again contemplated, but this time the services of J. P. Morgan & Co. were not required.

Stabilization loans were arranged in the 1920s for Austria and Hungary under League of Nations auspices, and for a succession of central banks in Eastern Europe under various arrangements with London, Paris, and New York. Perhaps the most widely known were the Dawes and Young loans, undertaken to recycle German reparations. The first had the fateful effect of stimulating U.S. foreign bond lending.

During the 1930s the suggestion was frequently put forward, with only partial irony, that what France needed—with the franc and the entire gold bloc overvalued as a consequence of successive devaluations of the pound, yen, and dollar, and the blocking of the mark and schilling—was a stabilization loan in gold. The gold, it was said, should be mounted in a transparent vehicle, like a glass hearse, and paraded through the streets of every town and village in France. This would convince the people that the authorities had an abundance of gold, and get them to dishoard from the *bas de laine* (wool sock) in which the Frenchman is said to keep his *louis d'or*.

1931

The rolling deflation of 1931 underlines the need for an international lender of last resort in a way that differs in scale and therefore in kind from previous episodes. I have written on

this in detail elsewhere, emphasizing the issues we have encountered earlier in various forms: the need for an adequate
amount of lending, the political character of the operation,
and the need for some country or countries to feel responsible
for the stability of the system, without which the system's
instability will run unchecked.[39] Others writing along similar
lines were Jørgen Pedersen and (unknown to me at the time)
R. G. Hawtrey and the British economists whose advice to
their government during the period is set out in Susan Howson
and Donald Winch's book *The Economic Advisory Council,
1930–1939.*

Hawtrey presents a cogent analysis of 1931:

The crisis of 1931 differed from earlier crises in its international
character. Earlier crises were international in that the fall of prices
and forced sales affected world markets. But only an unimportant
part of debts were due to foreign creditors. In 1931 the outstanding characteristic of the panic was that foreign creditors of Germany
and Eastern European debtors feared that the foreign exchange
market would break down *even if the debtors remained solvent.*
Against a panic-stricken withdrawal of foreign balances from
London, it [raising Bank rate] was too tardy a remedy. Such a
panic-stricken withdrawal *had never occurred before . . .* the
underlying cause of the trouble has been *monetary instability.* The
industrial depression, the insolvencies, the bank failures, budget
deficits and defaults, are all the natural outcome of a falling price
level. . . . The need arises for an *international lender of last resort.*
Perhaps some day the Bank for International Settlements. . . .
But as things are, the function can only be undertaken by a foreign
central bank or by a group of foreign central banks in co-opera-
tion.[40]

Quoting only the italicized passages makes the author
sound a little more breathless than he actually was. As we
shall see, Hawtrey was not fully cognizant of the difficulties
of discharging properly the role of the lender of last resort,
but his theoretical insight into limits was penetrating:

As a general rule, if credits are to be granted to a central bank
in difficulties at all, they should be granted up to the full amount

needed. There should be no limit. If the amount is inadequate, and the exchange gives way after all, the sums lent are completely wasted. . . . It can be argued in favor of unlimited credits, that if they *had* been granted, there would have been no withdrawal of funds at all. . . . either no credits to the Bank of England or unlimited. But there is some risk. Unlimited credits would have enabled the country to remain on the gold standard, prolonging conditions that were rapidly becoming intolerable . . . the lesson: if the country can maintain the monetary standard without undue strain, then grant unlimited credits; but if the effort of maintaining parity is excessive, no credits and allow the currency to depreciate.[41]

Howson and Winch set out a series of reports written by British economists to their government in the 1930s. Among them is a report of the Committee of Economists, which included Keynes as chairman and had Henderson, Pigou, Robbins, and Sir Josiah Stamp as members, with Hemming and Kahn as secretaries. It talked of general cooperation among central banks, preferably through the Bank for International Settlements, in funding short-term claims and in forming a pool for loans, first, to prevent currency debacles of the sort experienced in the early postwar period and, second, to restore "confidence in the financial stability of those many countries which are now the subject of distrust."[42] Nothing came of this rather vague recommendation.

In July 1932, after Britain had gone off gold but well before the World Economic Conference of 1933, the Cabinet Committee on Economic Information, with Stamp in the chair and including Citrine, Cole, Keynes, Sir Alfred Lewis, and Sir Frederick Leith-Ross, with Henderson and Hemming as secretaries, issued a report discussing the "international financial crisis." The document quotes Bagehot, cites the crises of 1825 and 1847, talks in terms of a lender-of-last-resort function that Britain could no longer discharge, and recommends developing the functions of the Bank for International Settlements through the issue of paper gold, to be called International Certificates, much like the Special Drawing Rights introduced

36 years later.[43] This, to be sure, was locking the barn after the horse was stolen.

The first opportunity to halt the international disintermediation came in May 1931 with the collapse of the Credit-Anstalt of Vienna. Publication of its statement on May 11 revealed that it had lost 140 million schillings, or all but 45 million schillings of its capital. The Austrian government turned for assistance to the League of Nations, which had organized the stabilization loans of a decade earlier, and the League turned instead to the new Bank for International Settlements, created under the Young Plan of 1930 to assist in the transfer of reparations. The Austrian government sought 150 million schillings (21 million). The BIS arranged for a loan of 100 million schillings from eleven countries, a process which took from May 14 to 31. By June 5 the credit was exhausted, and the Austrian National Bank requested another. This was arranged by June 14, subject to the condition that the Austrian government get a two- to three-year loan for 150 million. The French interposed a condition that the Austrian government renounce the customs union agreement with Germany, announced in March, but the Austrian government refused and fell. The Bank of England then offered a loan of 50 million schillings ($7 million) for a week.

The run shifted to Germany. The German banking position was weakened by excessive speculation, large securities write-offs, fraud, bankers' quarrels, banks supporting their own stock and depleting liquid reserves—the full range of classic troubles.[44] The outsider was Jacob Goldschmidt of the Danatbank,[45] the product of the merger of the Darmstädter and National banks. Other bankers such as Oskar Wasserman of the Deutsche Bank detested Goldschmidt and his aggressive tactics. In 1927 the Berlin Handelsgesellschaft had given up the business of the Norddeutsche-Wollkämmerei (Nordwolle), a thrusting firm in woolens. The Danatbank took it on. Nordwolle's failure, on June 17, 1931, brought down Danatbank; other banks were unwilling to save it because of their detesta-

tion of Goldschmidt. There were other complications, political
and financial, but the internal financial turmoil led to massive
withdrawals that were only briefly interrupted by the Hoover
moratorium. On June 25 a loan for $100 million was arranged,
including $25 million each from the Bank of England, the
Bank of France, the Federal Reserve Bank of New York, and
the Bank for International Settlements, for the period to July
16. Hans Luther, president of the Reichsbank, who had
wanted a larger amount, asked that the exact loan figures be
concealed, so the communiqué said merely that discount
facilities had been arranged in sufficient amount. When the
number was revealed in indiscretion (the source of which,
Born says, is not known), and when the Reichsbank statement
of June 23 showed that its reserve cover was at 40.4 percent,
scraping the bottom level of 40 percent, the motto became
"Devil take the hindmost" (in German, *Den letzten beissen
die Hunde*).[46]

New loans were discussed, but not forthcoming. The
Germans wanted $1 billion. The French were willing to
consider $500 million, but with political conditions. The
United States was worried about a prospective budget deficit
of $1.6 billion and thought it preposterous to expect Congress
to lend more money to Germany. It was willing to consider
stabilization of existing credits to Germany, something the
Reichsbank wanted as well as a loan. In Britain, Foreign
Secretary Arthur Henderson was attracted to the idea of a
loan, but Montagu Norman, governor of the Bank of England,
held that the Bank had "already lent quite as much as is entirely
convenient."[47] One argument against foreign loans was that
the crisis was believed to have been caused by a flight of
domestic capital rather than by foreign withdrawals. By July
20 the idea of a loan had been tacitly abandoned, "brushed
aside as impractical."[48] Instead, the Germans relied on internal
measures to halt the disintermediation at home, and on a
Standstill Agreement, imposed upon reluctant foreign bankers,
to halt the external drain.

Next Britain. The run began in mid-July, stimulated partly by losses on the Continent, but also fed by the May and Macmillan reports of the large prospective domestic budget deficit and the unexpectedly high estimate of foreign funds in London that might be withdrawn. Since 1927 the Bank of France had converted sterling to gold by a roundabout device, selling sterling to the market against purchases of forward sterling, then asking for gold against sterling as the forward contracts matured.[49] This made it look as though it was converting no old balances but only new acquisitions. But in the summer of 1931, the Bank of France cooperated fully, converting none of its sterling holdings. At the end of July, the Federal Reserve Bank of New York and the Bank of France each loaned the Bank of England $125 million. When this was gone, the British government contemplated a one-year loan from the New York and Paris markets. The Bank of England reported that foreign bankers would not lend Britain funds while it had such a large budget deficit because of the dole. The trade unions opposed a cut in relief to the unemployed and withdrew support from the Labor government, which fell on August 24. Four days later, after the formation of a new "national government" with MacDonald again as prime minister and Snowden as the chancellor of the exchequer, $200 million was borrowed from a Morgan syndicate in New York and another $200 million from a French syndicate in Paris. On one showing, the bankers held up the British government; their own explanation, echoing the Morgan statements to the French in the 1920s, and those of other lenders of last resort after World War II, was that they were not imposing political conditions, merely indicating the economic circumstances in which they felt they were justified in risking their own and their depositors' money. This included outlining the actions that would suffice to restore confidence in the currency.

On August 5, 1931, Keynes wrote to Prime Minister Mac-Donald, at the latter's request, to make a series of proposals for devaluation of the pound sterling and for the formation of a gold-based, fixed-exchange currency unit at least 25 percent below the old parity, to which all Empire countries, South America, Asia, Central Europe, Italy, and Spain—in fact, all countries—would be invited to join. This represented one of his frequent changes of opinion, for in July he had signed the Macmillan Report advocating adherence to the existing parity of sterling but a rise in tariffs. The letter, however, makes the telling point that if the pound cannot be successfully defended, it is foolish to continue to borrow foreign currencies to defend it.[50] This is equivalent in the lender-of-last-resort literature to unwillingness to make loans to insolvent firms and banks. Both the Labor government and its successor paid little attention to the point.

Loans of $400 million on top of $250 million were not enough, and the pound went off gold on September 21. The restraint that the Bank of France had shown to the British in the summer was not shown to the United States.* The Bank of France and the other members of the gold bloc converted $750 million of dollar deposits into gold. The deflationary pressure exerted by this reduction in reserves and by the appreciation of the dollar against sterling and its associated currencies were critical in undermining the U.S. banking system. The New York Fed did not ask for help or even for forbearance in conversion. The code of the central banker calls for a stiff upper lip, reminiscent of Walter Mitty refusing the blindfold before the firing squad. In 1929, when Harrison asked Norman whether the sterling the New York Bank had bought would be convertible into gold, he received the curt reply: "Of course the sterling is repayable in gold. That is the gold standard."[51] In 1931, Harrison in turn offered

---

* The French attitude toward Britain was not emulated by the Dutch, Swiss, or Belgians, who had no responsibility for the system and converted as much sterling to gold as they thought would not be too conspicuous.

to assist Moret in converting any or all of the Bank of France's dollars into gold.[52]

Five aspects of the 1931 story are especially striking: (1) the inability of Britain to act as a lender of last resort; (2) the unwillingness of the United States to do so, apart from the inadequate effort for Britain, the country of the "special relationship"; (3) the urge of France, with respect to Austria and Germany (but not to Britain, be it noted), to gain political ends; (4) the paranoia of Germany after 1923, preferring anything to a hint of inflation; and (5) the irresponsibility of the smaller countries.

Bretton Woods

The lesson of 1931 concerning the need for a lender of last resort was not learned. At Bretton Woods, the International Monetary Fund was created to finance current-account deficits, within moderate limits. Flows of hot money were left to be handled by capital controls. The IMF dealt in credits to be repaid, not in money creation; narrow limits were set by quotas, divided into four traches, no more than one of which could be used in a given year. Moreover, after the first gold tranche, access to credit was a matter of grace on the part of the Fund—not a matter of right, as the Keynes plan had provided. During the period of recovery, the Fund and the Bank were on the sidelines, as reconstruction finance was furnished by the Marshall Plan. It was not until 1958 with the devaluation of the franc and the convertibility of the pound that the Bretton Woods system can be said to have finally come into operation.

The inattention to financial flows soon had to be modified. It proved impossible to maintain convertibility on current account and controls over capital movements, since large capital transfers could take place through changes in the finance of exports and imports, the so-called leads and lags. A country called upon to pay cash for imports instead of getting three months' credit, and forced to extend six months' credit for exports instead of three months, could quickly lose the value of six months of the average of exports and imports. In 1960 the Articles of Agreement of the Fund were extended by the General Arrangements to Borrow (GAB), under which ten leading financial countries, the Group of Ten, or G-10, pledged an additional $6 billion on top of $14.4 billion of the Fund's quotas (up from $7.8 billion when the Fund started in 1946), to be made available through the IMF in case of perverse capital flows that could not be handled by a country's own reserves and IMF quota. These amounts proved inadequate. Moreover, the IMF was found not to work in timely fashion. Decisions were taken by weighted voting by directors, many of whom represented more than one country. To frame a proposal, obtain instructions, and arrive at a decision to help a country in crisis took as much as two weeks, an even longer lag than applied to an increase in that country's discount rate under the gold standard.

Hot money movements grew in size after World War II. Part of the increase was merely inflation, the rise of prices and the fall in the value of virtually all currencies. Part represented the increase in the ratio of money to national income in every country, which meant that liquid assets which could be transferred from one country to another were more plentiful. A third reason reflected the fact that horizons of owners of financial assets everywhere had been extended. Relatively few people in the United States (though not in Europe) contemplated foreign exchange as a liquid asset, or were inclined to speculate in favor of or against foreign exchange in the 1930s. Many more did in the 1950s, and a fortiori in the 1960s. Richard Cooper emphasizes the change:

A crude quantitative indicator of these developments is provided by contrasting the maximum daily speculation of under $100 million against the pound sterling, in the "massive" run of August 1947, with the maximum daily speculation of over $1.5 billion in favor of the German mark in May 1969, and the movement of over $1 billion into Germany in less than an hour in May 1971. Moreover, as the barriers of ignorance fall further, there is no reason why $1.5 billion should not rise to $15 billion, or even $50 billion a day.[53]

With the growth of hot money comes the need for new devices. There was considerable experimentation with defending a country by selling foreign exchange forward, which would satisfy the demand of speculators for a fixed price for foreign exchange, but not require the central bank to pay out reserves. In fact, if it sold enough foreign exchange forward, a country could gain spot reserves by driving the forward exchange rate so low that it would pay arbitrageurs to buy the local currency spot and hedge by selling it (buying foreign exchange) forward. A few observers believed that operations in the forward market could relieve central banks of the necessity to hold reserves: when the forward contracts matured, they could be rolled over and extended. But the experience of the British from 1964 to 1967 suggests limits to this dream, as to the hope of perpetual motion. By the time the Bank of England's forward commitments to deliver forward exchange amounted to several times its holdings of gold and dollars, the market was unwilling to continue to renew the old contracts and insisted on delivery. The devaluation which had been postponed from 1964 became inescapable in 1967.

Forward operations can be undertaken by a single central bank alone. The next lender-of-last-resort concept developed in the 1960s was the Basel agreement, including the swap network. This required multilateral cooperation. In 1961, when sterling was under attack, representatives of the major central banks, meeting at the Bank for International Settlements in Basel, Switzerland, put together a series of credits from different countries for Britain to draw upon, amounting

in all to $1 billion. Charles Coombs called it a major break-
through in international postwar finance.[54] The number was
large enough to reassure the market and to bring about the
return of most of the flight capital; what could not be paid
off from the reserves accumulated during the return flow was
funded through Britain's line of credit at the IMF. Thus, the
IMF sank back into the second line of defense, to tidy up
later. The first-line lender-of-last-resort, to indulge in oxy-
moron, was the central bankers' club, brought out on a
number of occasions: on behalf of Canada in June 1962, for
more than $1 billion; $1 billion in Italy in March 1963; $1
billion from the club and another $1 billion from the IMF for
Britain before the October 1964 British elections, extended
to $3 billion from the club alone after Labor won; then $1
billion for Britain, from all members of the club except France,
in September 1965; another $1 billion for Britain in April
1966;* a $1.3 billion package for France in July 1968, which
would have been extended to $2 billion in November for the
defense of the devalued franc, except that the French at the
last minute refused to devalue.[55] The French decision not to
help the British in September 1965 has been characterized
as a "shocking repudiation of the central-banking free-
masonry." The pressure to conform to the club, and the will
to be different as a matter of foreign policy, were doubtless
both intense. "It cut no ice. The British got the support
they wanted."[56]

The United States had taken a leadership role in the formation of Basel-club consortia. The whole experience showed
that the most effective device for providing credits was swaps,
as they were called—operations in which two central banks
wrote up equivalent amounts of foreign exchange as assets
and domestic currency as liabilities, the asset of one being the

* This time the French chose to participate not through the club,
since that credit looked to preserve sterling as a reserve currency, but
directly through a bilateral credit to the Bank of England, available
for any mutually agreed use.

liability of the other. This was instant money, albeit temporarily only, as most of the "swap lines" provided that the
swaps would be undone at the end of a period such as six
months. The technique was started by an arrangement between the Bank of France and the Federal Reserve Bank of
New York for the equivalent of $50 million in March 1962.
In June it was extended by swap lines of $50 million each with
the Dutch and Belgian central banks. The same month brought
Canada in for $250 million. By July the Swiss National Bank
had joined for $200 million. In October 1963 the total swap
network of the Federal Reserve Bank of New York comprised
$2 billion with eleven central banks. In September 1966 the
network expanded from $2.8 billion to $4.5 billion, and in
March 1968 (at the time of the dissolution of the gold pool
and the adoption of a separate, freely floating price for gold
outside the central banking system, i.e., the two-tier system)
to $9 billion. In July 1973, after much trauma and with the
dollar floating, the network was increased from $11.7 billion
to $18 billion.[57]

This was reliance on the lender-of-last-resort medicine with
a vengeance, and without consideration of the drawbacks:
postponement of fundamental correctives, weakening of incentives, loss of self-reliance. Coombs is a market man, and
enjoys taking advantage of an oversold market through a
squeeze on the shorts; he believes in resisting destabilizing
speculation that might push exchange rates, prices, inflation,
etc., beyond some point of ready snap-back. But fundamentals
count, too. Twice he states the market man's conviction that
a man can lose his shirt betting on fundamentals.[58] But his
only response to foreign-exchange crisis was to say: enlarge
the swap lines. It was not enough. The system broke down.

The proximate cause of the breakdown was an analytical
failure. Central bankers in the United States and in Germany
did not see that if their money markets were joined through
the Eurocurrency market and fixed exchange rates, as they
were after the Smithsonian accord of December 1971, the

two countries were committed to having joint monetary policies. The United States embarked on a policy of monetary expansion as the date for the 1972 presidential election approached. Meanwhile, West Germany, always fearful of inflation, kept interest rates high. The result was that funds poured out of the United States into Eurodollars in West Germany. In the end, the bigger battalions dominated: the Bundesbank was forced to lower its interest rates, though not before billions of dollars had spilled out on the world.

As in 1825, 1853, 1871, and 1885, the shock of lower interest rates led to relaxation of lending standards. Eurocurrency banks began lending freely to developing countries, virtually for the first time in the postwar period. Brazil, Mexico, South Korea, Zaïre, Peru, and others found themselves courted by Eurocurrency bankers, just as in the "good old days" of 1927. In addition, the Soviet Union and the Eastern bloc sought and obtained access to Western credits. On the whole, the base was small compared to what it would become after the OPEC oil price rise. It was a start.

Second, the great hemorrhaging of dollars over the world made it impossible to sustain the system of fixed exchange rates, even after the Smithsonian devaluation of the dollar. The United States made little or no effort to defend the new rate, but February-March 1973 speculation against the dollar had built up to the point where the Bundesbank and the Bank of Japan were unable to go on, and a system of floating exchange rates was forced on them when they stopped accumulating dollars.

Most economists, present company included, had thought that the adoption of floating exchange rates would kill the movement of interest-sensitive capital and make it possible for different countries to maintain independent monetary policies. There were differences of opinion over whether speculative capital movements would continue, and as to whether they would be stabilizing for the most part, or occasionally seriously destabilizing. But it was largely agreed that the world capital market would be broken up into national components, and that fear of exchange risks would keep most financial capital at home.

Under these new circumstances, the initial need for a lender of last resort proved to be domestic, though related to international finance. Floating exchange rates encouraged a certain amount of foreign-exchange speculation, and while many banks did well through buying low and selling high, not all did. The Herstatt Bank of Cologne and the Franklin National Bank of New York were among the most spectacular losers, each being forced to close its doors in June 1974. The Herstatt Bank went first, creating a problem when it was closed in the middle of the day in Europe, after it had collected sums due to it on exchange transactions but before it had paid out the DM counterpart. For a time, the consortium that guaranteed its liabilities was interested only in domestic German obligations, and was prepared to let the sums due to foreigners go unrequited. Second thought prevailed, however: the total liabilities of the bank were covered, foreign as well as domestic, and there was no shock wave felt abroad. The Federal Deposit Insurance Corporation took over Franklin National deposits up to the limit of $40,000, and the Federal Reserve System, acting as lender of last resort, guaranteed the remaining liabilities.

These episodes established the precedent in international banking that each country would take care of the problems of its own banks, including any damage done to foreign creditors, no matter where the bank happened to be located. There may someday be a residual question of who accepts responsibility for the liabilities of international banking groups. Fortunately, this issue has not arisen.

With the four- to fivefold rise in the price of oil following the Yom Kippur War, October 1973, a long list of countries found difficulty in paying their oil bills and turned to borrowing from the Eurocurrency market. The world recession caused by the high price of oil further complicated balances of payments. By September 1974, the U.S. comptroller of the currency "classified" Italy, serving notice on American banks to be careful in making additional loans to that country. Italy then turned to the European Economic Community for a loan of $5 billion. In the end, it received a $2 billion loan from West Germany alone, using its gold stock as collateral, valued at $75 an ounce. To meet the wider problem of financing oil imports, the United States proposed a new international mechanism for a lender of last resort, amounting to $25 billion and called the Financial Safety Net. This proved impossible to get through the U.S. Congress.

In the fall of 1976, Representative Henry S. Reuss, chairman of the House Banking and Currency Committee, said in London that the United States should not provide aid to Britain beyond the $3.9 billion it was already getting from the IMF with strong conditions.[59] If this were the statement of a Lord Liverpool or Napoleon III, seeking to deny to the world that there was a lender of last resort in order to strengthen British self-reliance, or if Representative Reuss thought that Britain was insolvent and took the Bagehot-Goschen view that no aid should be given to insolvent companies, his statement would be understandable. Reuss' remarks, however, seemed reminiscent of the 1931 attitude of the United States toward the lender-of-last-resort role in Europe: "Let someone else do it."

The OPEC price increase also led to increased bank lending to the oil-consuming LDCs and even to some OPEC countries that had spent funds on imports faster than oil receipts had accrued. By the end of 1976, the debts of 71 LDCs had risen to $157 billion from $107 billion at the end of 1974 and $132 billion at the end of 1975.[60] The United Nations Conference on Trade and Development requested worldwide rescheduling of debts at its Manila meeting in 1976. However, at the Conference on International Economic Cooperation, held in May and June 1977 and dealing with the Third World's proposals for a new international world order, the debt rescheduling proposal was dropped. And LDCs are not the only problem: another $50 billion is owed by the Soviet Union and the Eastern bloc.

Whether the world is in "distress" because of the large accumulation of claims of the LDCs and the Socialist countries is almost impossible to tell from the outside. Many banks show a cheerful face to the public; their private attitudes may or may not differ. Some public figures express concern. Is there a lender of last resort in case of trouble? Who is it? Does he or it know it? What sort of collateral does the lender demand, and how much does it rely on character? What conditions should be imposed? How is self-reliance preserved in the system? Is it possible artistically to threaten no rescue, while actually rescuing at the last minute, as in the New York crisis—that is, to keep the others honest but not to suffer the spreading collapse of a major failure or failures?

The interest of this study is historical. Luckily.

CHAPTER 11

Conclusion:
The Lessons of History

It is time to draw the threads of the argument together. But before we do, there is one unanswered question: Does it make a difference if there is no lender of last resort? This happens to be a difficult question to answer. For one thing, for most of the financial crises covered from 1720 to 1975, both national and international, a lender of last resort did swing into action, in response to the pressures of the market, often protesting all the way. The role was not always dispatched with efficiency, so that a refined analysis would categorize the aftermath of crises not only by the presence or absence of a lender of last resort, but also by how well the role was discharged. Second, the aftermath of a depression depends not just on how the crisis was handled but on a host of other variables, especially the factors affecting long-term investment: population growth, the existence of a frontier, demands arising from war, exports, the presence or absence of innovations that are not fully exploited, and the like. A speculative crisis like that of 1847 in England was likely in any event to be pulled quickly back into prosperity by renewed investment in railroads, whether or not the Bank of England suspended the Bank Act of 1844 and stood ready to provide liquidity to all borrowers with sound collateral.

Despite these difficulties, we are prepared to make the case, tentatively, that a lender of last resort does shorten the business depression that follows financial crisis. The evidence turns mainly on 1720, 1873, 1882 in France, 1921, and 1929. In none of these was a lender of last resort effectively present. The depressions that followed them were much longer and deeper than others. Those of the 1870s and 1930s were both known as "Great Depressions."

It is sometimes claimed that recovery after other crises has been unusually delayed, but the contentions are hard to sustain. Wiseley mentions in a new book that recovery from the panic of 1826 was slow; contemporary observation makes it difficult to accept the verdict.[1] Thomas Tooke stated that by the end of the year—the panic took place in January—"trade and manufacture resumed their normal course and hardly any trace remained of their having been disturbed in their progress."[2] Leone Levi wrote that the "crisis of 1825–26 like all other crises was momentary and transient."[3] Van Vleck asserts that recovery in the United States was slow after the panic of 1857, but he is virtually alone among economic historians in this view, as he himself recognizes.[4] When a lender of last resort comes to the rescue, even maladroitly, recovery after the panic is seen to be momentary, transient, ephemeral, episodic, slowing the economy down only briefly and marking in many instances the peak of a normal cycle with a recovery period of about two years, but without deeper significance. Not so, it is claimed, with 1720, 1873, 1882 in France, 1921, and 1929.

Large claims are made by Carswell for the importance of the South Sea bubble and its collapse. He asserts that these events marked the climax of the Commercial Revolution, its fatal end, and were responsible for the lull of forty to fifty years between the Commercial Revolution and the Industrial Revolution. Without the traumatic episode, he suggests, the two revolutions might have shaded into one another without the long pause. In addition, the collapse led Britain to abandon for twenty years the pretensions of Marlborough and Stanhope to the leadership of Europe.[5] In contrast to this view is that of Schumpeter, who characterizes the South Sea bubble as nothing more than an excess and breakdown of speculation.[6]

Carswell's contention is not equivalent to a claim that with a lender of last resort the Industrial Revolution would have occurred in the 1720s or 1730s rather than in 1766–76. His interest is in the whole episode, not merely in the deflation which followed collapse. One might argue that the Bank of England did in fact act as a lender of last resort in taking over the stock of the South Sea Company. It originally contracted to do so at 400, later reneged when the Bank itself came close to collapsing, and finally converted the stock only a little above the market when South Sea stock had sunk to 135.[7]

In any event, it is hard to take the Carswell view seriously as bearing on the question under discussion. Judged by the bankruptcies—220 in 1720, 288 in 1721, 240 in 1722—the depression ran the normal two-year course.[8] Ashton puts 1722 as the bottom and 1724–25 as the peak of the next cycle, with a new, milder crisis from October to December 1726.[9] Carswell's contention that the South Sea bubble marked a turning point may be justified, but it does not bear on our narrow claim that a lender of last resort shortens the recovery time.

The eighteenth century in France may be more revelant to our claim. There the trauma of the Mississippi bubble and the collapse of John Law's system slowed down the development of banking and the expansion of industry. Together with the collapse of the Assignats during the Directorate in the 1790s, it made the French for years neurotic about banking, or even paranoid, just as the Germans were rendered paranoid about

inflation by the inflation of 1923, and the British about un-
employment after their experiences during the 1920s.

We are left then with 1873, 1882 in France, 1921, and 1929.
There was no lender of last resort in 1873 in Vienna, Berlin,
and New York, the storm centers of the crash. In London there
was no panic, hence no need for a lender of last resort. The
French let the Union Générale go to the wall in 1882 with
minimal intervention. In 1929 the lender-of-last-resort function was inadequately performed in New York (as I attempted
to show earlier, though the verdict does not command general
agreement), and in 1931 international operations to halt the
spread of collapse and the decline of prices, and to restore
business confidence, were notoriously feeble. On every other
occasion from 1763 to 1914, more or less effective steps were
taken. It would be helpful if one could discriminate carefully
among the rescue operations, to determine which were more
and which less adroit, and to compare them separately with
the extent in various dimensions of the depressions that
followed. Unhappily, we discriminate only crudely, if at all,
limiting the analysis to whether recovery was fast or slow.

There can be little doubt that the depression of the 1870s
was severe. After 1857 and 1866 (1864 in France), prices declined for two years and then picked up. After 1873, however,
they declined for six years to 1879.[10] In the United States
there was a severe recession through 1874, and then five long
years of severe depression.[11] This would appear to support
the hypothesis. But one is given pause by an explicit statement
in McCartney that this was the result primarily of a breakdown in basic industries, rather than of the disruption of
financial machinery.[12] There is no need to identify the entire
"Great Depression" from 1873 to 1896 with the absence of
lenders of last resort in Berlin, Vienna, and New York—at
least one writer doubts whether it was a depression at all,
rather than merely profitless prosperity.[13] My inclination,
however, is to associate the extended depression of the 1870s
in Central Europe, the United States, and by propagation in

Britain, with the sharpness of the collapse of prices and the absence of a lender of last resort. This is far from an irrefutable case.

In 1882 in France, the speculative banks of Lyons were allowed to fail, with only limited assistance to mitigate some of the disastrous consequences for the brokers who had supported the speculators. Recovery in France was long drawn out, conditioned partly by the slowness of recovery in Britain, the United States, and most of the Continent.[14]

In 1920 and 1921 there was no lender of last resort because the recession was deliberately engineered—by Britain, as a step on the route back to the gold standard, and by the Federal Reserve System in the United States, in order to halt inflation. The United States recovered "fairly quickly," but the abrupt fall in prices and output in Britain "hastily spread to a number of other highly industrial countries and developed into a depression of extreme severity and duration."[15] Pedersen speaks of "the quasi-permanent depression inaugurated in 1920," although he does not associate the extent of the decline with the absence of a lender of last resort, and he allows, as he should, for the importance attached by the British authorities to a return to gold. He blames the American authorities, however, for deflationary policies that prevented European countries from returning to gold:

The authorities seem to have been guided by a somewhat vague idea that conditions were unsound, that prices were too high, that the budget should be balanced, that things would not correct themselves, and that some action "cleaning up" the aftermath of the unsound wartime policy was necessary.

Now it is my thesis that this state of mind and the action which it engendered was fateful, because so much depended on the policy carried out in the U.S.A. . . .

. . . For these reasons I think it safe to conclude that the U.S.A. monetary authorities by stimulating demand in the spring of 1920 instead of contracting it could have prevented the permanent depression of the countries struggling to return to gold, mitigated inflation in a number of countries, and made the attempt of monetary reconstruction of the countries easier, and diminished the structural fall in the prices of primary and agricultural products.[16]

The argument that the depression of the 1930s was exacerbated by the lack of effective lenders of last resort— domestically in 1929 in the United States, worldwide in 1931 —has been dealt with at length above, in a number of places.

This by no means constitutes a conclusive demonstration that intervention of a lender of last resort in a panic softens the depression that follows. Too many other factors are at work, both long- and short-term, and the occasions when a panic has been allowed to run its course are so few that the material is not abundant enough for strong conclusions. At most there remains a presumption, but perhaps not a strong one, that halting a cumulative deflation helps shorten the depression that follows.

Does the Lender of Last Resort Forestall Crises?

We should recognize the fact that a wider claim is made for the lender of last resort: that its existence makes it possible to avoid crises altogether. In the arguments of the nineteenth century, this was entirely unacceptable. Lord Liverpool in 1825, Lord Lidderdale in 1890, not to mention dozens of others, claimed that the presence of a lender of last resort weakened the self-reliance of the banking system and increased its likelihood of falling into excesses of overtrading, revulsion, and discredit. We have not sought to contravert their case, although it has overtones of the conservative argument that relief for the poor will make them unwilling to work, and that there is no use providing the poor with housing since they will only keep coal in the bathtub. Nonetheless, it is worth noting that domestic crises, or at least panics, have declined in the latter third of our period both in frequency and in intensity.

One basis for this last statement is a moderation in rhetoric. From 1772 to 1929 it is easy to find hyperbolic statements about separate crises:

1772   Britain: "One of the fiercest financial storms of the century."[17]

1825   Britain: "A panic seized upon the public such had never been witnessed before."[18]

1837   United States: "One of the most disastrous [panics] this nation ever experienced."[19]

1847   Britain: "In the last nine months more reckless and hazardous speculation than any other known in modern times."[20]

1847   Britain: "It may safely be affirmed, that since the fall of Napoleon, the City has never been in a state of greater excitement."[21]

1857   Britain: "Crisis of 1857 the most severe that England or any other nation has ever encountered."[22]

1857   Hamburg: "So complete and classic a panic has never been seen before as now in Hamburg."[23]

1857   Hamburg: Panic "of a violence hitherto unknown."[24]

1866   Britain: "Crisis of 1866 most serious in modern times."[25]

1866   Britain: "Wilder than any since 1825."[26]

1873   Germany: "In 56 years, no such protracted crisis."[27]

1882   France: "Never have I seen an equal catastrophe."[28]

1929   United States: "The greatest cycle of speculative boom and collapse in modern times—since, in fact, the South Sea Bubble."[29]

This is not a systematic list, as collecting began late in the research and no organized effort was made to go back and comb for statements.

In general, however, it would appear that panics were fewer after 1866 in Britain and after 1929 in the United States (and on the Continent), and milder as well. One possible explanation is the decline of the usury laws, which were finally abandoned in the middle of the nineteenth century, although they had fallen into disuse earlier. This would imply a substantial element of truth in the Fisher-Brown thesis, dismissed in Chapter 4, that speculation led the economy into trouble when interest rates were held too low, and that credit could be restricted only through rationing. Ashton comments that on occasion, under the usury laws (which were removed for the Bank of England in 1833, and for the economy as a whole in 1854), refusing loans to needy applicants because of the necessity to ration precipitated panics that everyone was anxious to avoid.[30] This would fit a hypothesis that the Bank of England's clumsiness in using its rediscount rate in the 1830s and 1840s contributed to manias and crashes, whereas success in avoiding panic in Britain in 1873 and after came from a greater readiness to use Bank rate. (It will be recalled that Bank rate was changed twenty-four times in twelve months in 1872–73.) But the case is not compelling. Usury laws were widely evaded in early times, especially in chains of discount bills where the face amount of the bill was changed rather than interest charged. The United States had no restriction of a similar sort; widely ranging interest rates, sometimes reaching 5 percent per day (as a premium for short-term liquidity), did not noticeably reduce the number of panics. At the other end of the spectrum, moreover, the French had a strong reluctance to change their rates of interest, and did not exhibit a clearly higher propensity to overtrading than did the British.

A second possible reason lies in the capacity of markets to learn, in rational fashion, that overtrading leads to trouble, and hence to abstain from excessive speculation. But the record of overtrading hardly shows significant diminution. The 1960s and early 1970s in the United States, for example, show a long list of mini-manias. These arose successively and declined simultaneously in 1969–71, with a near crisis, but no panic.[31]

Our third hypothesis is that the expectation that a lender

of last resort will come to the rescue does not, in fact, increase speculation and overtrading so much as it calms anxieties when overtrading occurs. This view was put forth by a group of distinguished economists in the 1930s, and again more recently. It runs diametrically counter to the usual view that the known existence of such an institution exacerbates the tendency to overtrade.

In July 1932 the Committee on Economic Information, a high-powered group consisting of Sir Josiah Stamp (as chairman), G. D. H. Cole, J. M. Keynes, Sir Alfred Lewis, Sir Arthur Salter, Sir Frederick Leith-Ross, with H. D. Henderson and A. F. Hemming as joint secretaries, wrote the following:

As the [19th] century wore on, the knowledge that the Bank Act would be suspended in case of need, and that, as a consequence, harassed debtors with good security to offer would be able to obtain advances from the Bank, sufficed to prevent panics from arising.[32]

This group of economists, advising the British cabinet, was advocating an international lender of last resort, and may have exaggerated the effectiveness of suspending the Bank Act. The committee further seemed to overlook the fact that suspension of the Bank Act had not been a certainty, as Lord Lidderdale went to great lengths to demonstrate in 1890, concerned as he was about the subversive effects of continuous suspensions.

Minsky, who believes the United States banking system is fragile rather than robust, points to "near panics" in 1966 ("The Crunch"), in 1969–70 ("The Second Crunch"), and in 1974–75, when the OPEC oil price rise coincided with speculation in foreign exchange that brought failure to the Herstatt and the Franklin National banks, and calls them "incipient crises." The last of these, says Minsky, was narrowly averted by "crudely apt fiscal policy—money was literally thrown at the economy—combined with successful lender-of-last-resort operations."[33]

But if domestic financial crises have dwindled in number

and intensity, the same is not true for international ones. On the contrary, these have increased in frequency. Starting only with the completion of recovery and the reestablishment of convertibility after World War II in 1958, there have been crises in 1958, 1961, 1962, 1963, 1964, 1967, and 1968, not to mention 1971, 1973, 1974–75, et al. The reasons are readily adduced. Since the collapse of the gold standard, the major countries of the world have coordinated their macroeconomic policies less closely, with the result that exchange rates have deviated more frequently from equilibrium rates. With fixed exchange rates, this has been the result of differing monetary and fiscal policies. The adoption of floating exchange rates in 1973, with or without managed intervention, has not justified the simple-minded faith of many economists that exchange rates would automatically move to equilbrium levels to produce automatic balance-of-payments equilibrium or autonomously chosen, independent domestic policies: capital movements still responded to differences in interest rates to a degree, and speculation proved not always to be stabilizing.

Greater frequency of foreign-exchange crises now than in the nineteenth century may be due in part to improved communications—transoceanic telephones, telex, jet aircraft, and the like. A hundred years ago it took time for differences in interest rates, exchange rates, prices, expectations of exchange rates, price levels, etc., to communicate themselves internationally. These lags slowed down the contribution that stabilizing capital movements could make in overcoming domestic financial crises, but they limited the sensitivity of the system to disparate monetary and fiscal conditions in different countries. Today's troubles travel instantaneously.[34]

Even if domestic crises are fewer and less acute, the prevalence of international financial crises makes it important for us to underline the lessons of this historical study as to the ambiguities of the role of the lender of last resort. This is not to endorse the views of the panic-mongers, the Janeways,

and Barracloughs.[35] We need not take seriously novelists like
Erdman, nor accept uncritically the predictions of Minsky. I
do not forecast world economic collapse, because I think that
our profession of economics does not know the dynamics of
the system well enough to do so. At the same time, the international lender of last resort seems worth thinking about, if
only for contingency planning. I focus on the international
scene because this is where there is both the greatest possible
need and the least consensus on who should do what to whom
when.

Do We Need an International Lender of Last Resort?

Is there need for an international lender of last resort? My
answer is yes. Floating exchange rates do not reduce the
necessity for such a stabilizing entity, and may even increase
it. It seems evident that the remedy of letting the fires burn
out, the flood subside of its own accord, is not satisfactory.
Responsibility for stability is a public good. Public goods,
though notoriously difficult to produce, are nonetheless called
for. One must recognize that the stronger the provision of
public benefits, the less the incentive to produce them privately—in stability as in welfare, social security, housing, or
hospital care. True, self-reliance is undermined by reliance on
others. Self-reliance itself is a weak reed, however, in a world
of contagion. It is not a contradiction simultaneously to emphasize the importance of personal health care and to work
on public health problems. Both preventive medicine and
epidemic control are important.

The medical metaphor leads to an analogy that I have used
before in discussing this subject. The matter is somewhat
delicate, and I hope no one will be offended by it. The monetarists are to the market what Christian Science is to the

body.* They think the market is never wrong; the Christian Scientists think the body is never sick. In my judgment, the monetarists and Christian Science are more right than those who take the diametrically opposed positions: the pill poppers and hypochondriacs, who think the body is never right; and the Socialists and planners, who think the market is never right, and prefer to substitute government direction of resources and consumption through planning. But there is an intermediate position between these extremes. The body can be mostly right, but occasionally sick; the market can be mostly right, but occasionally break down. When the body does not function correctly, we take it to the doctor; when the market breaks down on occasion, we may need the medicine of a lender of last resort.

Along these same lines, and in fairness to opposing viewpoints, I quote from a recent article on the progress of medicine:

Then, sometime in the early nineteenth century, it was realized by a few of the leading figures in medicine that almost all of the complicated treatments then available for disease did not really work, and the suggestion was made by several courageous physicians, here and abroad, that most of them actually did more harm than good. Simultaneously, the surprising discovery was made that

* Most monetarists I know repudiate the notion of having a lender of last resort, and I assume from various positions he has taken that Milton Friedman subscribes to this view. There are a few passages in Friedman and Schwartz, however, that might lead one to think otherwise, especially this one:

The detailed story of every banking crisis in our history shows how much depends on the presence of one or more outstanding individuals willing to assume responsibility and leadership. . . .
Economic collapse often has the characteristic of a cumulative process. Let it go beyond a certain point, and it will tend for a time to gain strength from its own development. . . . Because no great strength would be required to hold back the rock that starts a landslide, it does not follow that the landslide will not be of major proportions.

See Milton Friedman and Anna J. Schwartz, A Monetary History of the United States, 1867–1960 (Princeton: Princeton University Press, 1965), pp. 418–19.

certain diseases were self-limited, got better by themselves, pos-
sessed, so to speak, a 'natural history.' . . . In a sober essay
written on this topic in 1876, Professor Edward H. Clarke of
Harvard reviewed what he regarded as the major scientific accom-
plishment of medicine in the preceding fifty years, which consisted
of studies proving that patients with typhoid and typhus fever
could recover all by themselves, without medical intervention, and
often did better for being untreated than when they received
bizarre herbs, heavy metals and fomentations that were popular
at the time. . . .[36]

Assume, if you will, that the lender of last resort is not a
witch doctor, and that Bagehot's prescription does not fall
into the category of "bizarre herbs, heavy metals and fomentations." How does the Bagehot rule apply in international
foreign-exchange crises today? What does it tell us about the
respective roles of the International Monetary Fund, the
central-bank swap network, the oil "safety net" proposed by
Henry Kissinger when he was secretary of state under
President Nixon, and the Witteveen facility for extending the
IMF, which now stands on the international financial agenda?

The rule, let us recall quickly, was that in crisis the lender
of last resort should seek to halt the panic and restore confidence by discounting freely at a penalty rate. The liberal
provision of cash for other assets, or even the readiness to do
so, halted the Gadarene flight from less liquid assets into
money. The penalty rate ensured that no one would borrow
to get cash who did not really need it. "Discount freely" did
not embrace lending to insolvent debtors or relaxing requirements for good collateral, although as we have seen, there
were occasions when the strict rules were impossible to maintain in the smoke of battle. It did mean, however, that the
lender of last resort—typically the central bank—was not to
restrict its aid to a chosen group of insiders, nor to discriminate against those outside the pale. (This rule, too, was occasionally honored in the breach.)

In today's world of foreign-exchange crises, lending freely
has several aspects that bear on who should be the lender of

last resort. One is the question of insolvent applicants, or those with inadequate collateral. Others relate to speed and limits.

Decisions by lenders as to who is solvent and who is insolvent in a domestic situation gave rise on occasion to accusations of insider preference. In international rescue operations a political may be substituted for a social test, e.g., the French refusals to repeat the rescue loans for the Credit-Anstalt, or to join in a big operation for Germany in 1931, or to go along in the $1 billion swap operation for Britain in September 1965. Even when there is no evident political bias in a decision to withhold lending, it will often be impossible to avoid accusations of favoritism, whether the lender of last resort is a rich country (Basel-type) club or an international body like the IMF. There may also be occasions when the accusation is justified, at the subconscious if not the conscious level. I see no way to ensure that international rescue operations can be scrubbed clean of all taint of political bias. Nevertheless, the role of the lender of last resort is to provide the public good of stability, rather than to serve a class, caste, national, or private purpose.

When it comes to speed and limits, the International Monetary Fund does badly on both scores. The IMF takes weeks to make decisions. A proposal has to go to the directors in Washington; they appeal to their governments for instructions. Resolving the conflicts between governmental points of view takes more time. Yet a lender of last resort must act within days, often within hours, to halt and with luck reverse a speculative attack on a currency. In the domestic history of the Bank of England, it was more than once said that the Bank had swung into action before the chancellor of the exchequer or some other individual was out of bed.[37] In March 1961 the central bankers' club was able to agree on the telephone and to enter the market on the side of stability in a matter of hours—and without instructions from politically constituted authority. There seems little likelihood that the extension of the IMF through the Witteveen facility or the OECD safety net could overcome this handicap in rescue operations when time is of the essence. On the contrary, since under the Witteveen facility a given country can choose to withhold its proportionate contribution from a given loan, more rather than less decision-making time is required: each country must decide first on the operation, then on the extent to which it will participate, while the needy country and the market are left in doubt as to whether the rediscounting, if undertaken at all, will be sufficient.

Freely also refers to limits. Suspension of the Bank Act in 1847 and 1866 alleviated panic, without the need to issue bank notes in excess of the limit. Limits excite, as noted earlier (see page 101); in moments of stress, the existence of a limit increases the alarm. When the market feels that there may not be enough to go around, the rush to get there first is exacerbated. The IMF was originally unusable for financial crises because quotas were limited and divided in tranches; the amount of credit that any needy country could obtain in a given twelve months was limited to one tranche, equal to a fourth of the national quota. In contrast to the White Plan which formed the core of the IMF, the Keynes Plan set limits so high ($35 billion overall, in 1944 dollars) that they were thought not to constitute a limit at all. The contrast today runs between the Witteveen facility, of roughly $10 million, and the moribund safety net of $25 billion. It seems likely that even $25 billion would not be enough to convey fully the impression that in financial crisis there would be enough for all in trouble. The $10 billion of the Witteveen facility clearly seems too small, especially if the fact that Saudi Arabia is the largest contributor means that a substantial part of it will be reserved to finance deficits among friendly LDCs rather than to counter speculation.

The Bagehot rule calls for lending at penalty rates. In 1873 this meant at a high discount rate; as noted earlier, the letters of suspension of the Bank Act decreed a specific Bank rate that the Bank of England was expected to sustain. In today's world, the penalty represented by a high rate of interest is less sobering. Countries, like firms and individuals, expect *in extremis* to add the interest to the debt, if they cannot pay it. The swap arrangements had no interest charge, but were expected to be reversed at maturity, if necessary by international borrowing under less critical circumstances from the IMF. The stiff central-bank code was sufficient to ensure that this was done.

The penalty imposed by the Fund goes by the name of "conditionality," and consists in the agreement by the rescued to implement certain policy steps designed to remedy the underlying position. Similar conditions were imposed by bankers making private stabilization loans—to France in 1924, to Britain in 1931—not because they claimed to know best what the borrowing country should do, but because, if they were going to sell bonds to the public, the public would need to be reassured that the steps necessary to make interest and amortization service certain would be taken. Again, there is room for misunderstanding, or perhaps it would be better to say difference of opinion. The British Labor Party regarded the conditions "imposed" by the bankers in August 1931 as a "bankers' ramp." The bankers doubtless felt they were only safeguarding their depositors' money. More recently, the International Monetary Fund imposed conditions on rescue operations in Peru, that provoked rioting among the Peruvians. Economists from developing countries feel in some instances that the IMF personnel's conservative advice embodies a sadistic streak. The IMF staff, in turn, doubtless feels it is setting out minimal conditions necessary to make the rescue operation successful. An international body helps to diffuse the political sensitivity inherent in countries borrowing under stress, but it does not do so completely.

The swap network, then, is better at lending freely, with its speed in decision making and elastic limits. It lacks the penalty rate, but among the close-knit insider group of the Bank for

International Settlements the chances of abuse seems minimal. The International Monetary Fund has effective sanctions in "conditionality" to limit unnecessary borrowing—*vide* the anguish of the British in accepting IMF views on domestic macroeconomic policy—but it is slow in emergencies, and over the years to date, and prospectively for the future, suffers from narrow limits that violate Bagehot's admonition to lend freely.

What is intolerable, however, is for world stability to be underproduced while the Basel group and the IMF try to hand off the responsibility to each other. There must be a lender of last resort for emergencies. It is useful for the world to have doubts on this score, to encourage self-reliance, but it is not useful for national and international leaders to urge the role on others. When Congressman Henry Reuss states that the United States should not act as lender of last resort for countries in trouble, or when Arthur F. Burns as Chairman of the Board of Governors of the Federal Reserve System insists that the United States should have a smaller role and the IMF a larger one, they may be dissembling in order to extend the desirable illusion of uncertainty. The danger is that they mean what they say, and that in a future crisis, as in 1931, countries and international organizations will try to shrug the responsibility for international stability off onto others.

NOTES

Chapter 1

1. Charles P. Kindleberger, *The World in Depression, 1929–1939* (Berkeley: University of California Press, 1973).
2. For a particularly vigorous challenge on the economics, see Anna J. Schwartz's review, *Journal of Political Economy* 88 (April 1975): 231–37. David Calleo's essay in B. M. Rowland, ed., *Balance of Power vs. Hegemony: The Interwar Monetary System* (New York: New York University Press, 1976), disagrees with the political analysis.
3. Thomas Joplin, *Case for Parliamentary Inquiry into the Circumstances of the Panic, in a letter to Thomas Gisbourne, Esq., M.P.* (London: F. Ridgeway & Sons, n.d. [after 1832]), p. 29.
4. Franco Bonelli, *La crisi del 1907: una tappa dello sviluppo industriale in Italia* (Turin: Fondazione Luigi Einaudi, 1971).
5. E. E. de Jong-Keesing, *De economische Crisis van 1763 te Amsterdam* (Amsterdam, 1939).

Chapter 2

1. Joseph A. Schumpeter, *Business Cycles: A Theoretical, Historical and Statistical Analysis of the Capitalist Process* (New York: McGraw-Hill, 1939) vol. 1, chap. 4, esp. pp. 161ff.
2. Hyman P. Minsky, "Financial Stability Revisited: The Economics of Disaster," in Board of Governors of the Federal Reserve System, *Reappraisal of the Federal Reserve Discount Mechanism* (Washington, D.C., June 1972), vol. 3, pp. 95–136. A detailed list of Minsky's writings on financial crises is given by Allen Sinai in his comment on Minsky's paper "A Theory of Systematic Fragility," in Edward I. Altman and Arnold W. Sametz, eds., *Financial Crises: Institutions and Markets in a Fragile Environment* (New York: Wiley-International, 1977), p. 196.
3. See R. C. O. Matthews, "Public Policy and Monetary Expenditure," in Thomas Wilson and Andrew S. Skinner, eds., *The Market and the State: Essays in Honour of Adam Smith* (Oxford: Oxford University Press, Clarendon Press, 1976), p. 336.
4. M. J. Gordon, "Toward a Theory of Financial Distress," *Journal of Finance* 26 (May 1971): 347–56.

5. See C. P. Kindleberger, *The World in Depression, 1929–1939* (Berkeley: University of California Press, 1973), pp. 19–21.

6. Alvin Hansen, *Business Cycles and National Income* (New York: W. W. Norton, 1957), p. 226.

Chapter 3

1. John F. Muth, "Rational Expectations and the Theory of Price Movements" *Econometrica* 29 (July 1961): 315–35.

2. Harry G. Johnson, "The Role of Networks of Economists in International Monetary Reform," paper prepared for the University of Pennsylvania Conference on International Scientific and Professional Associations and the International System, Philadelphia, November 12–13, 1976, p. 16.

3. Milton Friedman, "The Case for Flexible Exchange Rates," in *Essays in Positive Economics* (Chicago: University of Chicago Press, 1953).

4. Harry G. Johnson, "Destabilizing Speculation: A General Equilibrium Approach," *Journal of Political Economy* 84 (February 1976): 101.

5. Milton Friedman, "Discussion" of C. P. Kindleberger, "The Case for Fixed Exchange Rates, 1969," in Federal Reserve Bank of Boston, *The International Adjustment Mechanism* (Boston, 1970), pp. 114–15.

6. H. M. Hyndman, *Commercial Crises of the Nineteenth Century* (1892; 2nd ed. [1932], reprinted, New York: Augustus M. Kelley, 1967), p. 96.

7. Walter Bagehot, *Lombard Street: A Description of the Money Market* (1873; reprint ed., London: John Murray, 1917), p. 18.

8. Sir John Clapham, *The Bank of England: A History* (Cambridge: Cambridge University Press, 1945), vol. 2, p. 326.

9. Adam Smith, *An Inquiry into the Nature and Causes of the Wealth of Nations* (1776; reprint ed., New York: Modern Library, 1937), pp. 703–4.

10. G. LeBon, *The Crowd: A Study of the Popular Mind* (London: T. Fisher, Unwin, 1922).

11. Charles MacKay, *Memoirs of Extraordinary Delusions and the Madness of Crowds* (1914; reprint ed., Boston: L. C. Page Co., 1932).

12. John Carswell, *The South Sea Bubble* (London: Cresset Press, 1960), p. 161.

13. Irving Fisher, *The Purchasing Power of Money: Its Determination and Relation to Credit, Interest and Crises*, 2nd ed. (New York: Macmillan, 1911), esp. chap. 1, dealing with crises.

14. Bagehot, *Lombard Street*, pp. 131–32.

15. George W. Van Vleck, *The Panic of 1857: An Analytical Study* (New York: Columbia University Press, 1953), p. 31.

16. R. C. O. Matthews, *A Study in Trade-Cycle History: Economic Fluctuations in Great Britain, 1832–1842* (Cambridge: Cambridge University Press, 1954), pp. 49, 110–1.

17. Max Wirth, *Geschichte der Handelskrisen*, 4th ed. (1890, reprint ed., New York: Burt Franklin, 1968), p. 480.

18. Ilse Mintz, *Deterioration in the Quality of Bonds Issued in the United States, 1920–1930* (New York: National Bureau of Economic Research, 1951).

19. William J. Baumol, "Speculation and Profitability of Stability," *Review of Economics and Statistics* 39 (August 1957): 263–71; L. G. Telser, "A Theory of Speculation Relating Profitability and Stability," *Review of Economics and Statistics* 41 (August 1959): 295–302.

20. Johnson, "Destabilizing Speculation," 101.

21. Larry T. Wimmer, "The Gold Crisis of 1869: Stabilizing or Destabilizing Speculation under Floating Exchange Rates," *Explorations in Economic History* 12 (1975): 105–22.

22. Christina Stead, *House of All Nations* (New York: Knopf, 1938).

23. Carswell, *South Sea Bubble*, pp. 131, 199.

24. Ibid., p. 120.

25. Clapham, *Bank of England*, vol. 2, p. 20.

26. William Smart, *Economic Annals of the Nineteenth Century* (1911; reprint ed., New York, Augustus M. Kelley, 1964), vol. 2, p. 292.

27. Matthews, *Trade-Cycle History*, p. 25.

28. D. Morier Evans, *The History of the Commercial Crisis, 1857–1858, and the Stock Exchange Panic of 1859* (1859; reprint ed., New York: Augustus M. Kelley, 1969), p. 102.

29. Max Wirth, "The Crisis of 1890," *Journal of Political Economy* 1 (March 1893): 220.

30. A. C. Pigou, *Aspects of British Economic History, 1918–25* (London: Macmillan, 1948).

31. J. S. Mill, *Principles of Political Economy, with Some of Their Applications to Social Philosophy* (1848; 7th ed., reprint ed., London: Longmans, Green, 1929), p. 709.

32. Maurice Lévy-Leboyer, *Les Banques européennes et l'industrialisation internationale dans la première moitié du XIXᵉ siècle*, (Paris: Presses universitaires de France, 1964), p. 715.

33. Charles Wilson, *Anglo-Dutch Commerce and Finance in the Eighteenth Century* (Cambridge: Cambridge University Press, 1941), p. 25. For a series from the early seventeenth century, see J. G. Van Dillen, "The Bank of Amsterdam," in *History of the Principal Public Banks* (The Hague: Martinus Nijhoff, 1934), p. 95.

34. For 1822 and 1824, see Smart, *Economic Annals*, vol. 2, pp. 82, 215. For 1888, see W. Jett Lauck, *The Causes of the Panic of 1893* (Boston: Houghton Mifflin, 1907), p. 39.

35. A. Andréadès, *History of the Bank of England* (London: P. S. King, 1909), pp. 404–5. See also p. 249.

36. O. M. W. Sprague, *History of Crises Under the National Banking System* (1910; reprint ed., New York: Augustus M. Kelley, 1968), pp. 35–6.

37. Great Britain, *Parliamentary Papers (Monetary Policy, Commercial Distress)*, "Report of the Select Committee on the Operation of the

Bank Acts and the Causes of the Recent Commercial Distress, 1857–59"
(Shannon: Irish University Press, 1969), vol. 4; Consular report from
Hamburg, no. 7, January 27, 1858, p. 438.

38. This statement appears in italics in Donald H. Dunn's fictionalized book, *Ponzi, the Boston Swindler* (New York: McGraw-Hill, 1975),
p. 98.

39. Wirth, *Handelskrisen*, p. 109.

40. Wirth, "Crisis of 1890," cited, pp. 222–24; Alfred Pose, *La
Monnaie et ses institutions*, Paris, Presses universitaires de France,
1942, I, p. 215. W. J. Lauck puts the rescue operation as 25 million
from the leading banks and 100 million from the Bank of France; see
The Causes of the Panic of 1893 (Boston: Houghton Mifflin, 1907), p. 57.

41. Wirth, *Handelskrisen*, p. 519.

42. J. W. Beyen, *Money in a Maelstrom* (New York: Macmillan,
1949), p. 45.

43. William R. Scott, *The Constitution and Finance of English,
Scottish and Irish Joint Stock Companies to 1720*, 3 vols. (London,
1922), as summarized by J. A. Schumpeter, *Business Cycles* (New York:
McGraw-Hill, 1939) vol. 1, p. 250.

44. Carswell, *South Sea Bubble*, p. 139.

45. Hans Rosenberg, *Die Weltwirtschaftskrise von 1857–59* (Stuttgart-
Berlin: W. Kohlhammer, 1934), p. 114.

46. David Divine, *Indictment of Incompetence: Mutiny at Invergorden*
(London: MacDonald, 1970).

47. Wirth, *Handelskrisen*, p. 92.

48. Ibid., p. 458.

49. Bertrand Gille, *Le banque et le crédit en France de 1815 à 1848*
(Paris, Presses universitaires de France, 1959), p. 175.

50. Lévy-Leboyer, *Banques européennes*, p. 673.

51. Gille, *Banque et crédit*, p. 304.

52. Honoré de Balzac, *César Birotteau* (Paris: Livre de Poche, 1972),
esp., pp. 13–14.

53. Leland H. Jenks, *The Migration of British Capital to 1875* (New
York: Knopf, 1927), p. 34.

54. Rosenberg, *Weltwirtschaftskrise*, pp. 50, 100–1.

55. Carswell, *South Sea Bubble*, p. 171.

56. Ibid., pp. 140, 155.

57. Ibid., p. 159.

58. Clapham, *Bank of England*, vol. 2, p. 239.

59. T. S. Ashton, *Economic Fluctuations in England, 1700–1800*
(Oxford: Oxford University Press, Clarendon Press, 1959), p. 151.

60. Ibid., p. 127.

61. See the review of Johannes van der Voort, *De Westindische
Plantage van 1720 tot 1795* (Eindhoven: De Witte, 1973), in *Journal of
Economic History* 36 (June 1976): 519.

62. Wilson, *Anglo-Dutch Finance*, pp. 169–87, Ashton, *Economic
Fluctuations*, pp. 127–29; Clapham, *Bank of England*, vol. 1, 242–49;
Martin G. Buist, *At Spes non Fracta, Hope & Co., 1770–1815: Merchant
Bankers and Diplomats at Work* (The Hague: Martinus Nijhoff, 1974),
pp. 21ff.

63. Arthur D. Gayer, W. W. Rostow, and Anna J. Schwartz, *The

Growth and Fluctuation of the British Economy, 1790–1850 (Oxford: Oxford University Press, Clarendon Press, 1953), vol. 1, p. 92.

64. Clément Juglar, *Des crises commerciales et leur retour périodiques en France, en Angleterre et aux Etats-Unis,* 2nd ed. (1889; reprint ed., Augustus M. Kelley, New York: 1967).

65. Theodore E. Burton, *Financial Crises and Periods of Industrial and Commercial Depression* (New York: D. Appleton, 1902), pp. 39–41.

66. Francis W. Hirst, *The Six Panics and Other Essays* (London: Methuen, 1913), p. 2.

67. Ernst Baasch, *Holländische Wirtschaftsgeschichte* (Jena: Gustav Fischer, 1927), p. 240, quoting Büsch.

68. Andrèadés, *Bank of England,* p. 404.

69. Wilson, *Anglo-Dutch Finance,* p. 77, quoting Isaac de Pinto, *Jeu d'Actions* (eighteenth century).

70. Fritz Stern, *Gold and Iron: Bismarck, Bleichröder and the Building of German Empire* (London: Allen & Unwin, 1977), p. 500, quoting Constantin Franz in 1872.

71. Oskar Morgenstern, *International Financial Transactions and Business Cycles* (Princeton: Princeton University Press, 1959), p. 550.

72. Robert Bigo, *Les banques françaises au cours du XIX* siècle* (Paris, Sirey, 1947), p. 262.

73. Stead, *House of All Nations,* p. 233.

74. Ibid., p. 244.

Chapter 4

1. Max Wirth, *Geschichte der Handelskrisen,* 4th ed. (1890 reprint ed., New York: Burt Franklin, 1968), p. 22.

2. Peter Temin, *The Jacksonian Economy* (New York: Norton, 1969), pp. 79–82.

3. Jean Bouvier, *Le Krach de l'Union Générale, 1878–1885* (Paris: Presses universitaires de France, 1960), pp. 129–34.

4. Martin Mayer, *The Bankers* (New York: Ballantine Books, 1974), p. 197.

5. Wirth, *Handelskrisen,* p. 478.

6. J. G. Van Dillen, "The Bank of Amsterdam," in *History of the Principal Public Banks* (The Hague: Martinus Nijhoff, 1934), pp. 79–123.

7. Eli F. Heckscher, "The Bank of Sweden in Its Connection with the Bank of Amsterdam," in ibid., p. 169.

8. Milton Friedman, *The Optimum Quantity of Money and Other Essays* (Chicago: Aldine, 1969), p. 1–50.

9. Jacob Viner, *Studies in the Theory of International Trade* (New York: Harper, 1937), pp. 232–33.

10. Great Britain, Committee on the Working of the Monetary System, *Report* (Radcliffe Report), Cmnd 827 (London: H. M. Stationery Office, August 1959), pp. 133–34, ¶ 391–92.

11. Ibid., p. 134, ¶ 394.

12. James S. Gibbons, *The Banks of New York, Their Dealers, the Clearing House, and the Panic of 1857* (New York: D. Appleton, 1859), pp. 376–77.

13. J. S. Mill, in *Westminster Review* 41 (1844): 590–91, quoted in Jacob Viner, *Studies in International Trade*, p. 246.

14. Samuel L. Clemens [Mark Twain] and Charles Dudley Warner, *The Gilded Age: A Tale of Today* (1873; reprint ed., author's national ed., vol. 10, 1915), vol. 1, p. 263.

15. T. S. Ashton, "The Bill of Exchange and Private Banks in Lancashire, 1790–1830," in T. S. Ashton and R. S. Sayers, eds., *Papers in English Monetary History* (Oxford: Oxford University Press, Clarendon Press, 1953), pp. 37–38.

16. Francis C. Knowles, *The Monetary Crisis Considered* (1827), referring to the House of Lords Committee on Scottish and Irish Currency of 1826; quoted in J. R. T. Hughes, *Fluctuations in Trade, Industry and Finance: A Study of British Economic Development, 1850–1860* (Oxford: Oxford University Press, Clarendon Press, 1960), p. 267.

17. Ibid., p. 258.

18. Kurt Samuelsson, "International Payments and Credit Movements by Swedish Merchant Houses, 1730–1815," *Scandinavian Economic History Review* 3 (1955): 188.

19. R. G. Hawtrey, *The Art of Central Banking* (London: Longmans, Green, 1932), p. 128–29.

20. See Herman E. Krooss, ed., *Documentary History of Banking and Currency in the United States* (New York: Chelsea House, 1969), vol. 1, p. 31.

21. Viner, *Studies*, pp. 245ff, esp. pp. 249–50.

22. Adam Smith, *An Inquiry into the Nature and Causes of the Wealth of Nations* (1776; reprint ed., New York: Modern Library, 1937), pp. 293–97.

23. R. G. Hawtrey, *Currency and Credit*, 3rd ed. (New York: Longmans, Green, 1930), p. 224.

24. Arthur D. Gayer, W. W. Rostow, and Anna Jacobson Schwartz, *The Growth and Fluctuation of the British Economy, 1790–1850* (Oxford: Oxford University Press, Clarendon Press, 1953), vol. 1, p. 105.

25. Great Britain, *Parliamentary Papers (Monetary Policy, Commercial Distress)*, "Report of the Select Committee on the Operation of the Bank Acts and the Causes of the Recent Commercial Distress, with Proceedings, Minutes of Evidence, Appendix and Index, 1857–59" (Shannon: Irish University Press, 1969), vol. 4, p. 113, question 1661, and p. 115, question 1679.

26. Albert E. Fr. Schäfle, "Die Handelskrise von 1857 in Hamburg, mit besonderer Rucksicht auf das Bankwesen," in Schäffle, *Gesammelte Aufsätze* (Tübingen: H. Haupp'schen, 1885), vol. 2, p. 31.

27. Wirth, *Handelskrisen*, p. 91.

28. See my *The World in Depression, 1929–1939* (Berkeley: University of California Press, 1973), p. 141 and note.

29. Schumpeter, *Business Cycles*, p. 673. By 1914, according to E. V. Morgan, the amount was at least £350 million. See his *Studies in British Financial Policy, 1914–1925* (London: Macmillan, 1952), p. 3.

30. Bouvier, *Le Krach*, pp. 130–31.

31. Ibid., p. 131.

32. Ibid. For prices, see Tables 7 and 8, pp. 136 and 144. For the shortfall, see p. 144.

33. Ibid., tables 7 and 8, pp. 136, 144, 145.

34. John Carswell, *The South Sea Bubble* (London: Cresset Press, 1960), p. 171.

35. Bouvier, *Le Krach*, p. 112.

36. Ibid., p. 113.

37. Federal Reserve System, *Banking and Monetary Statistics* (Washington, D.C., 1943), p. 494.

38. Alexander Dana Noyes, *The Market Place: Reminiscences of a Financial Editor* (Boston: Little, Brown, 1937), p. 353.

39. Bouvier, *Le Krach*, pp. 175, 177.

40. Peter H. Lindert, *Key Currencies and Gold, 1900–1913,* Princeton Studies in International Finance no. 24 (August 1969).

41. Robert Triffin, *Gold and the Dollar Crisis: The Future of Convertibility* (New Haven: Yale University Press, 1960).

42. Jacques Rueff, *The Age of Inflation* (Chicago: H. Regnery, 1964); and with Fred Hirsch, *The Role and Rule of Gold: An Argument,* Princeton Essays in International Finance no. 47 (1967).

43. Jeffry G. Williamson, *American Growth and the Balance of Payments, 1830–1913: A Study of the Long Swing* (Chapel Hill: University of North Carolina Press, 1964).

44. Alvin H. Hansen, *Business Cycles and National Income* (New York: Norton, 1957), chaps. 13 and 15.

45. A. C. Pigou, *Industrial Fluctuations* (London: Macmillan, 1927), pt. 1, chap. 7, and p. 274.

46. Milton Friedman and Anna J. Schwartz, *A Monetary History of the United States, 1867–1960* (Princeton: Princeton University Press, 1963). Chapter 10 of the book is published separately as *The Great Contraction, 1929–1933* (Princeton: Princeton University Press, 1965).

47. This assertion was made by Thomas A. Mayer in a seminar on "Money and the Great Depression," University of California, Berkeley, May 11, 1977.

48. Peter Temin, *Did Monetary Forces Cause the Great Depression?* (New York: Norton, 1976), *passim.*

49. Friedman and Schwartz, *Monetary History,* diagram, p. 454.

50. Temin, *Monetary Forces,* p. 141.

51. Frederic S. Miskin, "Illiquidity, Consumer Durable Expenditure, and Monetary Policy," *American Economic Review* 66 (September 1976): 642–54.

52. See Minsky's review of Temin, in *Challenge,* September/October 1976, pp. 44–46.

53. See Milton Friedman, "The Monetary Theory and Policy of Henry Simons," in Friedman, *Optimum Quantity of Money,* pp. 81–93.

54. Henry Simons, *Economic Policy for a Free Society* (Chicago: University of Chicago Press, 1948).

55. Friedman, "Henry Simons," p. 83.

56. Gayer, Rostow, and Schwartz, *Growth and Fluctuation,* vol. 1, p. 300.

57. Hughes, *Fluctuations*, p. 12.

58. Ibid., p. 261.

59. Elmer Wood, *English Theories of Central Banking Control, 1819–1858, with Some Account of Contemporary Procedure* (Cambridge, Mass.: Harvard University Press, 1939), p. 147.

60. A. Andréadès, *History of the Bank of England* (London: P. S. King, 1909), pp. 356–57.

61. Wirth, *Handelskrisen*, p. 463.

62. Ibid., pp. 515–16.

63. E. Victor Morgan, *The Theory and Practice of Central Banking, 1797–1913* (Cambridge: Cambridge University Press, 1943), pp. 184–85.

64. O. M. W. Sprague, *History of Crises Under the National Banking System* (1910; reprint ed., New York: Augustus M. Kelley, 1968), p. 241.

65. Gibbons, *Banks of New York*, p. 375.

66. Gayer, Rostow, and Schwartz, *Growth and Fluctuation*, vol. 1, p. 205.

Chapter 5

1. Hyman P. Minsky, "Financial Resources in a Fragile Financial Environment," *Challenge* 18 (July/August 1975): 65.

2. Martin F. Hellwig, "A Model of Borrowing and Lending with Bankruptcy," Princeton University Econometric Research Program, Research Memorandum no. 177, April 1975, p. 1.

3. See Norman C. Miller, *The Great Salad Oil Swindle* (New York: Coward, McCann, 1965).

4. Daniel Defoe, *The Anatomy of Change-Alley* (London: E. Smith, 1719), p. 8. See also the title of Jean Carper's book on fraud, *Not with a Gun* (New York: Grossman, 1973).

5. Jacob van Klavaren, "Die historische Erscheinungen der Korruption," *Vierteljahrschrift für Sozial- und Wirtschaftsgeschichte* 44 (December 1957): 289–324; 45, (December 1958): 433–69, 469–504; 46 (June 1959): 204–31. See also "Fiskalismus—Mercantalismus—Korruption: Drei Aspecte der Finanz- und Wirtschaftspolitik während der Ancien Regime," ibid., 47 (September 1960): 333–53.

6. E. Ray McCartney, *The Crisis of 1873* (Minneapolis: Burgess, 1935), p. 15.

7. Alexander Gerschenkron, *Economic Backwardness in Historical Perspective* (Cambridge, Mass.: Harvard University Press, 1962).

8. John Carswell, *The South Sea Bubble* (London: Cresset, 1960), p. 13.

9. Maximillian E. Novak, *Economics and the Fiction of Daniel Defoe* (Berkeley: University of California Press, 1962), p. 103.

10. Bray Hammond, *Banks and Politics in America from the Revolution to the Civil War* (Princeton: Princeton University Press, 1957), p. 268.

11. Carswell, *South Sea Bubble*, pp. 222–24.

12. William G. Shepheard, Wall Street editor of *Business Week,* in preface to Donald H. Dunn, *Ponzi, the Boston Swindler* (New York: McGraw-Hill, 1975), p. x.

13. Milton Friedman, "In Defense of Destabilizing Speculation," in *The Optimum Quantity of Money and Other Essays* (Chicago: Aldine, 1969), p. 290.

14. Quoted in Max Winkler, *Foreign Bonds, an Autopsy: A Study of Defaults and Repudiations of Government Obligations* (Philadelphia: Roland Swain, 1933), p. 103.

15. W. C. T. King, *History of the London Discount Market* (London: George Routledge & Sons, 1936), pp. 246–55.

16. E. Victor Morgan, *The Theory and Practice of Central Banking, 1797–1913* (Cambridge: Cambridge University Press, 1943), p. 177.

17. Honoré de Balzac, *Melmoth réconcilié* (Geneva: Editions de Verbe, 1946), pp. 45–50.

18. Introduction by Robert Tracey to Anthony Trollope, *The Way We Live Now* (1874–75; reprint ed., New York: Bobbs-Merrill, 1974), p. xxv.

19. Dunn, *Ponzi,* p. 188.

20. Sir John Clapham, *The Bank of England: A History* (Cambridge: Cambridge University Press, 1945), vol. 1, p. 229.

21. Charles Wilson, *Anglo-Dutch Commerce and Finance in the Eighteenth Century* (Cambridge: Cambridge University Press, 1941), p. 170.

22. George W. Van Vleck, *The Panic of 1857, An Analytical Study* (New York: Columbia University Press, 1943), p. 65.

23. Earl J. Hamilton, "The Political Economy of France at the Time of John Law," *History of Political Economy* 1 (Spring 1969): 146.

24. Jacob van Klavaren, "Rue de Quincampoix und Exchange Alley: Die Spekulationsjähre 1719 und 1720 in Frankreich und England," *Vierteljahrschrift für Sozial- und Wirtschaftsgeschichte* 48 (October 1961): 329ff.

25. Dunn, *Ponzi,* p. 247.

26. Max Wirth, *Geschichte der Handelskrisen,* 4th ed., (1890; reprint ed., New York: Burt Franklin, 1968), p. 510.

27. William Robert Scott, *The Constitution and Finance of English, Scottish and Irish Joint-Stock Companies to 1720* (Cambridge: Cambridge University Press, 1911), vol. 3, pp. 449ff; and D. Morier Evans, *The Commercial Crisis, 1847–48,* 2nd ed., rev. (1849; reprint ed., New York: Augustus M. Kelley, 1969), pp. 33–34. A separate list for the South Sea bubble, prepared by a contemporary and less detailed, is set out in Wirth, *Handelskrisen,* pp. 67–79.

28. A. Andréadès, *History of the Bank of England* (London: P. S. King, 1909), p. 133.

29. Carswell, *South Sea Bubble,* p. 142.

30. Scott, *Joint-Stock Companies,* p. 450.

31. Hans Rosenberg, *Die Weltwirtschaftskrise von 1857–59* (Stuttgart: W. Kohlhammer, 1934), p. 103.

32. Wirth, *Handelskrisen,* p. 480.

33. Anthony Trollope, *The Three Clerks* (New York: Harper & Brothers, 1860), p. 346.

34. Carswell, *South Sea Bubble,* p. 177.

35. Fritz Stern, *Gold and Iron: Bismarck, Bleichröder, and the Build-ing of the German Empire* (London: Allen & Unwin, 1977), p. 358.
36. Ibid., pp. 396–97.
37. U.S. Senate, Committee on Finance, 72nd Cong., 1st sess., *Hear-ings on Sales of Foreign Bonds of Securities*, held December 18, 1931 to February 10, 1932, (Washington, D.C.: U.S. Government Printing Office, 1932).
38. O. M. W. Sprague, *History of Crises Under the National Banking System* (1910; reprint ed., New York: Augustus M. Kelley, 1968), p. 341.
39. Quoted in Wirth, *Handelskrisen*, p. 80.
40. Honoré de Balzac, *La Maison Nucingen*, in *Oeuvres complètes* (Paris: Calmann Lévy, 1892), p. 68.
41. Carswell, *South Sea Bubble*, pp. 176, 181.
42. Wirth, *Handelskrisen*, p. 491.
43. Émile Zola, *L'Argent* (Paris, Livre de Poche, n.d.) p. 125.
44. Wirth, *Handelskrisen*, p. 491.
45. Zola, *L'Argent*, p. 161.
46. Jean Bouvier, *Le Krach de l'Union Générale* (Paris: Presses Uni-versitaires de France, 1960), p. 36.
47. *Economist*, October 21, 1848, pp. 1186–88, quoted in Arthur D. Gayer, W. W. Rostow, and Anna J. Schwartz, *The Growth and Fluctua-tion of the British Economy, 1790–1850* (Oxford: Oxford University Press, Clarendon Press, 1953), p. 316.
48. Rosenberg, *Weltwirtschaftskrise*, p. 101.
49. Stern, *Gold and Iron*, chap. 10 ("Greed and Intrigue") and p. 364.
50. Novak, *Economics of Defoe*, pp. 14–15 and 160, note 35.
51. Ibid., p. 16, note 50.
52. Maurice Lévy-Leboyer, *Les banques européennes et l'industrial-isation internationale dans la première moitié du XIXe siècle* (Paris: Presses universitaires de France, 1964), pp. 632–33.
53. Ibid., p. 503, note 90.
54. Bouvier, *Le Krach*, p. 124.
55. Ibid., p. 161, note 50.
56. Stern, *Gold and Iron*, chap. 11.
57. Theodore Dreiser's *Trilogy of Desire* consists of three novels: *The Financier* (1912), *The Titan* (1914), and *The Stoic* (1947). See *The Titan* (New York: World, 1972), pp. 371–72.
58. Ibid., pp. 515–40.
59. Henry Grote Lewin, *The Railway Mania and Its Aftermath, 1845–1852* (1936; reprint ed., rev., New York: Augustus M. Kelley, 1968), pp. 262, 357–64.
60. See Paul W. Gates, *Illinois Central Railroad and Its Colonization Work* (Cambridge, Mass.: Harvard University Press, 1934, 1968), pp. 66, 75–76; John L. Weller, *The New Haven Railroad: The Rise and Fall* (New York: Hastings House, 1969), p. 37n; Van Vleck, *Panic of 1857*, p. 58. Professor David Donald of Harvard University started me off on the first of these citations.
61. See Williard L. Thorp, *Business Annals* (New York: National Bureau of Economic Research, 1926), p. 126.
62. Watson Washburn and Edmund S. Delong, *High and Low Financiers: Some Notorious Swindlers and their Abuses of Our Modern Stock Selling System*, Indianapolis, Bobbs-Merrill, 1932, p. 13.

63. Ibid., p. 83, 101, 144, 309.

64. Samuel L. Clemens [Mark Twain] and Charles Dudley Warner, *The Gilded Age: A Tale of Today* (1873; reprint ed., author's national ed., vol. 10, 1915), vol. 1, p. 146.

65. James S. Gibbons, *The Banks of New York, Their Dealers, the Clearing House, and the Panic of 1857* (New York: D. Appleton, 1859), p. 104.

66. Ibid., p. 277.

67. John Kenneth Galbraith, *The Great Crash, 1929*, 3rd ed. (Boston: Houghton Mifflin, 1972), pp. 133–35.

68. See Robert Shaplen, *Kreuger: Genius and Swindler* (New York: Knopf, 1960).

69. Carswell, *South Sea Bubble*, pp. 225, 265–66.

70. Bouvier, *Le Krach*, pp. 211, 219.

71. Herbert I. Bloom, *The Economic Activities of the Jews of Amsterdam in the Seventeenth and Nineteenth Centuries* (Williamsport, Pa.: Bayard Press, 1937), p. 199.

72. Carswell, *South Sea Bubble*, p. 210.

73. Dreiser, *The Titan*, p. 237.

74. Christina Stead, *House of All Nations, A Novel* (New York: Simon & Shuster, 1938), p. 643.

Chapter 6

1. Milton Friedman, "In Defense of Destabilizing Speculation," in *The Optimum Quantity of Money and Other Essays* (Chicago: Aldine, 1969), p. 288.

2. Harry G. Johnson, "The Case for Flexible Exchange Rates, 1969," in Federal Reserve Bank of St. Louis, *Review* 51 (June 1969): 17.

3. See A. Andréadès, *History of the Bank of England* (London: P. S. King, 1909), p. 136.

4. John Carswell, *The South Sea Bubble* (London: Cresset Press, 1960), p. 139.

5. W. R. Brock, *Lord Liverpool and Liberal Toryism, 1820–1827* (Cambridge: Cambridge University Press, 1941), p. 209.

6. R. C. O. Matthews, *A Study of Trade-Cycle History: Economic Fluctuations in Great Britain, 1832–1842* (Cambridge: Cambridge University Press, 1954), p. 162.

7. Maurice Lévy-Leboyer, *Les banques européennes et l'industrialisation internationale dans la première moitié du XIXᵉ siècle* (Paris: Presses universitaires de France, 1964), pp. 618–20.

8. Ibid., p. 713.

9. Wladimir d'Ormesson, *La grande crise mondiale de 1857: L'histoire recommence, les causes, les remèdes* (Paris-Suresnes: Maurice d'Hartoy, 1933), pp. 110ff.

10. Hans Rosenberg, *Die Weltwirtschaftskrise von 1857–59* (Stuttgart/Berlin: Verlag von W. Kohlhammer, 1934), p. 210.

11. Max Wirth, *Geschichte der Handelskrisen*, 4th ed. (1890; reprint ed., New York: Burt Franklin, 1968), p. 463.

12. Fritz Stern, *Gold and Iron: Bismarck, Bleichröder, and the Building of the German Empire* (London: Allen & Unwin, 1977), p. 242.

13. *Economist*, April 21, 1888, p. 500. This citation and the following one were brought to my attention by Richard C. Marston.

14. Ibid., May 5, 1888, pp. 570–71.

15. M. J. Gordon, "Towards a Theory of Financial Distress," *Journal of Finance* 26 (May 1971): 348.

16. Carswell, *South Sea Bubble*, p. 170.

17. Sir John Clapham, *The Bank of England: A History* (Cambridge: Cambridge University Press, 1945), vol. 2, p. 257.

18. Jean Bouvier, *Le Krach de l'Union Générale* (Paris: Presses universitaires de France, 1960) pp. 129, 133, 137.

19. Wirth, *Handelskrisen*, p. 508.

20. D. Mortier Evans, *The History of the Commercial Crisis, 1857–1858, and the Stock Exchange Panic of 1859* (1859; reprint ed., New York: Augustus M. Kelley, 1969), p. 203.

21. Stephen A. Schuker, *The End of French Predominance in Europe, The Financial Crisis of 1924 and the Adoption of the Dawes Plan* (Chapel Hill: University of North Carolina Press, 1976), pp. 87, 104.

22. Arthur D. Gayer, W. W. Rostow, and Anna J. Schwartz, *The Growth and Fluctuation of the British Economy, 1790–1850* (Oxford: Oxford University Press, Clarendon Press, 1953), vol. 1, p. 190.

23. Ibid., p. 312.

24. Bouvier, *Le Krach*, pp. 29, 130.

25. James G. Gibbons, *The Banks of New York, Their Dealers, the Clearing House and the Panic of 1857* (New York: D. Appleton, 1859), p. 94.

26. See Clément Juglar, *Des crises commerciales et de leur retour périodique en France, en Angleterre et aux Etats Unis*, 2nd ed. (1889; reprint ed., New York: Augustus M. Kelley, 1967), p. 427.

27. W. T. C. King, *History of the London Discount Market* (London: George Routledge & Sons, 1936), p. 232.

28. O. M. W. Sprague, *History of Crises Under the National Banking System* (1910; reprint ed., New York: Augustus M. Kelley, 1968), p. 127.

29. Ibid., p. 33.

30. Ibid., p. 36.

31. Bouvier, *Le Krach*, p. 133.

32. Sprague, *History of Crises*, pp. 237–53.

33. Carswell, *South Sea Bubble*, pp. 136–37, 158.

34. Evans, *Commercial Crisis*, p. 13.

35. Gayer, Rostow, and Schwartz, *Growth and Fluctuation*, p. 307.

36. W. Jett Lauck, *The Causes of the Panic of 1893* (Boston: Houghton, Mifflin, 1907), p. 59–60.

37. Oskar Morgenstern, *International Financial Transactions and Business Cycles* (Princeton: Princeton University Press, 1959), p. 523.

38. Johan Åkerman, *Structure et cycles économiques* (Paris: Presses universitaires de France, 1955–57), vol. 2, p. 292.

39. E. Ray McCartney, *Crisis of 1873* (Minneapolis: Burgess Publishing Co., 1935), pp. 58, 71.

40. Wirth, *Handelskrisen*, p. 110.

41. George W. Van Vleck, *The Panic of 1857: An Analytical Study* (New York: Columbia University Press, 1943), p. 68.

42. H. S. Foxwell, introduction to A. Andréadès, *History of the Bank of England*, p. xvii.

43. E. Victor Morgan, *The Theory and Practice of Central Banking, 1797–1913* (Cambridge: Cambridge University Press, 1943), p. 109.

44. Elmer Wood, *English Theories of Central Banking Control, 1819–1858* (Cambridge, Mass.: Harvard University Press, 1939), p. 183.

45. R. G. Hawtrey, *Currency and Credit*, 3rd ed. (New York: Longmans, Green, 1927), p. 28.

46. Clapham, *Bank of England*, vol. 2, p. 153.

47. Leone Levi, *History of British Commerce* (London: John Murray, 1872), p. 233.

48. Milton Friedman and Anna J. Schwartz, *A Monetary History of the United States, 1867–1960* (Princeton: Princeton University Press, 1963), p. 339.

49. Lauck, *Panic of 1893*, chap. 7.

50. Sprague, *History of Crises*, p. 253.

51. Thomas Joplin, *Case for Parliamentary Inquiry into the Circumstances of the Panic, in a Letter to Thomas Gisbourne, Esq. M.P.* (London: F. Ridgeway & Sons, n.d. [after 1832]), pp. 14–15.

52. Robert Baxter, *The Panic of 1866, with Its Lessons on the Currency Act* (1866; reprint ed., New York: Burt Franklin, 1969), pp. 4, 26.

53. Clapham, *Bank of England*, vol. 2, p. 101.

54. Ibid., p. 100.

55. Rosenberg, *Weltwirtschaftskrise*, p. 118.

56. Van Vleck, *Panic of 1857*, p. 74.

57. Rosenberg, *Weltwirtschaftskrise*, p. 121.

58. Sprague, *History of Crises*, p. 113.

59. Alvin H. Hansen, *Cycles of Prosperity and Depression in the United States, Great Britain and Germany: A Study of Monthly Data, 1902–1908* (Madison: University of Wisconsin, 1921), p. 13.

60. H. S. Foxwell, "The American Crisis of 1907," in *Papers in Current Finance* (London: Macmillan, 1919), pp. 202–3.

Chapter 7

1. Herbert Hoover, *The Memoirs of Herbert Hoover* (New York: Macmillan, 1952), vol. 3, pp. 61–62.

2. Milton Friedman and Anna J. Schwartz, *A Monetary History of the United States, 1867–1960* (Princeton: Princeton University Press, 1963), pp. 359–60.

3. Quoted in Leone Levi, *History of British Commerce* (London: John Murray, 1872), p. 234.

4. S. Saunders, quoted in D. Morier Evans, *The History of the Commercial Crisis, 1857–1858, and the Stock-Exchange Panic of 1859* (1859; reprint ed., New York: Augustus M. Kelley, 1969), p. 13.

5. R. C. O. Matthews, *A Study in Trade-Cycle History: Economic Fluctuations in Great Britain, 1832–1842* (Cambridge: Cambridge University Press, 1954), p. 69.

6. Friedman and Schwartz, *Monetary History*, p. 360.

7. Jørgen Pedersen, "Some Notes on the Economic Policy of the United States during the Period 1919–1932," in Hugo Hegelund, ed., *Money, Growth and Methodology: Papers in Honor of Johan Åkerman* (Lund: Lund Social Science Studies, 1961); reprinted in J. Pedersen, *Essays in Monetary Theory and Related Subjects* (Copenhagen: Samfunsvidenskabeligt Forlag, 1975), p. 189.

8. R. T. Naylor, *The History of Canadian Business, 1867–1914*, vol. 1, *The Banks and Finance Capital*, (Toronto: James Lorimer & Co., 1975), p. 130.

9. Clément Juglar, *Des crises commerciales et de leur retour périodique en France, en Angleterre et aux Etats-Unis*, 2nd ed. (1889; reprint ed., New York: Augustus M. Kelley, 1967), pp. xiv, 17, 47, 149, and passim.

10. Wesley C. Mitchell, introduction to Willard L. Thorp, *Business Annals* (New York: National Bureau of Economic Research, 1926), pp. 88–97.

11. Oskar Morgenstern, *International Financial Transactions and Business Cycles* (Princeton: Princeton University Press, 1959), chap. 1, esp. sec. 6, On international stock exchange panics from 1893 to 1931, see table 139, pp. 546–47 and chart 72, p. 548.

12. Friedman and Schwartz, *Monetary History*, p. 360.

13. Ibid., p. 308.

14. Johan Åkerman, *Structure et cycles économiques* (Paris: Presses universitaires de France, 1957) vol. 2, pp. 247, 255.

15. John Carswell, *The South Sea Bubble* (London: Cresset Press, 1960), pp. 84, 94, 100, 101.

16. Ibid., pp. 151, 160–1, 166.

17. Charles Wilson, *Anglo-Dutch Commerce and Finance in the Eighteenth Century* (Cambridge: Cambridge University Press, 1941), pp. 103, 124.

18. Carswell, *South Sea Bubble*, p. 167.

19. Ibid., pp. 179, 199.

20. T. S. Ashton, *Economic Fluctuations in England, 1700–1800* (Oxford: Oxford University Press, Clarendon Press, 1959), p. 120.

21. George Chalmers, *The Comparative Strength of Great Britain*, p. 141, quoted in Ashton, *Economic Fluctuations*, p. 151.

22. E. E. de Jong-Keesing, *De Economische Crisis van 1763 te Amsterdam* (Amsterdam, 1939), pp. 216–17.

23. Wilson, *Anglo-Dutch Commerce*, p. 168.

24. De Jong-Keesing, *Economische Crisis van 1763*, p. 217.

25. Ernst Baasch, *Hollandische Wirtschaftsgeschichte* (Jena: Gustav Fischer, 1927).

26. Max Wirth, *Geschichte der Handelskrisen*, 4th ed. (1890, reprint ed., New York: Burt Franklin, 1968), p. 87.

27. Stephan Skalweit, *Die Berliner Wirtschaftskrise von 1763 und ihre Hintergrunde* (Stuttgart/Berlin: Verlag W. Kohlhammer, 1937), p. 50.

28. Wilson, *Anglo-Dutch Commerce*, p. 168; Alice Clare Carter,

Getting, Spending and Investing in Early Modern Times: Essays on Dutch, English and Huguenot Economic History (Assen: Van Gorcum, 1975), p. 63.

29. William Smart, *Economic Annals of the Nineteenth Century* (1911; reprint ed., New York: Augustus M. Kelley, 1964), pp. 529–30.

30. Arthur D. Gayer, W. W. Rostow, Anna J. Schwartz, *The Growth and Fluctuation of the British Economy, 1790–1850* (Oxford: Oxford University Press, Clarendon Press, 1953), vol. 1, p. 159.

31. Smart, *Economic Annals*, vol. 1, chap. xxxi.

32. Murray N. Rothbard, *The Panic of 1819: Reactions and Policies* (New York: Columbia University Press, 1962), p. 11.

33. Bray Hammond, *Banks and Politics in America from the Revolution to the Civil War* (Princeton: Princeton University Press, 1957), chap. x, esp. pp. 253–62.

34. Maurice Lévy-Leboyer, *Les Banques européennes et l'industrialisation internationale dans la première moitié du XIX* siècle* (Paris: Presses universitaires de France, 1964), pp. 464–79.

35. Åkerman, *Structure et cycles économiques*, p. 294.

36. R. G. Hawtrey, *Currency and Credit*, 3rd ed. (New York: Longmans, Green, 1927), p. 177.

37. Lévy-Leboyer, *Banques européennes*, pp. 570–83.

38. Juglar, *Crises commerciales*, p. 414.

39. Richard Tilly, *Financial Institutions and Industrialization in the Rhineland, 1815–1870* (Madison: University of Wisconsin Press, 1970), p. 112.

40. Alfred Krüger, *Das Kölner Bankiergewerbe vom Ende des 18. Jahrhunderts bis 1875* (Essen: G. D. Baedeker Verlag, 1925), pp. 12–13, 35, 49, 55–56, 202–3. Professor Richard Tilly kindly gave me this reference.

41. This is discussed in a Swedish study of the crisis of 1857 that I am unable to read: P. E. Bergfalk, *Bidrag till de under de sista hundrade aren inträffade handelskrisers-historia* (Upsala: Edquist, 1859), referred to in Theodore E. Burton, *Financial Crises and Periods of Industrial and Commercial Depression* (New York: Appleton, 1902), p. 128–29.

42. Sir John Clapham, *The Bank of England: A History* (Cambridge: Cambridge University Press, 1945), vol. 2, p. 226.

43. Hans Rosenberg, *Die Weltwirtschaftskrise von 1857–1859* (Stuttgart/Berlin: Verlag von W. Kohlhammer, 1934), p. 136.

44. Åkerman, *Structure et cycles*, p. 323.

45. Clapham, *Bank of England*, vol. 2, p. 268. R. G. Hawtrey makes the point that the crisis was not isolated but a sequel to the Continental crisis of 1864. See *Currency and Credit*, 3rd ed. (New York: Longmans, Green, 1930), p. 177.

46. Shepard B. Clough, *The Economic History of Modern Italy* (New York: Columbia University Press, 1964), p. 53.

47. David S. Landes, *Bankers and Pashas: International Finance and Economic Imperialism in Egypt* (Cambridge, Mass.: Harvard University Press, 1958), p. 287.

48. Jürgen Schuchardt, "Die Wirtschaftskrise vom Jahre 1866 in Deutschland," in *Jahrbuch für Wirtschaftsgeschichte* (East Berlin, 1962), pp. 107, 109, 133.

49. Wirth, *Handelskrisen,* pp. 462–63.

50. Larry T. Wimmer, "The Gold Crisis of 1869: A Problem in Domestic Economic Policy and International Trade Theory," Ph.D. dissertation in economics, University of Chicago, August 1968; U.S., Congress, House, *Gold Panic Investigation,* 41st Cong., 2nd sess., H. Rept. 31, March 1, 1870.

51. Wirth, *Handelskrisen,* p. 464.

52. U.S., Congress, House, *Gold Panic Investigation,* p. 132.

53. R. Ray McCartney, *Crisis of 1873* (Minneapolis: Burgess, 1935), p. 85.

54. Morgenstern, *International Financial Transactions,* p. 546.

55. Fritz Stern, *Gold and Iron: Bismarck, Bleichröder and the Building of the German Empire* (London: Allen & Unwin, 1977), p. 189.

56. Morgenstern, *International Financial Transactions,* p. 548.

57. O. M. W. Sprague, *History of Crises Under the National Banking System* (1910; reprint ed., New York: Augustus M. Kelley, 1968), p. 132.

58. Franco Bonelli, *La crisi del 1907: una tappa dello sviluppo industriale in Italia* (Turin: Fondazione Luigi Einaudi, 1971).

59. Ibid., pp. 31–32.

60. Ibid., p. 34.

61. Ibid., pp. 42–43.

62. Frank Vanderlip, "The Panic as a World Phenomenon," in *Annals of the American Academy of Political and Social Science* 31 (January–June 1908): 303.

63. C. P. Kindleberger, *The World in Depression, 1929–1939* (Berkeley: University of California Press, 1973), esp. chap. 7.

Chapter 8

1. Thomas Joplin, *Case for Parliamentary Inquiry into the Circumstances of the Panic, in a Letter to Thomas Gisborne, Esq., M.P.* (London: F. Ridgeway & Sons, n.d. [after 1832]), p. 10 (apropos the panic of 1825).

2. Sir John Clapham, *The Bank of England: A History* (Cambridge: Cambridge University Press, 1945), vol. 2, p. 236 (apropos the panic of 1847).

3. E. Victor Morgan, *The Theory and Practice of Central Banking, 1797–1913* (Cambridge: Cambridge University Press, 1943), p. 133.

4. The episode is noted in A. Andréadès, *History of the Bank of England* (London: P. S. King, 1909), p. 334.

5. "The Revulsion of 1857—Its Causes and Results," *The New York Herald,* n.d., quoted in D. Morier Evans, *The History of the Commercial Crisis, 1857–1858, and the Stock Exchange Panic of 1859* (1859; reprint ed., New York: Augustus M. Kelley, 1969), p. 121.

6. Herbert Hoover, *The Memoirs of Herbert Hoover* (New York: Macmillan & Co., 1952), vol. 3; p. 30; quoted by William Wiseley,

A Tool of Power: The Political History of Money (New York: Wiley-Interscience, 1977), p. 118.

7. Ernst Baasch, *Holländische Wirtschaftsgeschichte* (Jena: Gustav Fischer, 1927), p. 238.

8. Joplin, *Parliamentary Inquiry*, pp. 14–15.

9. Great Britain, *Parliamentary Papers (Monetary Policy, Commercial Distress)*, (Shannon: Irish University Press, 1969), vol. 1, pp. 427, 431.

10. D. Morier Evans, *The Commercial Crisis, 1847–1848*, 2nd ed. (1849; reprint ed., New York: Augustus M. Kelley, 1969), p. 89[n] (note begins p. 84).

11. Evans, *Commercial Crisis, 1857–1858*, p. 181.

12. Parliamentary Papers, *Commercial Distress*, p. xii.

13. Ibid., vol. 4, appendix 20; *Foreign Communications Relative to the Commercial Crisis of 1857*, Hamburg consular circular no. 76, November 23, 1857, pp. 435, 440, 441.

14. W. C. T. King, *History of the London Discount Market* (London: George Routledge & Sons, 1936), p. 243.

15. Theodore Dreiser, *The Financier* (1912), in *Trilogy of Desire* (New York: World Publishing, 1972), p. 491.

16. W. Jett Lauck, *The Causes of the Panic of 1893* (Boston: Houghton, Mifflin, 1907), p. 102.

17. *The Commercial and Financial Chronicle*, May 16, 1884, p. 589; quoted in O. M. W. Sprague, *History of Crises Under the National Banking System* (1910; reprint ed., New York: Augustus M. Kelley, 1968), p. 112.

18. W. R. Brock, *Lord Liverpool and Liberal Toryism, 1820–1827* (Cambridge: Cambridge University Press, 1941), pp. 209–10 (cited by Clapham, *Bank of England*, vol. 2, p. 108).

19. Clapham, *Bank of England*, vol. 2, p. 332.

20. Stephan Skalweit, *Die Berliner Wirtschaftskrise von 1763 und ihre Hintergründe* (Stuttgart/Berlin: Verlag W. Kohlhammer, 1937), pp. 49–73.

21. Larry T. Wimmer, "The Gold Crisis of 1869: A Problem of Domestic Economic Policy and International Trade Theory," Ph.D. dissertation in economics, University of Chicago, August 1968, p. 79.

22. Arthur D. Gayer, W. W. Rostow, and Anna J. Schwartz, *The Growth and Fluctuation of the British Economy, 1790–1850* (Oxford: Oxford University Press, Clarendon Press, 1953), vol. 1, p. 272.

23. Andréadès, *Bank of England*, p. 137, citing McLeod, 3rd ed., p. 428.

24. John Carswell, *The South Sea Bubble* (London: Cresset Press, 1960), p. 184.

25. Andréadès, *Bank of England*, p. 151.

26. Alexander Dana Noyes, *The Market Place: Reminiscences of a Financial Editor* (Boston: Little, Brown, 1938), p. 333.

27. Sprague, *History of Crises*, p. 259.

28. Ibid., p. 259.

29. Ibid., p. 181.

30. Max Wirth, *Geschichte der Handelskrisen*, 4th ed. (1890, reprint ed., New York: Burt Franklin, 1968), p. 521.

31. Maurice Lévy-Leboyer, *Les banques européennes et l'industriali-*

sation internationale dans la première moitié du XIXe siècle (Paris: Presses universitaires de France, 1964), p. 480, text and note 5.

32. George W. Van Vleck, *The Panic of 1857: An Analytical Study* (New York: Columbia University Press, 1943), p. 80.

33. Sprague, *History of Crises*, pp. 120, 182–83.

34. Ibid., pp. 75, 291–92.

35. Jacob H. Schiff, "Relation of a Central Bank to the Elasticity of the Currency," *Annals of the American Academy of Political and Social Science* 31 (January–June 1908): 375.

36. Myron T. Herrick, "The Panic of 1907 and Some of its Lessons," in ibid., 309.

37. John Kenneth Galbraith, *The Great Crash, 1929*, 3rd ed. (Boston: Houghton Mifflin, 1972), pp. 107–08.

38. Lévy-Leboyer, *Banques européennes*, pp. 470–71.

39. Bertrand Gille, *La Banque en France au XIXe siècle* (Paris: Droz, 1970), p. 93.

40. Parliamentary Papers, *Commercial Distress*, vol. 4, appendix, consular dispatch from Hamburg no. 75, p. 434.

41. Ibid., p. 435.

42. Hans Rosenberg, *Die Weltwirtschaftskrise von 1857–1859* (Stuttgart/Berlin: Verlag von W. Kohlhammer, 1934), p. 129.

43. Parliamentary Papers, *Commercial Distress*, vol. 4, appendix, consular dispatches from Hamburg nos. 77, 80, 81, 82, 84, 86.

44. Albert E. Fr. Schäffle, "Die Handelskrise von 1857 in Hamburg, mit besonderer Rücksicht auf das Bankwesen," in *Gesammelte Aufsätze* (Tübingen: H. Raupp'schen, 1885), vol. 2, pp. 44, 45, 52, 53.

45. Clapham, *Bank of England*, vol. 2, p. 156.

46. Ibid., vol. 2., p. 331. My account of the allaying of a possible Baring Brothers panic relies heavily on Clapham, but also on a term paper of December 1976 by J. David Germany, an M.I.T. graduate student in economics, who used Clapham extensively along with many other sources.

47. Diary of John Biddulph Martin, in George Chandler, *Four Centuries of Banking* (London: B. J. Batsford, 1964), vol. 1, p. 330.

48. Ellis T. Powell, *The Evolution of the Money Market (1384–1915): An Historical and Analytical Study of the Rise and Development of Finance as a Central Coordinated Force* (1915; reprint ed., New York: Augustus M. Kelley, 1966), p. 528.

49. Ibid., p. 525.

50. *Memoirs of Herbert Hoover*, pp. 211–12.

51. "F.D.I.C. Is Carrying Eight Major Banks on a Problem List," *New York Times*, November 3, 1976.

52. Wirth, *Handelskrisen*, p. 100.

53. Andréadès, *Bank of England*, pp. 187–89; Clapham, *Bank of England*, vol. 1, pp. 263–65.

54. Gayer, Rostow, and Schwartz, *Growth and Fluctuation*, vol. 1, p. 34.

55. William Smart, *Economic Annals of the Nineteenth Century* (1911; reprint ed., New York: Augustus M. Kelley, 1964), vol. 1, pp. 267–68.

56. Ibid., p. 271.

57. Wirth, *Geschichte der Handelskrisen*, pp. 110–111.

Chapter 9

1. T. S. Ashton, *Economic Fluctuations in England, 1700–1800* (Oxford: Oxford University Press, Clarendon Press, 1959), p. 112.
2. Ibid., p. 111.
3. E. Victor Morgan, *The Theory and Practice of Central Banking, 1797–1913* (Cambridge: Cambridge University Press, 1943), p. 240.
4. Maurice Lévy-Leboyer, *Les banques européennes et l'industrialisation internationale dans la première moitié du XIXᵉ siècle* (Paris: Presses universitaires de France, 1964), p. 490.
5. Thomas Joplin, *Case for Parliamentary Inquiry into the Circumstances of the Panic, in a Letter to Thomas Gisborne, Esq., M.P.* (London: P. Ridgeway & Sons, n.d. [after 1832]), p. 29.
6. Jacob Viner, *Studies in the Theory of International Trade* (New York: Harpers & Bros., 1937), p. 233.
7. Walter Bagehot, *Lombard Street: A Description of the Money Market* (1873, reprint ed., London: John Murray, 1917), p. 160.
8. Elmer Wood, *English Theories of Central Banking Control, 1819–1858* (Cambridge, Mass.: Harvard University Press, 1939), p. 147.
9. J. H. Clapham, *The Bank of England: A History* (Cambridge: Cambridge University Press, 1945), vol. 2, p. 289.
10. Bagehot, *Lombard Street*, pp. 161–62.
11. Clapham, *Bank of England*, vol. 2, p. 108.
12. Bertrand Gille, *La banque en France au XIXᵉ siècle: Recherches historiques* (Geneva: Librairie Droz, 1970), p. 32.
13. Bertrand Gille, *La banque et le crédit en France de 1815 à 1848* (Paris: Presses universitaires de France, 1959), p. 367.
14. Jean Bouvier, *Un siècle de banque française* (Paris: Hachette Littérature, 1973), pp. 83–84.
15. See Rondo Cameron, *France and the Economic Development of Europe, 1800–1914* (Princeton: Princeton University Press, 1961), pp. 191ff.
16. Maurice Lévy-Leboyer, *Histoire économique et sociale de la France depuis 1848* (Paris: Les Cours de Droit, Institut d'Etudes Poliques, 1951–52), p. 121.
17. Cameron, *France and Europe*, p. 117.
18. Alfred Pose, *La monnaie et ses institutions* (Paris: Presses universitaires de France, 1942), p. 215.
19. Jean Bouvier, *La Krach de l'Union Générale* (Paris: Presses universitaires de France, 1960), pp. 150, 152–53.
20. Esther Rogoff Taus, *Central Banking Functions of the United States Treasury, 1789–1941* (New York: Columbia University Press, 1943), pp. 22, 23, 29.
21. Ibid., pp. 39–131.
22. C. A. E. Goodhart, *The New York Money Market and the Finance of Trade, 1900–1913* (Cambridge, Mass.: Harvard University Press, 1969), p. 120.
23. George W. Van Vleck, *The Panic of 1857: An Analytical Study* (New York: Columbia University Press, 1943), p. 106.

24. O. M. W. Sprague, *History of Crises Under the National Banking System* (1910; reprint ed., New York: Augustus M. Kelley, 1968).

25. Myron T. Herrick, "The Panic of 1907 and Some of Its Lessons," *Annals of the American Academy of Political and Social Science* 31 (January–June 1908): 324.

26. Ridgely's essay in *Annals* was more narrowly entitled "An Elastic Credit Currency as a Preventive for Panics," but the papers of the others, except for Seligman, were unqualified in their advocacy of central-bank currency elasticity.

27. Wood, *English Central Banking Control*, pp. 169–70.

28. Franco Bonelli, *La crisi del 1907: una tappa dello sviluppo industriala in Italia* (Turin: Fondazione Luigi Einaudi, 1971), passim. and esp. p. 165.

29. Leone Levi, *History of British Commerce, 1763–1870*, 2nd ed. (London: John Murray, 1872), pp. 311–12.

30. Great Britain, *Parliamentary Papers, Monetary Policy, Commercial Distress* (1857; Shannon: Irish University Press, 1969), vol. 3, p. xxix.

31. Bouvier, *Le Krach*, chap. v.

32. Charles Wilson, *Anglo-Dutch Commerce and Finance in the Eighteenth Century* (Cambridge: Cambridge University Press, 1941), pp. 176–77.

33. Milton Friedman and Anna J. Schwartz, *A Monetary History of the United States, 1867–1960* (Princeton: Princeton University Press, 1963), pp. 309 and esp. note, pp. 309–10.

34. Clapham, *Bank of England*, vol. 1, p. 261; vol. 2, p. 58.

35. Ibid., vol. 2, pp. 59–60.

36. Ibid., vol. 1, p. 249.

37. Ibid., vol. 2, pp. 82–84.

38. Ibid., vol. 2, p. 145.

39. A. Dauphin-Meunier, *La Banque de France* (Paris: Gallimard, 1936), p. 100.

40. Bagehot, *Lombard Street*, p. 195.

41. Clapham, *Bank of England*, vol. 2, p. 59.

42. Ibid., vol. 2, pp. 206–7.

43. Ibid., vol. 1, p. 261.

44. D. Morier Evans, *The History of the Commercial Crisis, 1857–1858, and the Stock Exchange Panic of 1859* (1859; reprint ed., New York: Augustus M. Kelley, 1969), p. 80.

45. Lévy-Leboyer, *Banques européennes*, p. 559.

46. Ibid., p. 647.

47. Ibid., p. 492.

48. Evans, *Commercial Crisis, 1857–1858*, pp. i–ii, vi–xviii.

49. A. Andréadès, *History of the Bank of England* (London: P. S. King, 1909), p. 266.

50. Clapham, *Bank of England*, vol. 2, p. 157. He refers to it later as "the long drawn out W bank affair" (ibid., p. 337).

51. R. C. O. Matthews, *A Study in Trade-Cycle History: Economic Fluctuations in Great Britain, 1832–1842* (Cambridge: Cambridge University Press, 1954), p. 173.

52. Clapham, *Bank of England*, vol. 1, p. 245.

53. H. S. Foxwell, preface to Andréadès, *Bank of England*, p. xvii.

54. Clapham, *Bank of England*, vol. 1, p. 256.
55. See Friedman and Schwartz, *Monetary History*, pp. 339, 363–67.
56. Ibid., p. 395.
57. Ibid., p. 339.
58. See Milton Friedman, "Rediscounting," in *A Program for Monetary Stability* (New York: Fordham University Press, 1960), pp. 35–36.
59. Friedman and Schwartz, *Monetary History*, pp. 334–35.
60. Clapham, *Bank of England*, vol. 2, p. 102.
61. Evans, *Commercial Crisis, 1857–1858*, p. 207.
62. Taus, *Central Banking*, pp. 55, 70.
63. Sprague, *History of Crises*, p. 256.

Chapter 10

1. R. D. Richards, "The First Fifty Years of the Bank of England, 1694–1744," in *History of the Principal Public Banks*, compiled by J. G. Van Dillen (The Hague: Martinus Nijhoff, 1934), p. 234.
2. Charles Wilson, *Anglo-Dutch Commerce and Finance in the Eighteenth Century* (Cambridge: Cambridge University Press, 1941), pp. 168–69.
3. Ibid., p. 176.
4. Sir John Clapham, *The Bank of England: A History* (Cambridge: Cambridge University Press, 1945), vol. 1, p. 249.
5. Ibid., vol. 2, pp. 100–1.
6. Knut Wicksell, *Lectures on Political Economy* (New York: Macmillan, 1935), vol. 2, pp. 37–38.
7. Jacob Viner, *Studies in the Theory of International Trade* (New York: Harper, 1937), p. 273; Clapham, *Bank of England*, vol. 2, p. 169.
8. Clapham, *Bank of England*, vol. 2, pp. 164–65.
9. Clément Juglar, *Des crises commerciales et de leur rétour périodique en France, en Angleterre et aux Etats-units*, 2nd ed. (1889; reprint ed., New York: Augustus M. Kelley, 1967), p. 417.
10. E. Victor Morgan, *The Theory and Practice of Central Banking, 1797–1913* (Cambridge: Cambridge University Press, 1943), p. 148.
11. Arthur D. Gayer, W. W. Rostow, and Anna J. Schwartz, *The Growth and Fluctuation of the British Economy, 1790–1850* (Oxford: Oxford University Press, Clarendon Press, 1953), vol. 1, p. 333.
12. British Parliamentary Papers, *Causes of Commercial Distress: Monetary Policy* (Shannon: Irish University Press, 1969), vol. 1, p. 153, question 2018.
13. Viner, *Theory of International Trade*, p. 273.
14. Clapham, *Bank of England*, vol. 2, p. 170.
15. Bertrand Gille, *La banque et le crédit en France de 1818 à 1848* (Paris: Presses universitaires de France, 1959), p. 377.
16. Clapham, *Bank of England*, vol. 2, p. 229.
17. Helmut Böhme, *Frankfurt und Hamburg. Des Deutsches Reiches*

Silber- und Goldloch und die Allerenglishste Stadt des Kontinents (Frankfurt-am-Main: Europaïsche Verlagsanstalt, 1968), pp. 255–68.

18. Ibid., pp. 267–74.

19. Parliamentary Papers, *Commercial Distress*, vol. 4, appendix 20, consular dispatch no. 7, January 27, 1858, p. 441.

20. Ibid., dispatch no. 393 from Berlin, December 29, 1857, pp. 450–51.

21. Clapham, *Bank of England*, vol. 2, p. 234.

22. Morgan, *Theory and Practice of Central Banking*, p. 176.

23. Clapham, *Bank of England*, vol. 2, pp. 291–94.

24. Ibid., pp. 329–30, 344.

25. R. S. Sayers, *Bank of England Operations, 1890–1914* (London: P. S. King & Sons, 1936), chap. 5, esp. pp. 104–12.

26. J.-L. Billoret, "Système bancaire et dynamique économique dans un pays à monnaie stable: France, 1896–1914," unpublished thesis, Faculty of Law and Economic Science, Nancy, October 1969; quoted in Jean Bouvier, *Un siècle de banque française* (Paris: Hachette Littérature, 1973), p. 240.

27. Hans Rosenberg, *Die Weltwirtschaftskrise von 1857–1859* (Stuttgart/Berlin: Verlag von W. Kohlhammer, 1834), p. 38.

28. George W. Van Vleck, *The Panic of 1857: An Analytical Study* (New York: Columbia University Press, 1943), p. 42.

29. Billoret, "Système bancaire," as quoted in Bouvier, *Un siècle de banque française*, p. 238.

30. Walter Bagehot, *Lombard Street: A Description of the Money Market* (1873; reprint ed., London: John Murray, 1917), pp. 32–34.

31. O. M. W. Sprague, *History of Crises Under the National Banking System* (1910; reprint ed., New York: Augustus M. Kelley, 1968), pp. 248–85.

32. Franco Bonelli, *La crisi del 1907: una tappa dello sviluppo industriale in Italia* (Turin: Fondazione Luigi Einaudi, 1971), p. 42.

33. Oskar Morgenstern, *International Financial Transactions and Business Cycles* (Princeton: Princeton University Press, 1959), pp. 128–37.

34. See League of Nations, *The Course and Control of Inflation After World War I* (Princeton: League of Nations, 1945).

35. Paul E. Erdman, *The Crash of '79* (New York: Simon & Schuster, 1976).

36. Stephen A. Schuker, *The End of French Predominance in Europe: The Financial Crisis of 1924 and the Adoption of the Dawes Plan* (Chapel Hill: University of North Carolina Press, 1976), p. 67.

37. Ibid., chap. 4.

38. Ibid., p. 111.

39. C. P. Kindleberger, *The World in Depression, 1929–1939* (Berkeley: University of California Press, 1973), esp. chaps. 7, 14.

40. R. G. Hawtrey, *The Art of Central Banking* (London: Longmans, Green, 1932), pp. 220–24; all italics are in the original.

41. Ibid., pp 229–32; italics in the original.

42. Susan Howson and Donald Winch, *The Economic Advisory Council, 1930–1939: A Study in Economic Advice During Depression and Recovery* (Cambridge: Cambridge University Press, 1977), pp.

188–89. The personnel of the various committees are given in ibid., appendix 1, pp. 354–70.

43. Ibid., pp. 272–81.

44. This discussion is largely based on Karl Erich Born, *Die deutsche Bankenkrise, 1931: Finanzen und Politik* (Munich: R. Piper & Co. Verlag, 1967).

45. Ibid., p. 86.

46. Ibid., p. 83.

47. Norman to Harrison, cable, July 3, 1931, in Federal Reserve Bank of New York files.

48. Stephen V. O. Clarke, *Central Bank Cooperation, 1924–31* (New York: Federal Reserve Bank of New York, 1967), p. 44.

49. Clarke, *Central Bank Cooperation*, pp. 121, 148.

50. Howson and Winch, *Economic Advisory Council*, pp. 88–89.

51. Ibid., p. 162.

52. Kindleberger, *World in Depression*, pp. 168, 184.

53. Richard N. Cooper, "Economic Interdependence and Foreign Policy in the Seventies," *World Politics* 24 (January 1972), 167.

54. Charles A. Coombs, *The Arena of International Finance* (New York: Wiley, 1976), p. 37.

55. Ibid., pp. 81, 85, 111, 121, 127, 134, 181, 185.

56. Susan Strange, "International Monetary Relations," in Andrew Shonfield, ed., *International Economic Relations of the Western World, 1959–71* (Oxford: Oxford University Press, for the Royal Institute of International Affairs, 1976), vol. 2, p. 136.

57. Coombs, *Arena*, pp. 77, 79, 81, 83, 195, 202, 292.

58. Ibid., pp. 116, 235.

59. "Reuss Says Idea of Massive Aid from U.S. to Britain is Mistaken," *New York Times*, November 29, 1976.

60. See "The I.M.F. and the Debts of Poor Nations," *New York Times*, March 28, 1977.

Chapter 11

1. William Wiseley, *A Tool of Power: The Political History of Money* (New York: Wiley-Interscience, 1977), p. 41.

2. As quoted in William Smart, *Economic Annals of the Nineteenth Century* (1912; reprint ed., New York: Augustus M. Kelley, 1964), vol. 2, p. 328.

3. Leone Levi, *History of British Commerce* (London: John Murray, 1872), p. 182.

4. George W. Van Vleck, *The Panic of 1857: An Analytical Study* (New York: Columbia University Press, 1943), pp. 83, 106.

5. John Carswell, *The South Sea Bubble* (London: Cresset Press, 1960), pp. 271–72.

6. Joseph A. Schumpeter, *Business Cycles: A Theoretical, Historical and Statistical Analysis of the Capitalist Process* (New York: McGraw-Hill, 1939), vol. 1, pp. 250–51.

7. Carswell, *South Sea Bubble*, pp. 184, 205, 213.

8. T. S. Ashton, *Economic Fluctuations in England, 1700–1800* (Oxford: Oxford University Press, Clarendon Press, 1959), p. 121.

9. Ibid., p. 172.

10. Clément Juglar, *Les crises commerciales et de leur rétour périodique en France, en Angleterre et aux Etats-Unis*, 2nd ed. (1889; reprint ed., New York: Augustus M. Kelley, 1967), p. 99.

11. E. Ray McCartney, *Crisis of 1873* (Minneapolis: Burgess, 1935), pp. 113, 117.

12. Ibid., p. 117.

13. S. B. Saul, *The Myth of the Great Depression* (New York: St. Martin's Press, 1969).

14. W. Jett Lauck, *The Causes of the Panic of 1893* (Boston: Houghton, Mifflin, 1907), p. 55.

15. Jørgen Pedersen, "Some Notes on the Economic Policy of the United States During the Period 1919–1932," in Hugo Hegelund, ed., *Money, Growth and Methodology* (Lund: Lund Social Science Studies, 1961), reprinted in J. Pedersen, *Essays in Monetary Theory and Related Subjects* (Copenhagen: Samfunsvidenskabeligt Forlag, 1975), p. 188.

16. Ibid., pp. 193–94.

17. Ashton, *Economic Fluctuations*, p. 127.

18. Thomas Joplin, *Case for Parliamentary Inquiry into the Circumstances of the Panic, in a Letter to Thomas Gisborne, Esq., M.P.* (London: F. Ridgeway and Sons, n.d. [after 1832]), p. 14.

19. Reginald Charles McGrane, *The Panic of 1837: Some Financial Problems of the Jacksonian Era* (1924; reprint ed., New York: Russell and Russell, 1965), p. 1.

20. James Wilson, *Capital, Currency and Banking* (London: Economist, 1847), p. 1101.

21. D. Morier Evans, *The Commercial Crisis, 1847–48*, 2nd ed. (1849; reprint ed., New York: Augustus M. Kelley, 1968), p. 111.

22. D. Morier Evans, *The History of the Commercial Crisis, 1857–1858, and the Stock Exchange Panic of 1859* (1859; reprint ed., New York: Augustus M. Kelley, 1969), p. v.

23. Fred Oelssner, *Die Wirtschaftskrisen. Erster Band: Die Krisen in vormonopolistischen Kapitalismus* (Berlin: Dietz Verlag), p. 237, quoting Friedrich Engels.

24. Albert E. Fr. Schäffle, "Die Handelskrise von 1857 in Hamburg, mit besondered Rucksicht auf das Bankwesen," quoted in Wladimir d'Ormesson, *La Grande crise mondiale de 1857: L'histoire recommence, les causes, les remèdes* (Paris-Suresnes: Maurice d'Hartoy, 1933), p. 119.

25. A. Andréadès, *History of the Bank of England* (London: P. S. King, 1909), p. 357.

26. E. Victor Morgan, *The Theory and Practice of Central Banking, 1797–1913* (Cambridge: Cambridge University Press, 1943), p. 177.

27. Fritz Stern, *Gold and Iron: Bismarck, Bleichröder and the Building of the German Empire* (London: Allen & Unwin, 1977), p. 189,

quoting a letter of October 1875 from Baron Abraham von Oppenheim to Bleichröder.

28. Jean Bouvier, *Le Krach de l'Union Générale* (Paris: Presses universitaires de France, 1960), p. 145, quoting a director of the Crédit Lyonnais.

29. John Kenneth Galbraith, *The Great Crash, 1929*, 3rd ed. (Boston: Houghton-Mifflin, 1972), p. vii.

30. Ashton, *Economic Fluctuations*, p. 176.

31. Burton G. Malkiel, *A Random Walk Down Wall Street*, rev ed. (New York: W. W. Norton, 1973), chap. 3.

32. Fourth Report of the Committee on Economc Information, "Survey of the Economic Situation, July, 1932," in Susan Howson and Donald Winch, *The Economic Advisory Council, 1930–1939: A Study in Economic Advice During Depression and Recovery* (Cambridge: Cambridge University Press, 1977), pp. 277–78.

33. Hyman P. Minsky, "A Theory of Systemic Fragility," in Edward I. Altman and Arnold W. Sametz, ed., *Financial Crises: Institutions and Markets in a Fragile Financial Environment* (New York: Wiley-Interscience, 1977), p. 139.

34. Martin Mayer, *Today and Tomorrow in America* (New York: Harper and Row, 1976), p. 113–14.

35. This refers to a new book by Geoffrey Barraclough, *The World Crash* (London, 1977), notice of which I have seen, but not the book.

36. Lewis Thomas, "Biomedical Science and Human Health: The Long-Range Prospect," *Daedalus* 106, no. 3 (Summer 1977), pp. 164–65.

37. Sir John Clapham, *The Bank of England: A History* (Cambridge: Cambridge University Press, 1945), vol. 2, p. 283.

A Stylized Outline of Financial Crises, 1720–1975

Year	1720		1763	1772	
	England	France	Amsterdam	Britain	Amsterdam
Countries (city)	England	France	Amsterdam	Britain	Amsterdam
Related to	Treaty of Utrecht, 1713	Death of Louis XIV, 1715	End of Seven Years War	Seven Years War (10 years after)	
Preceding speculation in	South Sea Company stock; government debt	Mississippi Company, Banque générale, Banque royale	Commodities, esp. sugar (?)	Housing, turn-pikes, canals	East India Co.
Monetary Expansion from	Sword Blade Bank	John Law Banks	*Wisselruitij* (chain of accommodation bills)	Ayr Bank; country banks	*Wisselruitij*; Bank of Amsterdam
Speculative peak	Apr. 1720	Dec. 1719	Jan. 1763	June 1772	
Crisis (crash, panic)	Sept. 1720	May 1720	Sept. 1763	Jan. 1773	
Lender of last resort	Bank of England (??)	None	Bank of England	Bank of England	City of Amsterdam

A Stylized Outline of Financial Crises, 1720–1975 (continued)

Year	1793	1797	1799	1810	1815–16
Countries (city)	England	England	Hamburg	England	England
Related to	Reign of Terror (France)	Collapse of Assignats; French landing, Fishguard	Break in Continental blockade	Wellington's peninsula campaign	End of Napoleonic War
Preceding speculation in	Canal mania	Securities, canals	Commodities	Exports to Brazil (and Scandinavia)	Export commodities, Continent and U.S.
Monetary expansion from	Capital flows from France	Country banks	*Wechselreiterei*	Country banks	Banks
Speculative peak	Nov. 1792	1796	1799	1809	1815
Crisis (crash, panic)	Feb. 1793	Feb.-June 1797	Aug.-Nov. 1799	1810, Jan. 1811	1816
Lender of last resort	Exchequer bills	Exchequer bills, abandon gold	Admiralty bills	Exchequer bills	?

Year	1819		1825	1828	1836	1837	1838
Countries (city)	England	U.S.	England	France	England	U.S.	France
Related to	Waterloo (five years after)		Success of Baring loan; decline in interest rates	Decline in interest rates	Textile boom	Jackson presidency	July 1830 Monarchy
Preceding speculation in	Commodities, securities	Manufacturing behind embargo	Latin American bonds, mines, cotton	Canals, cotton, building sites	Cotton, railroads	Cotton, land	Cotton, building sites
Monetary expansion from	Banks generally	Bank of the U.S.	bonds sold in installments County banks,	Paris banks	Joint-stock banks	Wildcat banks; retention of silver	Regional banks
Speculative peak	Dec. 1818	Aug. 1818	Early 1825		Apr. 1836		Nov. 1836
Crisis (crash, panic)	None	Nov. 1818 to June 1819	Dec. 1825	Dec. 1827	Dec. 1836	Sept. 1837	June 1837
Lender of last resort	None needed	Treasury specie deposits	Bank of England	Paris, Basel banks, Bank of France	Bank of France and Bank of Hamburg helped Bank of England		

A Stylized Outline of Financial Crises, 1720–1975 (continued)

Year	1847	1848	1857		
	England	Continent	U.S.	England	Continent
Countries (city)	England	Continent	U.S.	England	Continent
Related to		1846 potato blight, wheat failure			End of Crimean War
Preceding speculation in	Railways, wheat	Railways, wheat, building (Cologne)	Railroads, public land	Railroads, wheat	Railroads, heavy industry
Monetary expansion from	Installment sale of railway securities	Regional banks	Gold discoveries, clearinghouses	Bank mergers, clearinghouse	Credit Mobilier, new German banks
Speculative peak	Jan. 1947		End of 1856		March 1857
Crisis (crash, panic)	Oct. 1847	Mar. 1848	Aug. 1857	Oct. 1857	Nov. 1857
Lender of last resort	Suspension of Bank Act of 1844	Bank of England loan to Bank of France; Russian purchase of French rentes	Capital inflow from England	Suspension of Bank Act of 1844	Silberzug (Hamburg)

Year	1864	1866	1873		1882
Countries (city)	France	England/Italy	Germany/Austria	U.S.	France
Related to	End of Civil War	General limited liability	Franco-Prussian indemnity	Fraud exposed in 1872 campaign	Expansion into southeastern Europe
Preceding speculation in		Cotton, shipping companies generally	Building sites, railroads, securities, commodities	Railroads, homesteading	Stocks of new banks, Lyons
Monetary expansion from	Credit Mobilier	Joint-stock discount houses	New industrial banks, broker banks, construction banks	Short-term credit; inflow of European capital	Securities bought on margin
Speculative peak	1863	July 1865	Fall 1872	March 1873	Dec. 1881
Crisis (crash, panic)	Jan. 1864	May 1866	May 1873	Sept. 1873	Jan. 1882
Lender of last resort	Maturities of bills extended	Suspension of Bank Act; Italy abandoned fixed parity	None	None	Limited help from Paris banks

A Stylized Outline of Financial Crises, 1720–1975 (continued)

Year	1890	1893	1907		1920–1921	
	England	U.S.	U.S.	France/Italy	Britain	U.S.
Countries (city)						
Related to	Argentine clearing of southern lands; prospective change in company law	Sherman Silver Act, 1890	Russo-Japanese war (?), San Francisco earthquake (??)		End of postwar boom	
Preceding speculation in	Argentine securities, private companies going public	Silver, gold	Coffee, Union Pacific	Industrial borrowing from banks	Securities, ships, commodities, inventories	
Monetary expansion from	Goschen conversion	Contraction	Trust companies	Società Bancaria Italiana	Banks	
Speculative peak	Aug. 1890	Dec. 1892	Early 1907	March 1906	Summer 1920	
Crisis (crash, panic)	Nov. 1890	May 1893	Oct. 1907	Aug. 1907	Spring 1921	
Lender of last resort	Baring liabilities guaranteed by Bank of France; Russian gold loans to Britain	Repeal of Sherman Silver Act, of Aug. 1893	$100 million inflow from Britain	?	None	

Year	1929	1931–33	1950s, 1960s	1974–75
Countries (city)	U.S.	Europe	Worldwide	U.S. Worldwide
Related to	End of extended postwar boom	Cutoff of U.S. foreign lending	Convertibility without macro-economic coor-dination	Collapse of Bretton Woods: OPEC price rise
Preceding speculation in	Land to 1925, stocks 1928–29	Not applicable	Foreign exchange	Stocks, REITS, office buildings, tankers, Boeing 747s
Monetary expansion from	Stocks bought on margin	U.S. lending	Not applicable	Eurodollar market
Speculative peak	Sept. 1929	1929	Speculation in currencies of:	1969
Crisis (crash, panic)	Oct. 1929	Austria, May 1931 Germany, June 1931 Britain, Sept. 1931 Japan, Dec. 1931 U.S., Mar. 1933	France, 1958 Canada, 1962 Italy, 1963 Britain, 1964 France, 1968 U.S., 1973, etc.	1974–75
Lender of last resort	FRBNY open-market operations (inadequate)	Feeble efforts in U.S., France	BIS swap network	BIS swap network

INDEX